P9-ECZ-313

The Saddest Country

THE SADDEST COUNTRY

ON ASSIGNMENT IN COLOMBIA

Nicholas Coghlan

McGill-Queen's University Press
Montreal & Kingston • London • Ithaca

ISBN 0-7735-2787-7

Legal deposit third quarter 2004
Bibliothèque nationale du Québec

Printed in Canada on acid-free paper

McGill-Queen's University Press acknowledges the support of the Canada Council for the Arts for our publishing program. We also acknowledge the financial support of the Government of Canada through the Book Publishing Industry Development Program (BPIDP) for our publishing activities.

National Library of Canada Cataloguing in Publication

Coghlan, Nicholas, 1954–
The saddest country: on assignment in Colombia / Nicholas Coghlan.
Includes index.
ISBN 0-7735-2787-7
1. Insurgency – Colombia. 2. Colombia – Politics and government – 1974–. 3. Human rights – Colombia. 4. Drug traffic – Colombia. I. Title.
F2279.C56 2004 986.106'35 C2004-902683-6

While the author remains an employee of the Department of Foreign Affairs Canada, the contents of this book reflect his own personal views and do not represent the position of the Government of Canada. They are observations of a particular period in Colombia (1997–2000) and may not be an accurate portrayal of the situation today. The author regrets any unintentional embarrassment or offence that any of the facts related in this book may cause to the individuals concerned.

Set in 10/13 Sabon and Helvetica Neue. Book design and typesetting by zijn digital.

Contents

Cartagena
Barranquilla
Panama
Magdalena R.
Mompox
Venezuela
Turbo
Apartadó
Barrancabermeja
Juradó
Bahía Cupica
Medellín
Quibdó
Bahía Solano
Nevado del Ruiz (5325m)
Puerto Carreño
El Tuparro
Bogotá
Atrato R.
Nevada del Tolima (5215m)
Villavicencio
Puerto Inírida
Cerros de Mavecuri
Neiva
DMZ
San Vicente
Larandia
Mocoa
Puerto Asís
Ecuador
Putumayo R.
Brazil
Peru
km
0
200
400

The Saddest Country

Prologue

A Day in the Life

FRIDAY, 15 AUGUST 1997, was just another day in Colombia. It was more violent than some, less so than others. From my desk at the Canadian Embassy, on Street 78 in Northern Bogotá, I reported briefly to Ottawa on some of the day's events with the aim of giving headquarters – Canada's Department of Foreign Affairs and International Trade – a glimpse of the morass of violence into which the country had sunk, depths from which at that time I sensed there was no prospect of release in the short to medium term. Here is my email of that day.

Late on Thursday night, ten workers at a sawmill 30 km from Medellín were shot dead, execution-style, by a gang of twenty armed men. Their bodies were found on Friday morning; no arrests have been made. There is speculation that the killers were right-wing paramilitaries, and that their victims were suspected of collaborating with the guerrilla, but the reverse might just as well be true. Also on Friday morning, coincidentally, the embassy received a plaintive letter from a

Medellín businessman, saying that he was receiving death threats from both the guerrillas and paramilitaries, each accusing him of collaborating with the other; the police, to whom he had made a formal denunciation, had sympathized but had just told him to "be careful." He was asking for refuge in Canada. Such letters are received at the embassy all too frequently.

The same morning, the family of city councillor José Ignacio González was burying him in a Medellín cemetery. Two days previously, he had been kidnapped by thirty armed men of Front 34 of the Fuerzas Armadas Revolucionarias de Colombia (FARC) and had died of a heart attack the same night.

Meanwhile, 100 km from Bogotá, Governor Leonor Serrano de Camargo was celebrating the 453rd anniversary of the foundation of the municipality of Bituima. Crossing a bridge, the second vehicle of her three-car convoy blew up, injuring her two bodyguards. All three cars were then fired upon but police fired back and the governor escaped with her life. She continued her round of visits.

In the city of Bucaramanga two bombs (described by the media as "of average size") went off at a trade fair, causing the fair's cancellation and US$2 million of damage. Meanwhile, in the Caribbean port city of Barranquilla, two more bombs destroyed the campaign headquarters of Virgilio Vizcaíno and Father Bernardo Hoyos, candidates (respectively) for the mayoralty of the city and governorship of the department.

In the remote Llanos village of Mapiripán, there was another chapter in the grisly saga that began on 20 July with the killing and decapitation of at least seven persons by right-wing paramilitaries. In a fierce gunbattle Thursday between the FARC and the Autodefensas Campesinas de Córdoba y Urabá (paramilitaries), an estimated forty people more were killed; twelve bodies were brought into Mapiripán on Thursday night. The village is now almost a ghost town, with 80 percent of its population having fled to join the approximately one million Colombians who have been displaced by violence. Military personnel based in Mapiripán were quoted as saying only "it's none of our business."

More kidnappings: also on Friday, a Canadian mining consultant began the second month of his captivity. He is being held by the ELN (Colombia's other guerrilla army) somewhere in Bolívar Department.

Near Cúcuta, the city where last week a senator was shot dead, Conservative politician and former Deputy Darío Alberto Ordóñez, a candidate for mayor in Sardinata municipality, was kidnapped by Front 33 of the FARC (this is not a new experience for Ordóñez; he was held for several months by the FARC in 1991). In the municipality of Simití, Bolívar Department, the entire town council (candidate for mayor, treasurer, and seven councillors) was kidnapped. The incumbent mayor had fled the town several days earlier following a FARC raid that left three police dead; he now says that he plans to "continue my holidays for at least two weeks more."

In Cartagena del Chaira, three candidates for mayor and twelve candidates for seats on the town council announced their withdrawal from the forthcoming October municipal elections; one of the candidates was quoted as saying "I received a message from the FARC saying I could not continue as a candidate. So I withdrew." In Gachalá, Cundinamarca Department, a community that on 3 August was briefly occupied in its entirety by some 250 FARC members, the last of the candidates for the mayoralty withdrew his name. At the last count, with the deadline for nominations having expired and elections due on 26 October, there were no candidates for mayor in fifty-eight of Colombia's one thousand municipalities.

Manuel Marulanda Vélez, FARC supreme commander, issued a statement saying that the FARC is looking for a "political way out from the social conflict" but insisted that the FARC would do all it could to destabilize the electoral cycle that begins in October. He said that "to speak of elections and democracy in the midst of state terror, paramilitarism, and special order zones is a contradiction in terms, a ploy to impose a neoliberal regime on political opponents such as the guerrillas." In an interview that also ran Friday, the locally based UN Human Rights Commissioner described Colombia as "feudal, Latin America's Bosnia."

Three years later, at the end of my assignment, I was in most ways equally pessimistic, but I had meanwhile become deeply attached to this beautiful, yet profoundly tragic, land. This account – of the saddest country – seeks to explain why Colombia deserves not just our horror but our sympathy.

1 Blood Canyon

Barrancabermeja

MAY 1999. IT'S 5:30 AM, and I'm waiting in the grey light of dawn on a Bucaramanga sidewalk, overnight bag at my feet. I'm not sure if El Zapato, the taxi driver with whom I met last night to negotiate a ride to Barrancabermeja, will turn up. He had been hesitant. "*Está delicadito*" – a little delicate – he'd said when we'd discussed the chances of getting held up on the two-hour trip: "*Mucha guerrilla, mucho paraco, mucha delincuencia* ..." But I'm paying him over the odds – nearly fifty dollars – and in five minutes, sure enough, here he is. Soon we are barrelling off through the empty streets, through the still sleeping suburbs and down through the rolling green hills that make up the foothills of the Eastern Cordillera of the Andes. After a couple of hours we're out of the mountains and into lush, flat country: the flood plains of the Magdalena. Even at this early hour I need the window fully open; it must be thirty-five degrees outside. We slow down when an Army patrol flags us down, but, after peering in briefly, they wave us on; El Zapato, visibly relieved, starts whistling quietly, and soon we're coming into Barrancabermeja.

The name of the town means "Red Canyon," after some low sandy cliffs on the Magdalena, but it might as well be Blood Canyon. In this, one of the two or three most violent countries in the world, Barrancabermeja (Barranca for short) is the most violent city by far, one whose name makes even the most inured of Colombians recoil at its mention.

Barranca's not in the least scenic: the only sights are the lights of the city's huge oil refinery at night, a bizarre Christ figure of wrought iron that, rising out of a lagoon by the refinery, spouts water from its fingertips, and the Conradian waterfront where passenger launches buzz in and out every few minutes, bound for Puerto Boyacá upriver or Puerto Wilches and San Pablo downriver. The climate is unrelentingly hot, windless, and sweaty, and I've never known the slightest breeze to waft up from the kilometre-wide muddy Magdalena.

But it's not the sights of Barranca that have brought me here five times in less than two years: as Political Counsellor at the Canadian Embassy in Bogotá, it's my job to understand and report on the politics of Colombia, the violence that wracks the country and the systemic abuses of human rights by all the "actors" (a uniquely Colombian euphemism that includes guerrillas, right-wing paramilitaries, and the legally constituted armed forces) in "the conflict" (another euphemism for what elsewhere would be known forthrightly as a war). There's no better place to start understanding than Barranca.

Flashback eighteen months, to October 1997. I'd been in the country only a couple of months. As they do everywhere (but usually without following their own advice) government figures and my colleagues on the Bogotá diplomatic circuit had insisted that I needed to get away from the capital to really understand what was going on in the country. "Colombia's a land of city states," the Colombian Ambassador had told me in Ottawa shortly before my departure. "Bogotá, Cali, Medellín, they are oases of civilization ... but the rest of the country is savage, untamed: the Barbarians at the Gates. You have to get out ..."

Later, I realized that when he said "You have to get out," he wasn't really encouraging me to visit rural Colombia: he meant get out to Miami, Cancún, even provincial but peaceful Quito. But now I rifled through the in-tray in my office at the embassy and fished out a standing invitation to visit Barranca, as a guest of Peace Brigades International (PBI). As good a place as any to start, I thought.

PBI is an international non-governmental organization (NGO) uniquely suited to the special needs of Colombia. Staffed by young volunteers from Europe and North America who serve usually for no more than one year, its mandate is simple: the volunteers provide "accompaniment" to human rights activists whose lives may be in danger, acting in effect as human shields. This means that they attend meetings of the national NGOs, accompany nationals when they travel to particularly risky areas, and, on occasion, sleep at the homes of their national counterparts. The theory is that individuals or groups who may have designs on the lives of the nationals they are accompanying will be deterred by the very presence of the international volunteers. To a point, this seems to work in the Colombian context, although PBI in turn very much appreciate periodic visits from diplomats and other foreigners as protection and as a public, visible validation of its work; hence my being invited.

Tomás, Paco (both from Spain), and Tessa (from the UK) met me at the airport and introduced me to our driver, a young man called Elkin. "*Es de confianza*," they explained, "he can be trusted." On cue, Elkin grinned broadly. He warned me not to trust any of the ordinary taxi drivers in the city: "You never know; most of them get paid for information from one side or the other ..."

As we drew up to PBI's one-storey house in a quiet suburb, I pointed out a small truck parked half a block away. Spray-painted all over its side, in red paint, was the slogan "We are Revolution – ELN." A common practice, explained Tessa. Vehicles that move through the guerrilla-dominated eastern barrios of the city are routinely pulled over by rebel ELN militia members and subject to spray painting. "It's a kind of forced advertising. The driver daren't erase the graffiti, and for weeks he must drive around the city advertising the ELN ..."

Barranca is a strategic city and always has been. With a population of nearly 300,000 it is, without being a provincial capital, the de facto capital of a large region in the heart of the country known as the Magdalena Medio, or Middle Magdalena. Since the time of the Conquest the river has been the easiest way of moving goods inland from the Caribbean ports of Cartagena and Barranquilla; Barranca grew up as a transshipment point; from here goods were offloaded from ships and onto land transport that either went southwest to Medellín, southeast to Bogotá, or east to Bucaramanga. More recently, the city's importance further grew with the construction of the country's largest oil

Mobile ELN graffiti, Barrancabermeja

refinery: several pipelines converge here. Up in the hills to the north, meanwhile, there are rich but only partially tapped gold deposits and large plots of the green gold that Colombia has begun to grow only over the last decade or so: coca.

It is common wisdom that guerrilla movements typically thrive on social discontent and that, therefore, they are typically found in the most benighted parts of the country. This may once have held true in Colombia, but the picture is no longer so simple: both the fifteen-thousand-strong Revolutionary Armed Forces of Colombia (FARC) and the smaller National Liberation Army (ELN) are strong not just where there is a restless proletariat but where there are sources of wealth which they can tap for their own profit: legal or illegal, oil or coca.

This is not to say both groups completely lack ideology. The ELN, for example, which has its roots partly in the Catholic Church and Liberation Theology and partly in classic Marxist doctrine, now kidnaps and kills with a most un-Christian zeal, but it has at least been ideologically consistent over the years on the question of the exploitation of natural resources, especially oil. In a word, the ELN is all for state control over oil exploration, extraction, and shipping.

The ELN finds in the Barranca region (and in the oil fields of Casanare and Arauca – two of its other strongholds) an industry to extort lucratively, pipelines to bomb in the name of anti-imperialism, and, in the powerful national oil workers' union (USO), a natural and broad base of support; USO is also strongly opposed to foreign participation in the industry. ELN units effectively dominate much of the countryside around here; their urban equivalents, known as militias, rule over at least half of Barranca, that is to say the eastern quarters where many of the refinery workers live.

For the past three years, some seventeen USO members had been jailed on charges of having conspired with the ELN so as to blow up pipelines (and then win the repair contracts for their own line gangs ...) and while USO President Hernando Hernández had earned himself a reputation as a tough but clean union boss, Hernández's brother, who also grew up in the oil industry, was a self-avowed senior ELN commander. It was difficult to escape the conclusion that there might be some truth to persistent allegations of USO-ELN links.

It was to the eastern barrios, a no-go area for the authorities, that PBI took me on that first morning, back in 1997. Sitting under a large thatched shelter in the grounds of a Franciscan mission we listened to the parish priest describe daily life in the barrio, while a huddle of townsfolk sat silently, occasionally nodding. You had to listen very carefully to understand what he was saying, not because his Spanish was difficult or his voice was low but because there was so much unspoken that you were expected to understand – things no-one would talk about openly.

What no-one would say was that ELN ruled this half of the city. Their slogans were everywhere – not graffiti, but professionally painted signs. They administered local justice – of a rough but effective kind: killings or kneecappings. There were a few small enclaves of Army and police here, protected with sandbags, anti-mortar nets and barbed wire, but neither force ventured out onto the streets except in their armoured personnel carriers.

But it was not the ELN rule that the local people were worried about – they had become used to them over the past twenty years and had learned to live with them. You cooperated or moved out. What they wanted to talk to me about, rather, was Army brutality, the "paras" (or "paracos"), and the Army's collusion with the latter.

The paras (paramilitaries) were not a new phenomenon in Colombia. They had their roots in the gangs set up by Pablo Escobar and other narco capos to provide protection for the drug industry and, a little more legitimately, in rural "self-defence" groups ("Autodefensas") established by landowners to protect their holdings from guerrilla depredations. In that the paras' enemy were the guerrillas (who competed with them for protection contracts from narcos and who stole cattle and land from their paymasters), they often enjoyed the tacit – and sometimes active – support of the Armed Forces.

It was para incursions into the traditional ELN stronghold of Barranca that had in the past few years dramatically ratcheted up the temperature in the city. Enjoying secret but growing public sympathy among the middle and upper classes, they had repeatedly made raids into the poorer eastern barrios like the one in which we now sat, dragging suspected ELN sympathizers from their homes, often shooting them on the spot or taking them away to a more grisly death. The paras, it seemed, deliberately tried to outdo the guerrillas in terms of horror: where the ELN kneecapped and shot in the back of the head, the paras slit throats and decapitated.

Often, the priest told us, the para raids were preceded by Army and police sweeps through the city blocks in question: a kind of softening up, it looked like. When the raid was under way, the Army and police were nowhere to be found and the paras were able to leave in complete impunity.

Today, the local people wanted to tell me about two particular incidents. In the first, heavily armed police equipped with warrants had arrived in the barrio and searched some ten or twelve homes. Only hours later, paras had come in and, apparently working from lists, had "hit" exactly the same homes, carrying three young men away with them. The collusion seemed obvious. In another apparently unrelated incident that took place in marshy open land close to where we sat, the Army had launched an operation aimed at rescuing a businessman whom the ELN had allegedly kidnapped and were holding in an abandoned farmhouse. The operation had freed the businessman concerned, but in the shootout a young child and a simple-minded deaf mute had inexplicably been killed: "How could they have been ELN members?" I was asked rhetorically.

At the end of our meeting, a barefoot twenty-five-year-old woman who had sat silently and expressionless throughout came and shook my hand. She was the mother of the little girl who had been shot dead only twenty-four hours before.

Back in town, in a set of hot first-floor offices overlooking the busy main street, I met with Osiris and Régulo, who jointly ran – on a shoestring – a non-governmental organization dedicated to the denunciation of human rights abuses in the region: CREDHOS, the Regional Council for the Defence of Human Rights. Both lived on the edge. Two years back, Osiris was receiving so many death threats that she had to flee to Spain for six months, "so as to let things cool down," as she said. Whom did these threats typically come from? She smiled at the innocence of my question. Usually they were anonymous, she said, but she had no doubt that they originated at police or Army headquarters or with the paras. "They think we're with the guerrillas ..."

Sometimes, the threats were quite cleverly managed. A few months after my first visit, I was horrified to read that the ELN had issued a press release announcing that Osiris had been awarded the ELN's highest military decoration, a de facto death sentence in polarized Barranca. I met Osiris in Bogotá on her way out of the country again. She showed me the ELN communiqué and a quite unconnected fax she had received about the same time from Barranca Army HQ: both showed the same originating fax number. It was a set-up. She's still out of the country.

Over at the Army base, where the Heroes of Majagual battalion was based, they had – not unexpectedly – a different slant on matters. The Colonel commanding insisted that, while he respected the right of CREDHOS to function and to denounce human rights abuses, the organization simply never denounced guerrilla atrocities. What about the para incursions into the barrios, couldn't the Army take action to stop them, or at least react to them? He smiled. "You've seen what it's like up there. Last time I sent a foot patrol in, two of my men were shot dead, in the back ..." And the botched kidnap rescue attempt? Yes, the deaths were regrettable. But even more regrettable was the ELN's having resorted to using innocent children and a deaf-mute as human shields.

In between more rounds – with the police commander, the mayor, members of USO's Human Rights Committee, and the chubby and worldly priest who runs the Jesuit Refugee Service – I spent a good amount of time drinking cold beer at the PBI house. I was impressed by the maturity, the professionalism, and the physical bravery of these young people. Not once did they seek to influence me by telling me "how it really is"; at every meeting they sat quietly and took notes, and it was evident by the way they were greeted that they commanded the respect of all players in this violent, conflictive context so different from the realities of the volunteers' home countries.

The last morning of my first visit to Barranca was doubly memorable. First, the PBI cat died, audibly, under Tessa's bed. This cast a pall over things, but we still went out for a farewell lunch, at a fish restaurant near the port.

The restaurant consisted of a few plastic tables under a corrugated tin roof in someone's backyard. It was 1:00 PM, the sun was beating down on the roof, but electric fans moved a little air around. We all ordered bagre, the Magdalena catfish.

As we waited for our lunch to arrive, I was introduced to a grizzled old man seated at the next table; he was well into his sixth or seventh Aguila beer. I forget his name now, but as I stood up and moved over to shake his hand, I realized he had lost both legs. Tomás explained to me quietly in English that he used to be a leading light in the Unión Patriótica (UP), the legal left-wing party that had formed as an offshoot of the rebel FARC some ten or twelve years back. But one day his small bar had been bombed, his wife killed, and his legs blown off. It was part of the unofficial nationwide campaign that saw at least three thousand UP members killed, maimed, or frightened out of politics in the space of a few years. This old fellow had been lucky: workmates and USO had clubbed together to send him to Cuba for surgery and rehabilitation. He'd survived other attempts on his life since and was still active in local politics, but, as Tomás said, "his story isn't exactly an incentive to the guerrillas to give up their weapons and go straight."

The fans started to slow down and soon creaked to a halt: there had been a power cut. Within a few minutes the place really felt like an oven. With sweat dripping onto our plates, we finished up as soon as we could and made ready to go. As I walked out, wiping my forehead with a paper towel, the old man pointed at the lapel of my short-sleeved shirt and asked me politely if I would give him my little maple-leaf pin as a souvenir of our meeting. As if apologizing, he said, "*Canadá es un gran amigo de Cuba, no?*"

16 May 1998. One morning a few months after my first visit to Barranca, the Bogotá newspapers confirmed the dramatic news I'd seen on last night's CM& 9:30 news program: paramilitaries had swept into

those eastern suburbs of Barranca, lists in hand, and had executed seven persons on the spot, carrying away a further twenty-five. The worst was feared.

Over the next few days, more and more details emerged. What was particularly shocking – and inexplicable – was how the paras had entered the barrio by driving right past a manned military checkpoint; the seven people they had killed had died in a clear line of sight of another military post and then the paras had to pass right by the first checkpoint again to make their getaway. Interviewed on TV, the regional Army commander had said that he only became aware of the massacre when watching TV in the officers' club next morning.

Canada issued press communiqués condemning the killings, one in Ottawa over the Foreign Minister's signature, another from the embassy in Bogotá. Other embassies followed suit, and the USA State Department spoke out strongly, calling for those responsible to be apprehended immediately. I received belated but forceful instructions to make an immediate verbal démarche at the highest possible level.

After many delays, some a natural result of cumbersome European Union bureaucracy, some placed in our path by a nervous Colombian Foreign Ministry, I was chosen to represent Canada on a five-nation, one-day "fact-finding" mission to Barranca. The point, in reality, was not to find out anything new – we knew that this would be most unlikely – but, by descending en masse and at the highest level possible, at least to display some collective displeasure and concern.

As current president of the EU, the United Kingdom Embassy took it upon itself to coordinate the mission. Rather strangely, it seemed to me, my colleague Russell insisted that we charter a plane for the exercise, even though there were regular scheduled flights direct to Barranca and the charter would cost us double the price of a normal ticket.

As we rolled to a halt at Barranca airport one morning some three weeks after the massacre, I realized why we had not flown commercial. Before any of us could even stand up in the cramped cabin of the ten-seater prop plane, the two anonymous-looking crewcut types in the back seats had leapt up, were already down the ramp, and were standing at either side of the exit, Rambo-style, light machine guns at the ready. The British Ambassador, for one, was taking no chances.

Nor was the Army. Although our ever-faithful friends from Peace Brigades had come out to meet us and had a small flotilla of *taxistas de confianza* waiting for us, we barely had time to wave to them before we had been bundled into a grey Bell 212 helicopter parked only a few metres away, rotors already turning. Buckled in but with the doors open we lurched up and away and, amid lame and shouted jokes about *Apocalypse Now*, were immediately en route to the city's main Army base, located in the heart of the refinery. We learned later that only two days ago the departmental governor had survived a landmine attack on the road one kilometre from the airport, but I suspect the Army would have laid this on anyway, partly out of genuine concern at losing five senior diplomats, no doubt, but partly to impress us with the gravity of the challenges the police and Army face in their everyday lives in Barranca.

Escorted throughout by phalanxes of heavily armed troops, we were hustled in armoured vehicles from place to place, meeting with the Army, the police, the mayor. A promised meeting with the victims of the dead and disappeared did not materialize. I was not surprised: they would have almost certainly been intimidated by the sheer amount of military hardware on display. A visit to the scene of the crime, as well, was clearly out of the question in such company as this and with all of the city's media trailing behind us.

In the days and weeks following, there were some further developments in the case of what had come to be known in the country as the Barranca Massacre, but few of them were good news. The locally dominant paramilitary group, the United Self-Defence Groups of Southern César, brazenly took responsibility for the seven shootings and added that the remaining twenty-five who had been carried off had been "tried" and executed, their bodies burned. The justification? All those killed, the paras affirmed, were either active ELN members or close collaborators with the guerrillas.

An Army Corporal by the name of Pérez was arrested for "crimes of omission" (i.e., having let the paras through), but the charges didn't stick and after six months he was out again. The Human Rights Unit of the Fiscalía (Attorney General's Office) launched an investigation, but its investigations slowed, then came to halt when the young female judge charged with the case began to receive death threats and sought political asylum in a friendly Western country.

My involvement was still not over. A coalition of local and international non-governmental organizations decided to take up the Barranca

Massacre as an emblematic cause. Why Barranca when there were no less than two hundred massacres in Colombia in 1998 (a massacre being defined, in Colombian terminology, as the killing of four or more persons at one time and in one place)? In part because of the dimensions and bloodthirstiness of this particular episode, but also in part because it seemed to be a particularly striking example of what, beyond the violence itself, is the single greatest ill in Colombia: impunity for crimes of all kinds, especially where it looks as though there may be state complicity of some sort. A call went out in the NGO world – via the internet, press releases, and public meetings – for the international community to mobilize and organize a set of "Tribunals of Opinion" on the Barranca massacre, to culminate in one grand tribunal to be held in Barranca itself on the first anniversary of the massacre.

Canadian NGOs rose to the occasion and organized two such tribunals, one in Toronto, one in Montreal. The idea, as the organizers explained, was to simulate as much as possible a real trial, but without actually seeking to supplant the Colombian justice system (such as it is). Bertrand Russell, it was explained to me, had founded the original such tribunal, in the dying years of the Vietnam War, the subject being the alleged abuses perpetrated by American troops and their government. It was the final Barranca tribunal, in the wake of the two Canadian tribunals, that drew me back to the city on 14 May 1999.

My driver, El Zapato, dropped me at the city's principal – and surprisingly luxurious – hotel: El Pipatón, on the banks of the Magdalena a few hundred metres upstream from the refinery. Checking in, I found myself in line behind Father Gabriel, a Jesuit priest and old friend from Bogotá who had flown up for the tribunal as well.

I couldn't help but hear him confirm that his room rate was about CDN$50, when I had been quoted what seemed to me to be a rather steep CDN$100. Once Gabriel was gone, I discreetly asked the clerk why this was so. "Oh. You'd like the discount, then?" she smiled. "Yes please. How much is it?" "50 percent, of course ..."

The tribunal was to take place at the city's other large hotel, the Bachué. In spite of the fact that the prospect of the tribunal had drawn the public ire of the country's military, of a host of conservative media columnists, and of the Foreign Ministry itself (all of whom dubbed it "unjustified interference in the internal affairs of the country"), the Army had not stinted on security for the event. For a block all around, the streets had been sealed off to vehicular traffic, there were soldiers on the rooftops, and everyone entering the hotel was subject to a careful body search. Participants from the Canadian tribunals who had come to observe the Colombian version were rather intimidated by this and were quoted on the front pages of national newspapers at home as being "afraid of the little green men" who seemed to be everywhere – failing, it seemed, to understand that they were ostensibly there for the visitors' protection.

As a trial, this tribunal left much to be desired. The eight-person international panel, none of whose members were experts on Colombia in any way, were inclined from the beginning to take the prosecution's word as gospel – and, indeed, there was no defence to put them right (who in their right mind would have tried to "defend" this case?). The tribunal president was a bizarre-looking hunchbacked Italian man in his seventies, with long grey hair to his shoulders, whose principal qualification as a judge (according to his official profile) was being "A Founding Member of the People's World Tribunal," whatever that is. Other members included two Spanish priests, a German member of an international development NGO, and a Canadian Franciscan Friar.

The top-floor conference room of the Bachué was jammed. Two hundred people sat in white plastic lawn chairs, while another two hundred sat in the aisles, stood at the back, or followed proceedings on a closed-circuit television in an adjoining room. The air conditioning did not work, and the only fan was monopolized by the two translators who sweated in a glass booth at the back. Throughout the crowded room circulated relatives of the dead and disappeared, distinguished by their white T-shirts with messages such as "Looking for my husband" or "Looking for my son." With only one exception, all were women: of the thirty-two dead and disappeared, thirty-one were men.

One by one, seven eye-witnesses, seated behind a screen that allowed them to be visible to the tribunal members but not to the public or to the TV cameras, gave their evidence. It was indeed damning insofar as state collusion was concerned. One spoke of having seen the paras' vehicles, several days before the massacre, parked at the local DAS (intelligence police) HQ. Two more said that there were men in black DAS waistcoats at the massacre scene itself. All described how their efforts to seek Army and police help in the minutes and hours following the massacre had been rebuffed, even mocked.

At one point, a special frisson went through the audience. One of the more perceptive judges was probing one of the witnesses as to the general ambience of the barrio in which she lived. "Yes," she said. "The ELN care for us, they look after us. They are our friends." There was a long silence; many in the audience looked at each other. I remembered my first day in Barranca, eighteen months previously: these things are known and understood, but it is dangerous to say them. The fact that the victims may indeed have been ELN sympathizers, even members, was of course hardly an excuse for the murders, but it seemed to me a very important piece of the complicated jigsaw that I had to put together to understand Barranca and, by extension, Colombia.

On the second morning, crammed into two small city buses, we took a macabre tour of the scene of the crime. One of the critical locations was a road junction known as "The Y." Here, on the night of the killings, there had been a military roadblock right by the side of the road, and yet the paras had passed without being stopped.

As we stood by the side of the road, with one of the relatives pointing out where the trucks had come from, where they went, and so on, a young Army corporal strolled up to one of our group and whispered a few words in his ear. "Let's sit down and have a beer," he said, turning to us. "We're going to have to wait a bit." Why? it transpired that landmines had been found in the bed of each branch of the "Y" ahead of us and the Army was about to detonate them. We were not to be alarmed when we heard two bangs ... and, indeed, no-one was.

Our visit was a moving one. The whole community was waiting for us. At one place, in the middle of the road, a middle-aged woman was patiently holding up a powerful, modern motorbike, evidently waiting for us. This, she explained, was where her son and his friend, who had been riding pillion, were stopped and pulled off their bike. With no sense of melodrama, but with a loud clatter, she let the bike fall. We stood in silence. She led us over to the sidewalk. This, she said with no apparent emotion, was where they died. "And there," she said while pointing to a building behind us, clearly visible across seventy metres of wasteland, "is the Army base."

In a re-creation of the crime organized by staff of the Procurator General's Office, we were told, soldiers had responded within ninety seconds to the sound of a single test shot loosed off here. But on that night several rounds of machine-gun fire had been completely ignored.

The verdict of the tribunal, unsurprisingly, was a ringing condemnation of the Colombian state for "crimes of omission and commission," both at the time of the massacre and in the course of subsequent investigations. Was this a valid exercise? As a simulacrum of a trial, no. In that it drew much needed renewed attention to the Barranca massacre and to the impunity that reigns in Colombia, yes; and in that it signalled to the world that there are crimes being committed in Colombia that are of such magnitude and horror that they are of legitimate interest to the international community and that indeed those responsible might eventually be subject to trial in a war crimes court, yes.

But only a couple of weeks after the tribunal had handed down its verdict I was again given food for thought. It was reported in the news that FARC units had conducted a set of drive-by shootings in Barranca, leaving twelve dead in only half an hour. The FARC had taken full responsibility, claiming that the victims were paramilitaries who had been extorting the local population in the name of the rebels and that "justice had been done." Next morning, at my computer terminal, I waited in vain for NGO denunciations of this latest war crime to plop into my electronic in-tray.

2 Down the Magdalena River

Puerto Wilches, San Pablo, Simití, Santa Rosa

IN *THE TIGER'S OTHER STRIPE*, Colombian historical novelist Pedro Gómez Valderrama describes the turbulent life and times of German colonist Geo von Lengerke in Santander Department in the early nineteenth century. The story begins with the long, exotic journey by paddle steamer from the Caribbean port of Barranquilla up the Magdalena to the first rapids at Honda, where the hero disembarks for Bogotá:

> It was still known then as the Río Grande de la Magdalena, as wide as death, the river of giant catfish and of turtles, of ferrymen and caymans, of straw huts from which half-naked people waved at the paddle-steamer while a plume of smoke rose into the desperately blue sky ...

Then, it would take ten days from the sea to Barrancabermeja, another four or five to Honda. There were frequent stops to cut and load firewood; the gentlemen would take advantage of the pauses to go hunting for tigres (jaguars) or would pass the time taking potshots at the caymans lying on the sandbanks.

As late as the early 1970s, cargo paddle steamers still plied the Lower Magdalena. Now most of the traffic consists of oil barges going laden downstream from Barranca then returning empty, small Navy gunboats on stretches of the river disputed by paras and guerrillas, and high-speed twenty-seater launches known as voladoras (flyers) plying between river towns. A few quite large ocean-going cargo ships use the artificial canal that has been dug between Cartagena and Barranquilla, but the main river is now too silted for them to venture far upstream.

At the voladora quay, on the Barranca waterfront, the scene is always a colourful one: twenty or thirty of the covered launches tied nose-to at the steps, their regular destinations – San Pablo, Puerto Wilches, Puerto Boyacá – painted on the side; young boys touting energetically for business, unfailingly promising departure within five minutes, while campesino families who have evidently been waiting an hour or more periodically move their possessions and livestock from one boat to another as they try to determine which launch is in fact about to leave. A row of stalls serves coffee, arepas, and that incomprehensible staple of the Colombian breakfast, *cuchuco de espinazo* (pig-spine soup).

One way or another, I've taken several voladora trips downstream from Barranca. My first, like most, saw me up at dawn: that way you avoided the worst of the heat on the river.

Only a few minutes out, just past the huge refinery on the east bank, we had to make our first stop: an obligatory check of papers at the small naval base that adjoined the refinery's northern edge. It was everybody off, a search of bags, and then a body search. Sometimes on these occasions, for form's sake, I protested – diplomats going about the course of their duties in the country of their accreditation are supposedly immune to such searches – but usually it seemed too much trouble. After a few moments of incomprehension, the young recruit would feel obliged to summon his superior, who must then get on the phone ... and so on. The delay wasn't worth it.

Sweeping out into the middle of the wide river as the sun came up, so as to gain maximum benefit from the current, we soon reached our top speed: an exhilarating thirty knots or so. Occasionally, the motorista would swerve to avoid some hidden sandbank. On either side, the banks were low and lush, with sugarcane growing right to the water's edge. Once or twice, a little back from the banks, I saw sets of "donkeys" – those small beam-engine oil pumps that are also part of the landscape

Stranded on a sandbank: the voladora to San Pablo

in Southern California or Alberta. Here they are known phonetically as "matcheenies." Only when I saw the word written did I realize that this was a Hispanized version of "machines"; the first oilmen hereabouts were English-speaking and much of their vocabulary lives on.

Thirty minutes downstream, we made a brief stop to pick up passengers at the waterfront of Cantagallo (Cock-crow). A large hoarding behind the floating wharf proclaimed Cantagallo as a "Haven of Peace" – an optimistic view of things and, I later learned, code for "In the hands of the paramilitaries." Another half-hour later, and we pulled up to the concrete-stepped waterfront of Puerto Wilches, on the east bank.

Wilches is a small town of one-storey whitewashed concrete buildings and mud tracks that become more well-trodden but muddier the closer they come to the water and fade away into sugar and palm plantations behind the town. It's reputed to be one of the hottest places in Colombia, with daytime temperatures regularly reaching 43°C in the shade.

It was local election time, and the people and politicians of Wilches were in a peculiarly difficult and Colombian bind. To begin with, most of the management team of the only significant industrial enterprise in the town – the palm-oil factory – had been kidnapped by the FARC for reasons that were still unclear. There were conflicting versions as to whether a ransom had been demanded or whether the rebels were just demanding better wages and working conditions for the field labourers. The factory had meanwhile closed down.

It was the main candidate for mayor whose story I found most interesting. He met me in his blessedly air-conditioned office (the only such place in town) and, after offering me coffee and a glass of cold water, explained his plight. The guerrillas (and this was a zone of FARC influence) were calling upon voters, as they were in much of the country, to boycott the municipal elections. All candidates for office had in fact been threatened with death should they stand, and even the town teachers and others charged with administering the election had been warned to stay away on election morning.

This was only half the story. As well as receiving a clear message from the guerrillas, the prospective mayor had received a quite contrary message from the local paramilitary commander, Camilo, warning him that if he did indeed cave to guerrilla threats and decline to stand, then the paras would "account for him." What did he intend to do, I asked? He shrugged and wrung his hands. His first plan had been to sell up his small farm and leave the area completely. Unsurprisingly given the local situation, he had found no buyers. Plan B was to stand for election but to try simultaneously to do some kind of deal with the guerrillas, without letting the paras know.

This seemed to me a risky strategy, and indeed, months later, I learned that the mayor (who had been elected unopposed, with about 5 percent of the eligible voters turning out) was in a bind again. He had been kidnapped by the FARC and held to ransom, but his wife had bravely offered to take his place while he was set free to raise the ransom money. But the real-estate market was no better now than it had been when I had first met him. The mayor was almost at his wits' end and even appeared on national TV to plead for help in raising the US $100,000 required. His appeal was featured at the end of the "Believe It or Not" section of the news. As far as I know, he never raised the money.

I paid a visit on the local police commander. The news here was also election related. The previous evening, the police had received an anonymous phone call tipping them off that there was a bomb in the main square. They had responded and had very cautiously opened a package they found in the place described. It turned out to contain a

At the police station, Puerto Wilches

cassette tape with a demand that the tape be played a certain number of times in the days ahead on the community radio station; failing this, the next package would indeed be explosive.

The police commander played the tape to me on his cassette recorder. It was FARC propaganda, but in the form of a set of raucous and sometimes amusing Vallenato songs, accompanied by accordion and guitar. The commander thought he would probably play the cassette as requested.

The next town downstream from Wilches is San Pablo, on the west bank and at the southeastern end of the San Lucas mountains. San Pablo was at first sight strangely prosperous for a river town that was not a port and whose only road led to an even smaller river town, Simití, then ended. The place positively bustled: Vallenato music blared out all hours, every day of the week from the bars that lined the main street, teenagers rode up and down on expensive motorbikes, and here and there were parked four-wheel-drive pickups that went for US $50,000 in Bogotá. The town's one hotel was full.

Then I started to notice what seemed to be an abnormal number of establishments selling gasoline, while in the windows of many houses were little handwritten signs saying "*Hay éter*" (We have ether). Another shop sold nothing but microwave ovens and had dozens in stock. The business that kept San Pablo alive was coca, grown and processed in small plots in the hinterland behind the town: gas, ether, and microwaves are all key to the refining of cocaine.

I went to San Pablo several times over the three years I was in Colombia and came to know the town well, but my most memorable visit was in June 1998, nearly a year after my earlier trip to Wilches. The local and national news were full of the massive displacement of campesinos provoked by paramilitary killings and threats in Southern Bolívar Department, and the first wave of several thousand displaced had several days previously reached San Pablo.

Under the coordination of the United Nations High Commission for Refugees, a small multi-agency team comprising other UN agencies, local and international NGOs, and two embassies (Switzerland and Canada) was assembled to take a quick look at the phenomenon and make recommendations as to appropriate responses, both by the national government and the international community. In our own chartered voladora from Barranca, we arrived at San Pablo at midmorning – to be met by a huge, banner-waving, and singing crowd that jammed the waterside steps and threatened to spill down into the water. Directed and escorted by megaphone-bearing ushers we were taken down the main street (lined with more banners and crowds on the sidewalk) to the main plaza, where a large stage and sound system awaited us. The crowds swayed to a Spanish version of "We Shall Overcome," occasionally interrupted by rhythmic shouts of "*El pueblo, unido, jamás será vencido*" (The people, united, will never be defeated). It seemed that there might be more to this displacement than met the eye – things just didn't look right, these people were too organized and too disciplined for a mass of humanity that had supposedly fled in fear and chaos from aggressive paras only two days previously.

The welcoming committee, San Pablo

Over the next thirty-six hours we met with community leaders throughout the town, in the many diverse locations where the five thousand to six thousand refugees were holed up – in the school, in the churchyard, under tarpaulins strung between trees in the main square, and (memorably) in the cockfighting stables where, every thirty seconds or so, we would have to wait while the permanent residents worked through a deafening collective crow. The stories of the displaced were consistent: they described in detail how the paras had made various incursions into their rural communities, threatening one here, evicting another there, and killing at least two persons. But what didn't hang together was that, in the Colombian context, a mere two killings would not normally account for a displacement of this size.

I remembered my first visit to San Pablo, when campesino leaders had listed to me a whole host of grievances that they had a few months previously presented to the government as part of a wave of social protests and marches (*Marchas campesinas*) across the country. At the heart of these grievances was a demand that the authorities not go ahead with their threatened campaign of massive aerial fumigation of

Displaced persons in the town square, San Pablo

coca fields, or at least that small farmers and landowners be given some means of alternative subsistence before the fumigation began.

The same demands, coupled with others relating to the paramilitary presence, were now being put forward again by the same campesino leaders. It seemed to me and to others on the delegation that this might be more protest march than displacement.

Strangely, there were few women and children among the displaced – it was ingenuously explained to us that they had been left behind to keep an eye on the fields and on the houses. For a two-day-old displacement, the whole affair was remarkably organized, with people arriving not on foot but in convoys of trucks, to be met by representatives of the health committee, the resettlement committee, and so on. The displaced had elected their own Central Committee, who took it upon itself to organize (and shadow) all our meetings.

Who was behind it and why? It had to be the guerrillas, tapping into the genuinely felt grievances of the rural population so as to step up pressure on the always faltering but now moribund Samper administration (due to leave office within days) and, hopefully, to bring the weight

The police station, San Pablo

of the state down on the guerrillas' biggest enemy in Southern Bolívar: the resurgent paramilitaries. None of this lessened in any way the real misery and fear of the thousands who had been displaced to San Pablo: they were indeed desperately afraid, but as much of the FARC as of the paras. While some of their leaders were no doubt FARC sympathizers, I am sure that most had simply been coerced and manipulated into making this march.

We visited the police station. San Pablo had over the past few years been taken by the FARC or ELN several times, and the police HQ was a fortress, a vision out of *Mad Max* with anti-rocket and anti-mortar nets festooned all over it and sandbagged emplacements on the roof. But a bright white banner happily proclaimed "*Cambiamos para servir a la gente!*" (We're changing to serve the people!).

The police detachment was commanded by a lieutenant who can have been at most twenty-one years old, and all the dozen or so of his men were younger. They had one Israeli-made Galil rifle apiece, each equipped with a grenade launcher, and there were two light machine guns mounted on the roof. In the daytime, they would patrol the town in groups of two or three, as fully prepared as two or three people can be against a possible guerrilla attack of several hundred, but at night they all holed up in the police HQ. They had no motor vehicle at their disposal. Although the Army base at Barranca had a couple of Hueys in service, the nearest offensively capable aircraft on which they could call (if their radio worked – the batteries were flat today) was at Yopal, approximately 300 km away.

The men were watching a soccer game on television, rifles propped up against the back of their plastic bar chairs; one was doing his washing in a sink in the corner. The lieutenant was polite, fatalistic. They had no orders to assist the displaced he said, and, in any case, what could he do? Yes, this was indeed a march, not a "real" displacement. The thing was, he said, that the people here had been living with the guerrillas for twenty or thirty years. They didn't necessarily like them, but the guerrillas did administer rough justice and you had to learn to get on with them if you wanted to survive. So when the FARC suggested it was time for a march, you obeyed.

And what about the paras? Did the police take them on? "Well of course," said the lieutenant, but he was starting to look a little shifty. Wasn't it hard to do that, I suggested, when the paras were themselves fighting the guerrillas, apparently with some success? "Yes, I suppose so ..." he finally answered, hesitantly.

Following our visit, the displaced in San Pablo reached a critical mass of ten thousand or so, then moved on upstream, in a huge flotilla of voladoras, to Barranca. There they remained in conditions of growing squalor for some weeks, while their leaders negotiated with government authorities a wide-ranging accord by which the government pledged again to postpone fumigation, promised massive social investment, and said formally it would clamp down on paramilitary activities in the region. Finally, the displaced returned home on great flat-bottomed barges.

By the end of my posting, San Pablo remained on the edge of a complicated social and military dynamic that had it coming first under para influence, then FARC or ELN; it would be only a matter of time before the next march descended on the town, for the government's promises were always too lavish ever to be kept. The police were still beleaguered in their fortress but periodically featured on the national news because San Pablo was always the bridgehead where government authorities came so as to try to negotiate something (e.g., the freeing of kidnap hostages) with the rebels or the paras; the steps on the waterfront were a favourite location for breathless taped accounts by news reporters who had just emerged from guerrilla-held territory.

Still further north and in the very heart of the conflict are the neighbouring settlements of Cerro de Burgos and Simití, 40 km downriver again from San Pablo. With hindsight, I realize that it was only because our informal commission in mid-1998 enjoyed the de facto blessing of the guerrillas (in that it suited their agenda to have para atrocities in the region and the plight of the civil population highlighted) that we made it in and out of these settlements intact – the villages subsequently reverted to their more normal status of war zone.

The river narrows a little above Cerro de Burgos and on the left one can clearly make out the high blue-looking hills of the Serranía de San Lucas. White egrets took wing from the reeds as our launch roared past. Occasionally, we would pass a couple of young men stringing fishing nets from their dugout, but they rarely looked up. Unlike in Lengerke's day, there was not a cayman to be seen.

At the head of an inlet just off the Magdalena, Cerro de Burgos spills prettily down a hillside, its fifty or so houses grouped around one main concrete street. There were ten or a dozen combat-ready army troops hanging around the muddy expanse that comprises the waterfront here; they shook our hands politely and seemed unfazed by this motley group of Westerners disembarking at this remote place.

It was here that had occurred one of the incidents that led to the massive movement of people to San Pablo. Up a side street, we contemplated a blackened pile of rubble that a week ago had been the local health promoter's house. That evening, his widow told us, three voladoras had tied up just where ours was and about fifty black-hooded men had got out. They had calmly walked up the main street, their rifles in their hands, and had politely knocked at several doors, asking for the health promoter.

Ruins of the health promoter's house, Cerro de Burgos

Someone had shouted a warning to him. He had barricaded himself into his house, but the paras had simply blasted the wall down with a rocket launcher. His widow showed us, room by room, inch by inch, how her husband had gradually found himself forced to the back of the house. "And here," she said, pointing to the concrete floor at the back door, "is where he died." The corrugated iron interior walls of the house were riddled with twenty or more bullet holes.

In any moderately peaceful country, Simití might have been an up-market ecotourism location. It is located on a large and tranquil lagoon well off the muddy Magdalena, surrounded by low green hills. At dusk – which is when we arrived from Cerro de Burgos – the fishermen are out on the lake in their dugouts, fishing by line or casting their unique disk-shaped diaphanous nets over the mirror-like waters. You can hear the bullfrogs and the crickets and occasionally the deep growl of a howler monkey.

The large and solidly built town church is sixteenth century, a time when, interestingly, Simití was relatively more accessible than it is today. Why did they build a town here, on this quiet backwater of the Mag-

The international commission arrives at Simití

dalena, before even Bogotá was founded? Wherever you are in Latin America and you're faced with a similar puzzle, chances are it's the same answer: gold (or maybe silver). The reserves in the Serranía de San Lucas are reputedly the richest in Colombia and among the richest in South America. Ore yields, a mining union executive told me, were better than on the Witwatersrand. But there are no roads to speak of, the country is rugged, and – more to the point – all of that gold has for the last thirty or forty years been under the feet of the guerrillas.

Simití was in a state of some tension when we arrived. We met with the town council who informed us matter-of-factly that the paras were camped very close by, just by the "Y" junction, three kilometres out of town on the dirt track to Santa Rosa. Their commander went by the name of Popeye; if we wanted, the mayor could arrange a meeting. Just give him ten minutes or so ... We politely declined.

That night we slept in bunk accommodation at the CLEBER, the Church-sponsored social development and agricultural centre that was established here some twenty years previously under the guidance of French-born Padre Clemente. There was a dramatic thunderstorm in the night, with flashes of lightning, great rolls of thunder and a torrential downpour. Some of our commission's members were in such a tense state that they initially mistook the thunder for a rocket attack and had us all hiding under our bunks before we realized what was really going on.

On my own, I met next morning with Pacho Martínez, head of Colombia's principal mining union, Sintramineralco. Pacho had some rather alarming allegations to recount to me.

The gist was that, given the mineral wealth in the region and the currently very primitive level of resource exploitation (most of the gold "mining" here was semi-illegal panning and/or pressure hosing of likely looking cliffs), a number of foreign multinationals were starting to become interested. Fair enough, Pacho said; in fact the region could do with some investment in modern technology.

But the problem was that, first, they wanted to clear out all the small-time miners working here and, specifically, their homegrown association that was affiliated to Sintramineralco. In order to achieve this, Pacho suggested, they were paying the paras.

He spread out reams of paperwork in front of me, mainly license applications that he had dredged up from the public records offices. Some of the license applications – and he ran his finger over them – were in the name of firms registered on Canadian stock exchanges. As I had no means of proving or disproving Pacho's fundamental allegation – that multinationals were paying off the paras – I decided to look into what should be easier to prove or disprove: the real identity and ownership of the companies he named.

Back in Bogotá I found myself plunged into the complex and ever-shifting world of Canadian junior mining companies, where companies change their names as often as their executives change their clothes, and where one telephone number in Vancouver or Calgary may admit to be the seat of any one of a dozen or more companies. It's a world where company names are deceptive – where, for example, Southern Bolívar Gold and Gran Colombia Gold will admit to operating in Chile or Peru but laugh incredulously when you ask if by any chance they have any operations in Southern Bolívar or in Colombia in general. There's an Archangel Mining registered in Canada, another in Medellín – but the former, it seems, operates only in Siberia and has never been anywhere near South America. And then there's Corona Gold – are they out of California, Vancouver, Calgary, or Medellín, and do they own any stakes in Southern Bolívar? Constantly, I had to remind myself that I should not be surprised by the shell games that seemed to confront me at every turn – this was the industry, after all, that had spawned Bre-X, a scandal that even Pacho had heard of. Eventually I was able to satisfy myself that no Canadian-controlled company was active in Southern Bolívar, and I presented Pacho with the proof of this. An unintended effect of my investigations was that, a month after my visit to Simití, miners camped out for several weeks outside the USA Embassy in Bogotá, having originally planned to target our own mission.

After we talked, Pacho asked me to escort him back to the little airstrip at Santa Rosa, up in the mountains, whence he would take a light plane to Bucaramanga. I assented because I knew that, although we differed on this particular issue, he was – as a union leader – likely high on the local paras' hit list. Coming to meet me, he said, he had several times had to leave the jeep in which he was riding to make a long detour on foot, so as to avoid para roadblocks.

Would I mind sitting on the roof, he said? That way, I would be more visible to anyone planning to stop us (i.e., a deterrent) and, if the worst came to the worst, it was easier to jump off the roof and head for the bush rather than climb out from the inside of the jeep. A bizarre feature of the jeep still sticks in my mind: a broken rear window had been replaced with a large X-ray photograph of somebody's chest. On a red dirt road, we wound up into ever more lush and cool mountains for nearly two hours, holding on hard to the roof rack on particularly tight bends, getting down once or twice to push when we bogged down in ruts.

The Santa Rosa airstrip was on a flattened hill top a little out of town. Three soldiers sat under a grass shelter, swatting flies. They body-searched Pacho then sent him to sit at the far end of the shack. Ten minutes later the only other passenger arrived – a very fat, sweating man in an open-necked shirt and wearing a large straw hat. A toothpick hung from his mouth and every so often he deftly shifted it with his tongue

Riding the jeep to Santa Rosa; the author (left) on the roof with Pacho Martinez; Luis van Isschot of Peace Brigades in the foreground

from one side of his mouth to the other. Almost hidden under his overhanging belly were the mother-of-pearl handles of a pair of revolvers stuck into the top of his trousers.

When the soldiers gestured to the guns, he never took his eyes off Pacho, but laconically handed the weapons over to have the bullets emptied out of their chambers. The soldiers would later give them to the pilot.

The plane was a WWII-vintage Junkers, with a corrugated hull. I'd only ever seen one of these in war movies. Waving goodbye, Pacho climbed on first. At the last minute, just when I thought the plane was going to leave him behind, the fat man got up, winked at the soldiers, and climbed on too. I was quite relieved to bump into Pacho a few weeks later in Bogotá, safe and sound.

3 Old Colombia

Mompox, El Banco, Cartagena, and Old Providence

EVERY YEAR, FOR TWO WEEKS just before Holy Week, all of Colombia lives and breathes the Reinado de Cartagena, literally, the "Kingdom of Cartagena." But this is no religious rite or tradition from the days when Cartagena was the jewel in the Spanish Crown. It is the annual Miss Colombia contest. Contestants from all thirty-two of Colombia's departments (i.e., provinces) converge on the city, each outfitted lavishly with a wardrobe of twenty or so outfits and with a train of camp followers.

In 1998 the governor of Bolívar Department (of which Cartagena is the capital) announced to great media interest that, given the state of war then extant in the southern part of his department and the large number of displaced persons that were draining departmental coffers, the department would only pay for one of Señorita Bolivar's dresses. However, no other department followed suit and the host city's candidate finished in the low twenties out of thirty-two.

Every day, national newspapers feature two or three of the candidates on their front pages and otherwise serious news magazines such as *Cambio* and *Semana* run special full-colour supplements. But it is on TV that the Reinado truly takes over the country.

News channels compete to attract former Miss Colombias as expert commentators. Many, such as the famously long-legged Viena Ruiz, now in fact have their own careers as newscasters or media personalities and regularly show up at social events rubbing shoulders with former presidents, industrial magnates, and figures from the artistic world, while others such as Lori Simpson (imagine Pamela Anderson in her late forties) are annually wheeled out just for the occasion.

Every evening these personages report from the floodlit ramparts of the Old City or the foyer of a luxury hotel, commenting on the day's developments: perhaps Miss Antioquía was voted Miss Photogenic, or Miss Caquetá was spotted having a tiff with Miss César. There is analysis every bit as serious and detailed as that which accompanies the fortunes of the Colombian soccer team at the World Cup: Miss Cundinamarca is reported as having the perfect stats (90-60-90), but it is noted that she has a touch of cellulitis on the back of her thighs; Miss Boyacá is reported to have surgically enhanced breasts, but will the judges be influenced by this?

Whatever else is happening in the country is relegated to the inner pages or to the second half of the newscast: fifteen killed in a massacre in Meta, a minister resigns, a congressman is imprisoned for corruption, this is hardly noticed. On the day when the queen herself is selected, there are special live newscasts and the following day, when she returns triumphant to her home department, it is a local holiday and the entire city turns out to give her a ticker-tape parade through the streets.

The politically correct are annually shocked at the frivolity of the whole show, at its degradation of women and pandering to machismo, but the truth is that their protests are hardly audible and are universally scorned. This is the one moment of the year when Colombia shakes off its collective gloom and navel-gazing to indulge in a fortnight of unashamed sexist bacchanalia. I'm tempted to say "good luck," because it sometimes seems there is little enough to celebrate here.

Just as the Reinado of Cartagena is Colombia's annual escape from reality, so is the city itself an oasis of tranquillity and genteel old-fashioned Latin America in a crime-racked and wartorn country. The glossy brochures of North American travel agencies frequently fail to acknowledge that Cartagena is in Colombia at all (lest the Colombia tag frighten off potential travellers), but many Colombians themselves also see the place as an escape from their own country, on a par with Miami, Aruba, and Cancún.

Mystifyingly, the narcos, the guerrillas, the paras – all of those bad people that infest the hinterland – seem to respect old Cartagena. It is as much on account of this de facto truce as the undeniable beauties of the city that the government invariably chooses it as the seat of international conferences it hosts – Iberoamerican Summits, for example, or the 1998 annual gathering of the Inter American Development Bank. In fact, of course, the place is not completely safe.

My first visit here was in July 1975. My wife-to-be Jenny and I were hitchhiking and bussing through South America, from Trinidad to as far as our money would last (Lake Titicaca, it turned out). Arriving by bus from Venezuela, we'd found ourselves a cheap hotel (hospital-green plywood cubicles with spy holes gouged in the walls and locked with your own padlock) in the Getsemaní district of town, then gone to relax for the afternoon on Bocagrande Beach. As the sun dipped and the shadows lengthened, we'd shifted a few feet away from our little pile of belongings ... an error.

Before we knew it, we were being swarmed by a group of six or eight teenage youths. They got away with our hotel key, our jeans, and my wristwatch, but, by a stroke of luck, the one whom I selected for a flying rugby tackle in the sand was the one who had our passports and precious Jetsave return air tickets from Port of Spain. Those twelve- and fourteen-year-old children are now no doubt the sharks who run illegal taxis and pickpocket gangs of their own at the airport.

In those days, the city's famous walled town was as quaint as it is now, but a lot more run down. The whole city was white, but the walls of the one-storey seventeenth- and eighteenth-century houses were invariably peeling, mildew stained. An unsightly web of electricity and telephone lines filled every street barely above head level and the huge encircling ramparts were generally crumbling, invariably stinking of urine. This was not a safe place to be at night.

One of the sights of the city in those days was the vast market on the waterfront, most of which was inside a huge corrugated iron shed. This was not for the faint of heart or stomach: sides of beef seethed with

Street scene, Cartagena

flies, blocks of ice were dragged back and forth through the gutters, eventually to be grated into your Passion Fruit juice, and dogs lifted a hind leg over the piled-up displays of fruit.

This at least has changed now, mostly, but not all, for the better. The market has gone, replaced by a modern Tropical/Soviet-style Convention Centre. At what one imagines to be great expense, all of those cables and wires in the Old City have been taken down and buried. The entire place now looks as if it has just been painted for the filming of a period-piece movie, and not just in white: there are houses in a tasteful old-gold colour, with their balcony railings picked out in white, while others are blue and red. Bougainvillaea trails from every balcony and shady courtyards shelter quietly rustling old stone fountains.

In the squares of the Old City, tables are set out Venetian style, their tablecloths denoting which café they belong to. You can eat out as the shadows lengthen and the four-hundred-year-old stone walls of the church turn through every shade of yellow and gold. It could be Seville or Córdoba.

Just off the shady Plaza de Bolívar is the Palace of the Inquisition, dating from 1710, its entrance an imposing stone gateway. Half of the palace's rooms are filled with nothing but piles of masonry, and, on account of missing planks, its magnificent main staircase requires careful negotiation, but there is an inquisitors' rack to be seen in one of the rooms (and furtively tested for size if the guard is at a safe distance) and in another is a pair of Witches' Scales. All of the explanatory notes attempt to minimize the actual number of people killed by the Inquisition in Cartagena (an admittedly modest total of four), but it is interesting to note that the list of Grand Inquisitors runs right into the twentieth century.

Also in the Old City is a large and unwittingly entertaining naval museum. This contains such exhibits as pieces of hardware chipped off modern naval patrol boats, Airfix models of famous vessels ranging from the Golden Hinde to the Bismark, unlabelled pieces of coral, and a series of models of the many great naval battles to which Cartagena was a witness. The models, I noted on my last visit, were financed with funds from the Spanish government; they seemed not to correspond with versions of the battles that I had read in English-language publications.

If you have the budget, you can stay at the beautifully and lavishly restored Santa Clara or Santa Teresa Hotels; in 1975 these were decaying and collapsing convents inhabited by a few dozen nuns in their dotage, but now they are five-star establishments where (in the case of the Santa Clara) one end of the Chapel is a bar.

It was at the Santa Clara, as half a dozen fellow guests will inform you over the course of a twenty-four-hour stay, that Gabriel García Márquez set his novel *Of Love and Other Demons*:

> It was October 26th 1949. The beautiful Chapel of the Convent of the Clarissas was virtually exposed to the elements on account of the steady collapse of its roof ... In the crypt were the remains of a Viceroy of Peru and his secret lover; don Toribio de Cáceres y Virtudes, Bishop of this Diocese; various Abbesses ... But the news was the third niche of the high altar, by the Evange-

list. The covering stone had broken at the first tap of the hammer and a great mane of hair, the colour of bright copper, poured out of the tomb. It measured twenty-two metres and eleven centimetres long ...

The old-world Santa Clara and its rival the Santa Teresa are the exceptions to the rule in Cartagena. South of the Old City, on the long and narrow strand that protects the lagoon of Cartagena from the open Caribbean, more and more high-rise hotels are crammed in every year. The oldest and stateliest is the Art Deco Hotel Caribe, where deer wander freely in the gardens and nibble at your breakfast rolls.

The beaches, to be honest, are nothing special. An off-white colour, they are none too clean; digging your toes into the sand you are more likely to encounter a cigarette end or bottletop than a shell. The craze is to have your hair braided Rasta-style, beads and all; every three or four minutes a young Black girl offers you a special price on this service or, when you demur, then at least a leg massage. But the forts still are special and must have been, in their day, one of the wonders of the world.

It is recounted that one day King Philip II of Spain, at an idle moment in a cabinet meeting at the Royal Castle of Segovia in the heartland of Castille, wandered over to a window, gazed intently out of it for some minutes, then summoned his Treasurer: "Mr Treasurer. Kindly explain to me how it is that, however hard I look, I cannot see the walls of Cartagena. For we have surely expended enough upon them for them to be visible from here ..."

Around the Old City, the walls of Cartagena are on average twelve metres high and seventeen metres thick. At the two points of the harbour most vulnerable to external attack – the narrow entrances of Bocagrande and Bocachica; Big Mouth and Small Mouth – there are, respectively, an underwater wall that rises to within two feet of the surface and a mechanism that allowed an enormous chain to be drawn all the way across the entrance. Protecting the city from land attacks is what at the time was the largest single fortress in the world, San Felipe de Barajas, with several miles of tunnels dug deep into its heart, permitting for successive abandonment of four circles of fortification.

Why all the effort? An excellent natural harbour, Cartagena stood at the northern end of the supply routes by which, for three hundred years, Spain shipped back most of the gold and silver of its South American Empire; a 160-kilometre-long canal eventually linked it to the Lower Magdalena, making it accessible from the interior not only by land but by water. While Portobello (in modern Panama) periodically competed with Cartagena as the prime depository of the Empire's wealth, this was a better harbour by far and two days' sailing closer to Spain; sooner or later Cartagena always regained its supremacy.

This strategic location made it a prime target for corsairs, buccaneers, and navies unfriendly to Spain. In the sixteenth century alone, Cartagena was besieged five times by pirate fleets; Francis Drake sacked the place in 1586 and agreed not to burn it down only when he was bought off with the enormous ransom of ten million pesos.

But the epic for which Cartagena is best known was the 1741 siege set by Edward Vernon. Vernon came with nearly two hundred ships, with an average of ten cannons apiece, and twenty-five thousand men. The city was defended heroically by the one-legged, one-armed, and one-eyed Blas de Lezo, who miraculously held Vernon off long enough for bad weather and yellow fever to decimate the English Admiral's fleet and cause him to withdraw. All the Colombian guidebooks proudly note that the arrogant English had been so confident in victory that they had already minted victory medallions prior to starting the siege.

A small plaque in an inconspicuous location on the walls refers to the siege and quotes from historian Arnold Toynbee: "Had these walls been any thinner, then Latin America would be English-speaking today." When I last checked out the plaque, a wit had scrawled beneath it, in chalk, the one word "Ojalá," which, roughly translated, means "Would that it were so." But to most Colombians Blas de Lezo nevertheless remains an icon.

24 December 1998. We'd squeezed into the last seats on a holiday charter flight from Bogotá to Cartagena. From Cartagena airport, we grabbed a taxi out to the bus station, through the surprisingly extensive and undistinguished suburbs of the city. "Maganguey," the taxi driver repeated to us as we neared the hangar-like bus station, "I think you've missed the last bus. You should try an Express Taxi ..." and he pulled up to a café at the roadside.

A handful of sharp-looking youths, all with greased-back hair and all clutching wads of banknotes, descended on us and began pulling us first one way then the other, all the time reeling off interior place names interrogatively. There weren't actually any taxis in sight – it was illegal to run such an operation out of anywhere rather than the bus station –

so it was a matter of judging whose uncle really *was* somewhere close by and who already had a clutch of passengers to fill the other seats.

Four in the back and three in the front passenger seat of a 1970s Toyota, we were soon haring off to the south, with the sun dipping low in the sky over the Caribbean to our right. "It's best if we try to get there before dark," shouted our fat driver over his shoulder, competing with the rushing wind. "That's when the paras come out." As he chortled, I glanced at my watch. It was 5:30, would be dark at 6:15, and, according to the map we'd consulted before setting off from Bogotá, it was 210 km to Maganguey.

Of course, we didn't make it in time, but we did drive fast enough to have given any slightly hesitant para (or guerrilla) second thoughts. For the last hour, the road reflectors hurtled out of the night towards us at over 100 km per hour, and we saw not a soul on the road, even though this was Christmas Eve.

There didn't seem to be much to recommend Maganguey. We stayed the night in an airless room at a hotel recommended to us by our taxi driver, above the bus terminal (rarely a good location if you want to sleep), and were up, hardly rested, at 5:30 on Christmas morning. The hotel owner treated us to a strong black coffee when we paid our ten-dollar hotel bill and waved us down to the waterfront: "The launches to Mompox are about every hour, starting at six ..." he said.

Mompox. One of the most evocative names in Colombian history. Founded in 1537 on the Lower Magdalena, this was for three centuries a great port, often a refuge for the traders and high society of Cartagena when that city was under siege. In 1810 it was the first city on the entire continent to proclaim its independence from Spain, and it was here that The Liberator, Simón Bolívar, recruited his finest troops, the men who freed South America.

In some ways, things have changed dramatically since those days, in other ways not at all. Mompox is a place name now hardly known outside Colombia, and, nearly two centuries after its glory days, it is still accessible only by river.

It took an hour and a half of the usual riverside uncertainty – finding a launch, waiting for the motorista, assembling a critical mass of passengers – before we were off, downstream along the slow Magdalena in still-pleasant temperatures, with the sun barely up. For forty minutes we swooshed our way along the Brazo del Lobo (Arm of the Wolf), then swung hard right into a network of creeks and swamps at the

Street scene, Mompox

north end of the huge island that temporarily forces the Magdalena into two arms.

At Bodega (Warehouse), we transferred to a jeep and a forty-minute ride through green meadows, where egrets stepped daintily in the footsteps of ponderous Brahmin cattle. We passed through a few tiny villages, scarcely more than three or four houses by the track, where it was evident that the local population was still sleeping off its Christmas Eve revels.

Mompox is a jewel: an almost perfectly preserved nineteenth-century colonial town, all low white buildings, old homes with courtyards and rocking chairs, wrought-iron lamps hanging on the walls, dark beauties lingering languidly in doorways or on balconies, and scarcely a car to be seen or heard: instead everyone rides bicycles.

Mompox owes its state of preservation to a freak of nature. In about 1870, the Brazo del Lobo began to silt up and virtually all the traffic on the Magdalena was diverted up the river's other arm, converting Mompox into a backwater that has been untouched by history or commerce ever since. The mystery is how the town continues to live on at all. It

Waterfront scene, Mompox

has a reputation for producing the finest rocking chairs in Colombia, is home to a group of artisans who specialize in gold filigree, and attracts photographers from all over the country, but that's about it.

Then as now, such life as there is in Mompox revolves around the river. At the steps behind the Town Hall, small canoe freighters load and unload. Upstream, a narrow promenade, with the river on the left and seventeenth-century warehouses on the right, serves as the town's busiest street and favourite location for a stroll in the cool of the late afternoon. Much of the promenade is shaded by ancient fig trees in and out of which kingfishers and hummingbirds flit and where a small group of Capuchin monkeys comes down every morning out of the treetops to be fed fresh bananas by the compliant locals.

There's a small white monument here that in very simple terms commemorates the various visits paid by Bolívar to the town: one set of arrows points upstream, with dates, and another downstream. Elsewhere in the town, there's a statue to him. It pays special tribute to the four hundred men of Mompox that formed the core of his first army, but I'm

The bus depot, Mompox

not convinced by the authenticity of the quotation: "To Caracas I owe my birth, but to Mompox I owe my glory." In the Plaza Bolívar in Cartagena, there's a very similar statue, with the word "Cartagena" replacing "Mompox." I wonder what the statues in Caracas say?

Still further upstream, the promenade widens: on the right you come to the unique Mompox Cathedral, with its oriental-looking hexagonal tower, and here's the town's bus station: a shop with a crude hand-chalked sign saying *La Veloz* and a few crates of Coca Cola inside it. There's a strip of concrete laid under the trees, and, that morning, the town's children were trying out what was evidently the Christmas present of 1998: rollerblades.

A little way back from the waterfront is the town cemetery. You can see that the town has had grander days: many of the vaults, brilliantly whitewashed under cypress trees, are as big as houses. But nearly all the graves with modern dates are much simpler, often only handwritten boards in the Columbarium. When we strolled around, there were two young men playing cards on a table-height marble tomb in the shade.

In the evening, amid the rustling and chirping of the cicadas and the less welcome blare of Vallenato music, little tar-paper stalls down by the waterfront sell Aguila beers to the domino-playing old men. Everything – other than the insistent music – is very peaceful, bucolic. The woes of urban Colombia seem to be a world away. There's really nothing to do here, and nothing ever happens – and that's why, in this country, this is such a delightful oasis.

On Boxing Day morning, before the sun was up, we caught another launch, upriver to El Banco. The ride is a beautiful one, with five or six stops at tiny riverside communities where campesinos with bunches of bananas climb on and off and students going back to the city after their Christmas visit home climb aboard with plastic bags bulging with gifts. You're not far from the birthplace of Gabriel García Márquez and the setting of *One Hundred Years of Solitude*: the then-and-now mythical Macondo.

But at El Banco – dirtier and noisier than Mompox, no doubt on account of its having road communication with the outside world – you could on this clear and still-cool morning see far to the south the blue hills of the Serranía de San Lucas. We were coming at the region from a different direction now, but we were on the northern edge of the Magdalena Medio; another three hours by fast launch upstream, and we'd be back at Simití, San Pablo, and finally Barrancabermeja.

El Banco is still quaint. There's a gambling stand on the waterfront manned by an eagle-faced man who could be one of those gypsies that brought the magic of ice to Macondo, and the local people fish the Magdalena River with huge Y-shaped hand nets that are apparently seen nowhere else in the world and give the men prodigious arm muscles.

But I was told that this was a para town, a forward base for their incursions into guerrilla territory further south. We had breakfast, a short wander around, then caught the first launch back downriver – to the otherworldly cocoon of Mompox.

September 1999. It fell to me to sit briefly beside the president at the formal closure of an international police conference in Cartagena that had brought together hundreds of criminal investigators from all over Colombia. Two homicide detectives from Vancouver had travelled from Canada to participate, although I wasn't sure how useful their talk had been in the Colombian context. In Vancouver, it seemed, ten or twelve detectives would routinely be assigned to a murder investigation, whereas in Colombia the reverse was more usually true: any one detective was running with ten or twelve murders at any one time.

It had been a long way to travel just to exchange pleasantries with the president for a few minutes, so I decided to make the most of what remained of the evening. At ten o'clock, Wilson Montaño and three friends of his picked me up at the Hotel Caribe and, in his battered old Mazda, we set off in the middle of a rainstorm, heading for the outskirts of Cartagena. I felt a little uneasy: it might be dangerous, and, God forbid, someone might take a picture of me ...

Wilson and a number of other young social workers run the Cartagena operation of a Bogotá-based Foundation called Renacer ("Rebirth"). Their prime objective is to entice underage hookers off the street and into more wholesome, healthier, and safer lines of business. They maintain a drop-in centre in the Getsemaní quarter of the old city and a small residential home in the country town of Turbaco, about half an hour's drive from Cartagena. As a tourist town, Cartagena has more than its share of young girls (and boys) engaged in prostitution, a business that is also fed in part by foreign tourists. What I would observe tonight, Wilson explained as we headed into ever more dimly lit industrial suburbs, was the most time- and patience-consuming phase of Renacer's work: the process of acercamiento, or trust-building, that is the prerequisite for persuading the young prostitutes to participate voluntarily in Renacer's education and rehabilitation programs.

Our first stop was a nightclub called The Pirate's Cave. Wilson knew the bouncer well and explained that only three of us – the three men – would be let in; the two female members of the group had burned themselves on an earlier visit to this location by letting the other patrons see what their purpose was; they would have to wait for us outside.

At a hole in a concrete wall, a woman wordlessly opened the door to us and gestured over to a low shed from which loud disco music was throbbing and outside which a flickering green and yellow Sprite sign told us that we had the right place. A burly Black man frisked us politely and ushered us in.

On the low wooden stage that ran the length of the opposite wall, a lithe mulatto woman was near the end of her show; stark naked, she was slowly and rhythmically caressing a post with her ginger-coloured pubic mound. She soon walked off languidly, to desultory applause from the dozen or so clients seated around tables in the dimly lit building. Nautical flags criss-crossed the room, and on the walls were a few glass fishing floats; the place looked disappointingly un-seedy, clean even.

In the long pause before the next show, as we lingered over a very expensive set of beers, Wilson clinically explained Renacer's procedures to me. Occasionally, tall, elegant Black women clad only in suspender belts would come and linger by the table: Wilson would press a wrapped condom into their hand, enquire cheerfully about business, and send them on their way. Then he pointed out to me in the gloom a female figure dancing cheek to cheek with a fat man whom I had earlier heard speaking Russian or Polish. I could only make her out because her lingerie was brilliant white against her dark skin and seemed to fluoresce in the dark. "Fourteen years old," he said laconically. "She won't talk to us yet. This one is going to take a while ..." "What's that on her hip?" I asked eventually, trying to sound equally unfazed. "A cellphone. That's how they get most of their business."

The bouncer nodded courteously as we left. We picked up the two Renacer women who had been patiently waiting in the dark on the steps on an abandoned factory, and we drove on to our next destination.

After we had parked and were picking our way across puddles in the unlit dirt street, Wilson explained: "This is a different kind of joint. It's called a Retirado. There's beer and music, but no shows. You come in, hang out for a while, then if you find someone you like, you pay the dueña her percentage and you take the girl off into one of the cubicles ..."

An unmarked narrow housefront led consecutively into four or five dimly lit rooms, in most of which there was a table or two and a stand-up fan that was at least as loud as the music. I tried not to stare, but it was evident that this was a much lower-class joint than The Pirate's Cave. The girls were short, chubby, excessively made-up, and stuffed into impossibly tight short velvet dresses; they seemed sober and surprisingly cheerful, which was more than could be said for the male clientele: dangerous-looking and muscular Black men with a frightening glazed look that I did my best to avoid. At the back was a large courtyard. Along the back wall were several doorways covered only with flimsy shower curtains.

I found it difficult to tell the age of the girls. Wilson nodded: "Most of them have false ID. The police do come in and check quite regularly, and there's not much they can do when the girls insist they're overage."

More condoms, more banter. A couple of the girls promised to come by to the drop-in centre; one asked after an old friend who, with Renacer's help, had gone straight and was now apprenticed as a hairdresser. A couple of girls ogled me and looked interrogatively at Wilson.

Back to the old city. At 2:00 AM in a street that I had earlier that day photographed as the epitome of colonial quaintness but which now had a different air, we bumped into a young gay couple, hand-in-hand, whom the Renacer team greeted as old friends. After months of delays, they'd finally agreed to have an AIDS test, they told Wilson, but they weren't sure if they wanted to go back to the clinic to learn the results.

Waving goodbye to them, we ducked under an old colonial doorway and, after the obligatory weapons-frisking, into a long dark room that reeked of beer; the floor was littered with discarded plastic cups. The music here was heavier than at either of the other two places we had visited, the atmosphere more sullen and threatening. I edged around one table at which sat an old man sobbing silently into his beer, while at the next an all-out brawl appeared to be imminent. Suddenly I found my shirt lapel being grabbed. A woman was yelling at me; I couldn't understand her over the din. "She wants you to pay in advance, then take your pick of the girls," Wilson shouted in my ear.

At our last stop of the night, on the steps of a disco in the modern hotel area of Bocagrande, we struck pay-dirt. Over a period of more than an hour, often barely able to follow what was going on, I watched Wilson and his team ever so carefully engage in casual conversation a four-foot-six girl who can have been no more than twelve. She was high on something, constantly dancing around like a boxer, her eyes flitting from one side to another.

There came a tense moment when a taxi cruised slowly up and the driver beckoned. She hesitated. Wilson said nothing, averted his eyes. After another moment of indecision, the girl waved the taxi driver away; the driver laughed and called out some unintelligible obscenity.

There was another interruption when a well-built and exceptionally pallid girl with a cow lick of hair falling over her forehead wandered up and began to hover around the group. It looked as though the younger girl's attention might again be lost. But it was an old friend. I realized after a few minutes that she wasn't really a girl at all but a transvestite, and her pallidness was in fact white makeup. All the regulars called her Michael Jackson. Wilson cheerily slapped a couple of condoms into her hand, and she wandered off.

In the end, the young hooker agreed to come to the drop-in centre. Perhaps tomorrow, perhaps the day after. It wasn't much but, as the Renacer team drove me back to the Caribe at 4:00 AM they agreed that it had been a good night.

Renacer functions in Bogotá, too. Under the direction of a near-legendary social worker called Stella, they trawl the rough streets of central Bogotá for hookers, drug addicts, and delinquent street children – and try to give them a home. It's a thankless job – the dropout rate is high – but over the years they have attracted a band of faithful supporters.

One such is a former BBC World Service correspondent, Timothy Ross, who met Stella while covering a demonstration by Bogotá prostitutes. Nowadays, he spends most of his time enthusiastically and tirelessly canvassing embassies and international organizations for funds to support Renacer. He has a store of breathtaking stories to tell of life on the streets and doesn't always endear himself to everyone: when he was briefly featured again on the BBC, shepherding ex-Monty Python star Michael Palin around, as part of the *Around the Rim* TV travel series, his revelations on camera to a shocked Palin prompted a diplomatic protest to Britain from the Government of Colombia.

Another supporter, and friend of Timothy's, is Andrew Loog Oldham. When Tim introduced me to the slightly unshaven Andrew, wearing a black polo neck and black woolly hat, the name seemed vaguely familiar to me. Later, I remembered. It was in the small print on my old 45 rpm version of "Satisfaction" – Loog Oldham was the Rolling Stones' producer. A longtime resident of Bogotá, he conducts business by email and is married to a Colombian ex-supermodel and good friend of Bianca Jagger. Riding into town one day from Renacer, Loog Oldham regaled me with stories of the Stones' concert in Toronto and of Keith Richards getting busted; he mused that helping Renacer out was one way for him to put something back into society, after so many years of living the high life.

And finally there was Nohra Puyana de Pastrana, wife of the president. A high-society girl and former Christian Dior model, Nohra seemed a little ill at ease the day we visited Renacer jointly with her and Canadian Foreign Minister Lloyd Axworthy, but she tackled it gamely and most of the children were literally awe inspired. Tim wisely did not offer to show her how Renacer demonstrates condom use to the girls –

with a larger than lifesize mock penis – as he once had done with a more junior Canadian minister.

March 2000. Gabriel García Márquez, these days, divides his days between his Bogotá apartment, a luxury home in Mexico City (where he spent many years in self-imposed exile), and a restored colonial house close to the Santa Clara in Cartagena. He is a familiar figure on the streets of the old city – where he is known as Don Nobel, or Don Premio – and rather enjoys being interviewed. Like many Latin American writers, notably his great friend and contemporary Carlos Fuentes of Mexico, García Márquez is taken (with questionable logic) as an authority not just on literature but on politics, both national and international. So, I thought, why not see if he would agree to meet with the Canadian Foreign Minister, myself, and Canadian ambassador Guill Rishchynski, taking advantage of a ministerial visit to Cartagena?

We arranged for breakfast in a cool and airy room off the main courtyard of the Hotel Santa Teresa – rival to the Santa Clara and another ex-convent, but lower down the price scale. The Great Man arrived a little late but with no fuss, wearing his trademark white trousers and white guayabera. As we sat down, I noticed the minister had a white plastic bag loaded with new paperbacks at his foot.

We spoke in French. García Márquez's was good (he studied at the Sorbonne), mine acceptable, the minister's poor – which allowed me and the ambassador to effectively monopolize the conversation, albeit at the possible expense of my career prospects. We began with small talk – "You can't imagine how hard it is to get up every day and discipline yourself to write for six hours," Márquez said as the juice arrived – but soon launched into Colombian politics.

From reading interviews with him, I had formed the impression that García Márquez was definitely left of centre, but his remarks were in fact balanced and within the mainstream of most informed commentary on Colombia. Referring to President Pastrana and the peace process, he was for example emphatic that, whatever misgivings one might have about the president, he fully deserved credit for having advanced discussions further than any preceding president and that the international community should support him unreservedly in this area. He added that "my great friend" Castro was genuinely anxious to be of assistance in this area, but that Fidel nevertheless had hoped that recent

ELN/Government of Colombia contacts in Havana would be kept secret. As for Hugo Chávez, president of neighbouring Venezuela and at that time something of a bogey man for Colombians, García Márquez felt that although his usefulness in the peace process might be limited, he had been demonized in Colombia: "he is no tyrant"; Colombia and the international community at large should not be overly alarmed at some of his verbal excesses.

Weaving life and literature together again, García Márquez mused that although *One Hundred Years of Solitude* was now over thirty years old, Colombia grows to resemble Macondo more and more. He related that when he travels in rural Colombia people often upbraid him with the comment that the "magic" happenings he recounts in his masterpieces are nothing compared with the experiences they have lived through; invariably, people will tell him that Colonel Aureliano Buendía is understated, not the reverse.

Nevertheless, the book that won him the Nobel is not his favourite; his own preference is for *Love in the Time of Cholera* (tourists are commonly seen wandering the streets of Cartagena, with a paperback edition, trying to find the different locations described). He confirmed that for twenty-five years he had actually forgotten where he had put the one million US dollars of the Nobel prize until, when he was looking for money to buy *Cambio* magazine, his wife reminded him that it was still sitting in a Swiss bank.

García Márquez felt that Canada was little known in Colombia, but that we deserve a higher profile and "can be very useful to Colombia" at the present juncture. What was needed, he said in a quietly jocular reference to his *News of a Kidnapping*, was *News of Canada*.

I was left with the impression of a gentle man, slightly vain but courtly in an old-fashioned manner; on politics, he had little new to say (what new is there to say about Colombia?), but he clearly neither expected nor was used to contradiction. He autographed the minister's pile of books with a wry smile, then came to the old Spanish-language copy of *One Hundred Years of Solitude* that I had brought with me. Asking me my name again, he commented that he had a grandfather of the same name and accordingly inscribed the title page: "*Para Nicolás, como mi abuelo.*"

Later, our little delegation dwarfed by a massive operation surrounding American Secretary of State Madeleine Albright, who was coincidentally in town at the same time (an operation which included a reported five thousand troops, as well as a destroyer parked offshore from the Santa Clara), we travelled by boat out to President Pastrana's private island for lunch with him and a few of the Americans. I sensed that the minister was having all of his worst expectations of Colombia confirmed when into our wake swung a navy launch armed with two heavy machine guns and a navy helicopter clattered overhead, but the event itself was low-key, informal, relaxing. Observing the president at close quarters – jovial, suntanned, bright-eyed – it was easy to forget the almost unimaginably heavy load he carried on his shoulders day to day, not the least heavy part of which must be fear for his own life. He offered the minister (who fancied himself a cigar connoisseur) a choice item, waited until he had had a half-dozen puffs then, with a mischievous smile, said: "I hope you're enjoying it ... it cost me a thousand dollars, and you've already smoked two hundred's worth."

Cartagena's a Caribbean city in most senses of the word, but some 500 km to the north, much closer to Nicaragua than Colombia but still a Colombian possession, is the historical throwback of Old Providence: a tiny tropical island whose population is entirely Black, where they speak Jamaican or Belizean English and where Reggae is the beat of preference. To reach Old Providence, you have to fly to the tacky, touristified, and overcrowded island of San Andrés by jet, and there change to a much smaller SAM Twin Otter for the half-hour flight still further north.

The airstrip is on the west side of the 7 km by 4 km hilly island, and you're usually met by a couple of laidback Black taxi drivers with 1960s Chevvies. They speak no Spanish, and their English is hard to follow; it all seems a bit like Jamaica in the 1960s (as judged from *Doctor No*).

One taxi drove us round the island to a small guesthouse near the village of Aguadulce – Sweetwater. Here we stayed for four or five days, eating seafood and West Indian concoctions familiar from visits to Belize, striving to understand our host and hostess. Like in Belize, 50 percent of every conversation seemed to consist of the words *fock* or *fockin*, but relations between the locals and outsiders nevertheless seemed a lot less edgy than they often are in the West Indies proper.

One day we took the hardly used tarmac road to the southern tip of the island to the settlement of Bottom House. Behind the houses, a narrow track led up into bright green meadows and forest and soon started

Old Providence

to climb steeply above a stream bed. Dazzling blue and green lizards flitted away from their sunlit spots as we approached, and unseen raucous birds called to one another high up in the canopy. After an hour's strenuous climbing we emerged on a breezy and grassy ridge at about 300 m and traversed over to the highest point on the island – known unimaginatively as El Pico. From here we could see the entire island and its fringing reef. The shallows were a brilliant turquoise: a diver's and snorkeller's paradise.

As we sat taking in the view, a noisy but cheerful group of pioneros – a kind of military sponsored boy- and girl-scout movement – clambered up and greeted us; behind them, puffing and sweating, came the lieutenant who had drawn this Saturday morning duty. The irrepressible children had unsurprisingly scattered potato-chip bags and empty Coke bottles all over the mountain top, but, to his credit, the young soldier insisted they pick everything up before heading down again – which they did with good grace.

Every evening we would wander a couple of hundred metres down the road to a small shack built out on stilts over a small cliff and the darkening sea below. It was lit only by a hurricane lamp and the decor was a few lumps of old coral and seashells strewn around; there were only two tables. We would sip a couple of Aguilas and watch the sun set in silence, then the old man would ask us in English if we wanted to listen to the radio. Once we did, but the news from Bogotá seemed as though it came from another planet; the next evening we politely indicated we would rather sit in silence.

4 Banana Country

Turbo, Apartadó, San José, Chigorodó, and Pavarandó

URABÁ, THE POINT AT WHICH the entire continent of South America abruptly spills out of the constriction of the Panama isthmus like toothpaste out of a tube, has long been a battleground, like Barrancabermeja, one of those place names that makes even war-jaded Colombians recoil in distaste.

The primary reason why the region has so long been fought over is its location. Anybody wishing to smuggle arms, drugs, cheap cigarettes, or people into or out of South America from or to Central and North America overland must be assured of safe passage through Urabá. The region also has one of the best ports on the entire Caribbean coast of South America – Turbo – which means that this is a favourite destination of maritime smugglers.

Urabá is also rich in its own right. The flat, near-swamp lands at the head of the shallow Gulf of Urabá (sometimes known unflatteringly on account of their humidity as "the armpit of the Americas") are prime banana-growing country. More speculatively, it is perennially rumoured that the Panamerican Highway joining Panama and Colombia is finally to be completed, necessarily passing through Urabá and/or that vast plans are being drawn up, by unnamed but surely US-controlled multinational companies, to drive a second transoceanic canal through from the Gulf of Urabá to the remote Pacific village of Juradó.

As and when these rumours gain credence, which is usually every couple of years, then Colombian violentologists, especially those who enjoy a good conspiracy, can be counted on to explain the latest upsurge in violence in Urabá by saying that it is due to land speculators whose object is to gain control of potentially valuable terrain unencumbered by inconvenient campesinos. This theory would be fine had not both scenarios been around, already, for nearly a century without a single investor ever having shown his face in Turbo. The fact is that, in the security climate that has long reigned in Urabá, anyone with a few billion dollars to invest would be mad to come here. But if part of your job is to cover human rights, the war, and internal displacement then, like Barranca, Urabá's one of the places to be.

The safest way here is unfortunately not the most picturesque. There is a fine new metalled road from Medellín north to Urabá's so-called Banana Axis: the three towns, strung out in a south-north line, of Chigorodó, Apartadó, and Turbo. Long-distance buses on this road are routinely hijacked and burned by the FARC, their passengers robbed or kidnapped; the FARC also like to try their skills as sappers by periodically blowing the key bridge near Mutatá, just as you would emerge from the mountains on your way north. Consequently, even persons of relatively modest income try to use the frequent light-plane routes operated by SAM and ACES (motto: "We respect you") that serve Urabá from Medellín's Olaya Herrera local airport.

As you walk to your Twin Otter from the terminal in Medellín, a sign reads (in English) "Have a Happy Fly." For novices to this route, the Fly is usually rather nerve-wracking for at least the first few minutes, as the plane climbs steeply out of the deep bowl in which Medellín lies (it's not for nothing that most services have been moved to Río Negro airport, an hour away on a high plain east of the city) and then struggles over the high and usually cloud-bound ridges to the north. But as you work your way north, the land starts to flatten and fall away, and

"Have a Happy Fly": arriving by air in Urabá

soon you are flying over nothing but mile upon mile of geometrically arranged banana plantations. As you disembark, the heat and humidity hit you like the opening of a sauna door.

Early on in my first visit to Urabá, I checked in with the mayor of the largest of the three towns of the Banana Axis: Apartadó. Four unshaven men in civilian clothing, each toting a machine pistol, escorted me to his office in the large, rundown municipal complex on the road to Turbo. The mayor welcomed me effusively, ordered me coffee and iced water, and without prompting volunteered the fact that he knew Canada well. "Oh, what part of Canada?" I asked. "Gander, Newfoundland," he said.

I must have looked a little nonplussed, for he immediately launched into a long explanation. For years, the mayor explained, he had been a member of the insurgent Ejército Popular de Liberación, or EPL (now almost extinct; always smaller and lesser known than the FARC and ELN). In fact, he said, he had been the senior rebel commander for most of the Urabá region. In this capacity, in the 1970s and early 80s, he had several times travelled to Tripoli "for training and instruction."

The most convenient route was via Havana, Gander, and Moscow, mostly on Aeroflot. He hadn't actually seen much of Gander, he admitted, except on one occasion in midwinter when a technical problem had kept the Aeroflot plane grounded for three days and he'd been lodged in a small motel on the edge of town.

"So what made you decide to leave the EPL?" I asked, after we had exhausted the topic of Gander. He laughed. One time, returning from Libya, he had taken a stopover in Amsterdam. After three hard and austere months in the Libyan desert, he said, the delights of Amsterdam, especially the red light district, had converted him "in a few days." Once back home, he promptly applied for the government's amnesty program, was accepted, and, a year or two later, decided to try his hand at more conventional means of achieving change: legitimate regional politics.

With almost childlike enthusiasm, the mayor pulled forward a blackboard and showed in the form of a diagram how many men, at the height of his power, he had commanded in the EPL: about six hundred. He then brandished a conveniently handy sheaf of paper on which were summarized the most recent municipal elections. With a crow of triumph he pointed to the figure "6,000" – the number of citizens who had voted for him as mayor. "See? By going into politics, my army is now ten times as big ..."

Later I learned that, for all his innocent charm, the mayor was reputed to have abandoned his former Marxist ideals to the extent of having gone over completely to the other side and joined the paramilitaries who now dominate urban Urabá. The accusation is not as far-fetched as it sounds: while many EPL members have banded together to form a more-or-less legitimate movement with the same initials (Esperanza, Paz y Libertad – Hope, Peace and Freedom) many more have indeed taken their only marketable skill (killing people) and offered it to the current best bidder in an increasingly large number of areas of northern Colombia: the paramilitaries. Still others are still out there, "fighting the good fight" and all the while hunting down their former colleagues, whom they see as the worst kind of traitors.

On all of my early visits to Urabá in 1997 and early 1998, a compulsory stop was the large refugee camp at Pavarandó, reached via a dirt track that led east for 30 km from the small roadside settlement of

Mutatá. This makeshift camp had come into being following a territorial war between paramilitaries and the FARC in the Middle Atrato region of Chocó Department. Over a period of several months, and as a result of massacres and threats uttered principally by the paras, five thousand persons had fled their remote riverside settlements and trekked through dense jungle eastward to the nearest roadhead at the thirty-house settlement of Pavarandó. Here Army units had blocked their onward progress to the main road at Mutatá and they had been forced to set up a town of makeshift shelters of palm leaves and bamboo on the edge of the tiny village.

My first visit, in late 1997, was at the invitation of Father Gabriel, the same Jesuit priest who at that time headed up a Bogotá NGO called CINEP, which also covered Barranca; he knew how to get cheap rates at the Pipatón. Working with the local diocese, Gabriel had been instrumental in arranging for initial humanitarian relief for the displaced and in encouraging community leaders to organize themselves.

The displaced of Pavarandó had since their arrival here gradually evolved their own version of a strategy that has been tried in locations as diverse as Ulster and Sierra Leone. With a view to their eventual return to their homes and recognizing that they would probably have to go back in the midst of continuing violence, they had concluded that the only viable survival strategy would be for them to proclaim themselves completely neutral in the conflict and have nothing to do with any of the "actors" – Army, police, FARC, or paramilitaries. They would formally declare themselves a "Community of Peace", and all their members would have to follow strict rules: no persons bearing arms would be admitted within village limits; no goods were to be sold, let alone given, to any of the "actors"; there would be no alcohol sales whatsoever within the Community; for the greater safety of all, the tending of fields outside of the village limits would be done communally; initially at least, only the principal village sites would be reoccupied and those who had previously worked outlying plots would be taken under the wing of the Community at large. The Community's logo, they determined, would be a yellow sun symbol: this they wore on T-shirts and on little plasticized ID cards worn around the neck, which also listed the basic rules of the Community. October 1997 would mark the formal declaration of the Community of Peace of Saint Francis of Assisi, and it would be done in style.

Ceremony and ritual are important for drifting communities of refugees such as this. Without formal structures, without regular mass meetings that follow strict procedural rules, without constant long speeches that ritually – almost biblically – recapitulate the tribulations of the community and their demands, then solidarity in this trying context quickly collapses, and such little hope as the displaced may have of gaining the attention of the authorities and of humanitarian agencies dissolves. In this sense and in the Colombian setting, displaced persons who either willingly or unwillingly are confined to one location and who are obliged to live hugger-mugger with other refugees tend to have a better chance of achieving the ultimate objective of most of the displaced within Colombia – a safe return home – more promptly than the vast majority who end up dispersed into city slums. Thus, for all the Rwanda-like squalor of Pavarandó, those who had forcibly been confined here were in some ways better off than those who had fled in other directions and who were now living on the fringes of Medellín or Bogotá.

After we had driven in from the airstrip at Apartadó, I spent the morning wandering around from one cambuche to another – a cambuche is typically a small makeshift shack, walled and roofed with palm leaves or, for the more affluent, with a black plastic tarpaulin. Everywhere, preparations were under way for the ceremonies to come. The settlement itself, I immediately learned, was geographically organized according to the thirty or so veredas (outlying settlements) from where the displaced had come: this morning, each vereda was preparing its placards for the marches that would take place later in the day. And each of these veredas had a representative on the camp's council, which met on a daily basis to discuss not only medium- to long-term plans, such as the eventual return home, but more immediate questions such as sewage, positions to be taken in discussions with the local authorities, and so on.

The nominal leadership of each vereda was constantly rotated. "But isn't that incredibly inefficient?" I asked. "After all, not everyone is cut out to be a leader ..."

"Yes, that's true. But what you have to understand is that nobody here wants to become identified as a leader. We have to accept that the camp is probably infiltrated by both guerrilla and para sympathizers – it's not good for anyone to emerge as a leader ..."

In addition to the plenary council, a number of other committees met regularly: the Health Committee, the Sports Committee, Education, Culture, and so on. The Culture Committee comprised principally the community elders: it was their mandate to keep alive the traditions of the community, to constantly remind them of where they had come from; this they did by storytelling sessions, by singsongs, even by joke-telling contests. The Education Committee had a more challenging mandate: with 60 percent of the displaced aged fifteen or under, they had to find enough volunteer teachers among their own ranks to maintain through the months – possibly years – of the displacement some kind of continuing education.

By noon, all of the children had finally been persuaded into their best clothes – surprisingly white, dazzling even – and each vereda had assembled itself with its placards and banners. At some unknown signal, the children made their way out of the narrow mud alleyways of the camp and out onto the wider main street of Pavarandó. The few animals – pigs, a handful of donkeys, and some roosters – that the displaced had managed to bring with them from the Middle Atrato were also given their place in the procession, giving it the air of a Nativity play. Each child carried either a white balloon or a white paper flag. Slowly and patiently, with Council members periodically giving instructions by megaphone and children repeatedly having to be hustled back into line, the procession of five thousand people made its way to the large open space, in front of a wooden platform, where the ceremonies would take place.

Over his jeans and T-shirt, Gabriel pulled on a surplice and, with the sound system periodically failing and obliging him to shout, said an abbreviated form of mass and formally blessed the new Community of Peace of Saint Francis of Assisi. All of the guests of honour – myself included – were invited to speak a few words and were thunderously applauded. To the rhythms of African-style drums, there was dancing and singing, and, finally, one of the diminutive grey-habited Clarita nuns who had been directing the cooking all morning gave the signal that the feast could begin.

All this time, the ten or twelve Army soldiers who control the track out to the main road kept their distance. Gabriel told me that they were friendly enough but that, understandably perhaps, they did resent the formal decision of the Community at large to have nothing to do with them. Indeed, when I checked in with the young lieutenant in command, he seemed frustrated: "We just want to do our duty and protect them ... but they won't even talk to us."

Six months later I was back in the region, accompanied by Sharon O'Regan, the desk officer from the Department of Foreign Affairs in Ottawa who was responsible at that time for Colombia. She had asked to see a little of the "real Colombia," away from government ministries in Bogotá, and a visit to Pavarandó seemed like a good idea. She had little idea what she was letting herself in for.

In Mutatá, down on the main road east of the camp, we checked in with the two Clarita Sisters who would accompany us out to Pavarandó. With their help, we chartered a Willy's Jeep; across the top of the windshield was emblazoned the slogan *El Ultimo Guerrero*, though the jeep's owner, who must have weighed 250 pounds and who could barely wedge himself behind his steering wheel, was not quite the prototypical Last Warrior.

There was no scheduled public transport out to Pavarandó, and days often went by without a single vehicle making the trip. So, as we bounced along the rutted track through the jungle, we were soon picking up people in ones and twos. Ninety minutes later, when we finally arrived at the familiar military checkpoint at the entrance to the camp, we had seventeen people on board, half of them hanging on to the roof.

We spent an hour or so moving through the camp, meeting with the current council members, hearing about different problems they were dealing with or about their plans for the long-awaited return. Then I heard a helicopter overhead. Nothing unusual – after all, we knew we were near areas in which confrontations between the FARC and the Army were frequent.

But the noise of distant rotors suddenly took on a different tone – a kind of deep-throated burp-burp-burp. Sharon and I looked at each other. We stepped out of the cambuche. About two kilometres to the west, just on the edge of the camp limits, the olive-green Huey was banked to one side, describing tight circles and machine-gunning the jungle. It looked to me to be too high to do much damage to its presumed target, but I was nevertheless slightly alarmed at the prospect of a FARC detachment apparently so close to the camp.

Most of the settlement was now out on the street, shading their eyes as they gazed high up at the Huey. The children had stopped playing football.

We walked quickly out to the Army checkpoint, intending to find out what was going on. Indeed, there was some action, but the situation was far from one of panic. Wandering in from the undergrowth around the checkpoint were half a dozen camouflage-painted and bandoleer-festooned soldiers, each carrying their mess kits – the incident, whatever it was, had apparently disturbed their lunch.

I approached the young lieutenant, whom I remembered from my previous visit; I opened my mouth to speak to him when there was a sudden loud peal of thunder. I turned around; the helicopter had gone, but two light bombers had replaced it. In ponderous, low-level runs, what I later learned were two OV-10s, known in the US Air Force as Broncos, came in time after time over the camp, then soared up two or three kilometres way. A full eight or ten seconds after they began to peel way, another roll of thunder would reach us.

The lieutenant was not in the least fazed. While continuing to talk to us quite casually, he occasionally interrupted himself to give orders to his ten or twelve men, who, having dumped their lunch plates, were now moving rather more purposefully and were picking up heavy weaponry and ammunition tins from here and there. "Yes, we think it's the FARC," he answered casually. "We've been picking up their radio transmissions all morning, so I decided to call in a bit of support; the OV-10s are from Medellín."

"The guerrillas – how many are they?"

"Well, from the fact that they've been transmitting from as many as eleven separate locations, we think there must be at least five hundred ..."

"And how far off?"

The lieutenant waved casually to the two-hundred-metre rise at the far end of the village. "Somewhere beyond that hill – two or three kilometres."

By now, the entire platoon had assembled in front of us, politely waiting for the lieutenant to finish his chat and give them some orders. He frowned for a moment and then, apologetically, asked if Sharon and I would mind him borrowing our jeep for a few minutes. We were hardly in a position to object, although I wasn't sure how the use to which it would now presumably be put would go down with the embassy accountant.

The Last Warrior; Pavarandó camp for the displaced

Our corpulent driver was rousted out from the shady spot where he was enjoying a warm Aguila. Truculently and muttering audibly, he lumbered up. He was unsurprised by the request the lieutenant made, but complained bitterly that this "happens every time I drive to this bloody place, and they never compensate me for it."

The Last Warrior and his steed spent the next two hours reluctantly ferrying soldiers and ammunition back and forth, mainly to and from the hill that was the centre of our attention. After a while the planes went away and the helicopter, presumably having refuelled at the nearby Carepa Army base, returned.

With our transport forcibly commandeered and the main road 30 km away, there seemed little else to do than sit and chat with the lieutenant, while listening with one ear to the occasional bang from the hill in the distance. He was twenty-one years old and had been posted here for the past nine months; in another three months he would be rotated out. The pay was quite good, he admitted: "You get more for being in a red zone like this." But he missed his young wife – he got out his wallet and showed us passport-sized black and white photos of her – and he'd like to be able to have her along on his next posting. I was conscious, all the while we spoke, that this was all rather surreal: it seemed entirely possible that in the very near future we would be overrun by a major FARC unit and a number of us might soon be dead. But, I told myself, there was little we could do about it; we might as well relax.

It was near dusk when the commotion began to settle down. The helicopter flew off; "They don't fly at night," the lieutenant said laconically. There had been no bangs for a while, although most of the soldiers would spend the night out in foxholes. I began to worry about something else. The lieutenant himself and all of the Community leaders had impressed upon us that we must not drive the Mutatá road after dark, and yet it was already half past five and would be completely dark within the hour.

The Last Warrior, who had finally been told his services would no longer be required, was keen to go for it. "After all," he said, "where would you stay in this dump?" The two Sisters shrugged their agreement: "We might as well."

Off we set, the Sisters jammed into the front passenger seat, hard against the large and sweating Last Warrior, myself and Sharon in the half-sized back seat. We said little on the way out. Soon, in the narrow tunnels formed by the dense jungle and overarching trees, it was utterly black, the headlights carving a path ahead. Once or twice we saw pairs of eyes transfixed by our beams. "Could be jaguar," said the driver laconically.

We were almost back at the main road when we rounded a bend and came up hard against it. A makeshift road block: a large log spanning the road, supported by oil drums. The driver cut the lights and the engine, and we sat for a full minute in utter silence.

"It could be a trap," he finally said, superfluously. He squinted out of his window, looking up the hillside. The Sister on the passenger side did the same. We waited some more. Finally, the more diminutive of the two tiny nuns said: "Well, are we going to wait here all night? Put on the lights."

Determinedly, she climbed out, laboriously pushed the log off the oil drums and to one side, and beckoned us forwards. We reached Mutatá without further incident, although the Sister did insist on accompanying us through the darkened backstreets of the small town to our little pension – the Hotel Bélgica. "You should be careful," she said earnestly. "Those people who we just saw sitting at that bar, the ones in the cowboy hats who wolf-whistled at me, they're paramilitaries. Don't even talk to them: they are very dangerous people. Lock your door. I'm not leaving until I hear you put the bolt across."

Late that night, I think it was after two, I was awakened by what sounded like fireworks. I got up and craned out of the window. Far to the west, in the direction of Pavarandó, there were flashes in the sky and an occasional white flare soared high then died. In the morning, as we were leaving Mutatá by taxi, a graffito on an abandoned shack caught my eye: *Kill; God is merciful.*

I always tried on field visits to hear as many points of view as possible. In the complicated context of Colombia, it was my experience that no one person held all the truth, but many had part of the truth. Hence, the Army and, if possible, the police were always on my agenda in places like Urabá.

The headquarters of the XVII Brigade are in Carepa, on the main highway between Apartadó and Chigorodó. Usually, my interlocutors here were General Orlando Carreño and, later, General Vargas, but if they were not available then a Colonel was always assigned to receive me, even at the shortest notice.

Carreño, who bore a striking resemblance to former President Carlos Salinas of Mexico (short, balding, with a neat moustache), was regarded as one of the rising young stars in the Colombian Armed Forces. He was posted to Urabá to succeed the bluff, hardline Rito Alejo del Río, whose uncompromising, even ruthless anti-guerrilla stances had won him a number of enemies in the human rights community and who was to be forcibly retired in early 1999 following repeated allegations of collusion with the paramilitaries.

Carreño was a sophisticated man, not at all the unthinking, brutal military man that, outside Colombia, is seen as the stereotypical Colombian Army Commander. Whenever I brought to his attention specific cases of alleged abuses by the men under his command, he invariably addressed my concerns seriously and thoughtfully. He also had much to say on the concept of Communities of Peace. "It's a fine model, in theory," he began.

"And in practice?"

"The practice is that in this war it is impossible truly to remain neutral. The guerrillas will be the first to tell you that. If you're not with them, you're against them. And you must see that, for my men, who have been told that their job is to protect the civilian community, it's very hard for them to understand when the people they are protecting won't even let them into their village, let alone sell them a Coke."

And there were questions of a more philosophical nature, he suggested. By excluding the legally constituted Armed Forces of a legally elected government, communities that proclaim their "neutrality" in this way are in a sense breaking away from the state: "And what about persons who have always lived in these new Communities of Peace but who do not wish to share in them?" he asked rhetorically. "What about the little storekeeper who wants to keep selling beer? What about the family that wants to farm their plot on their own, as they always have done? The law says they must be allowed to, and it is our job and that of the police to see that the law is respected ..."

"So will you respect the Communities?"

"Yes we will, but we have to reserve the right to go into the villages sometimes. For instance, if we believe that they are harbouring paramilitaries or guerrillas, or if there's a major disturbance, or a major crime has been committed ... then I have to go in."

Not all my discussions with Carreño were so serious. One evening, as a part of a larger delegation, I was meeting with him over the highly polished oak table that was the centrepiece of the base's well-appointed and air-conditioned conference room. It was after dark, and it began to rain very heavily. Soon, we heard peals of thunder; every two or three minutes there was a dramatic flash of lightning. The rain intensified, and now it was difficult to hold a conversation over the din of the rain on the roof. Then, abruptly, the lights went off, and the air conditioning whined down. We were almost shouting now, but still we kept talking, even though none of us could any longer see the papers on the table in front of us, or each other. After fifteen minutes of this, I noticed my feet were damp. I paid no attention, thinking there must be a leak in the roof just behind me – but they got wetter and wetter. Soon there seemed to be at least an inch of water on the floor. Someone eventually found a flashlight: the entire room was flooded, and a small carpet was floating precariously around, on the verge of sinking. We decided it was time to abandon the meeting.

The Community of Peace of Saint Francis of Assisi, founded within the confines of the Pavarandó Displaced Persons' camp but later functioning in situ in the Medio Atrato region, was not the only Community of Peace in the Urabá region. There existed a smaller such community at San José de Apartadó.

San José is located in low hills to the east of the much larger town of Apartadó itself and is reached via an often very difficult muddy and rutted track some 20 km long. Leaving Apartadó, the first "sight" is an open field to the left of the road, known as La Chinita. Here, a few years back, FARC units had massacred, in cold blood, at least thirty former EPL members who had abandoned guerrilla ranks to rejoin civilian life; the name La Chinita acquired a certain infamy at a national level. The second sight is a sharp bend in the track, a couple of hundred metres past a small Army post on the edge of San José. Here, up until at least mid-1998, the paramilitaries openly maintained a roadblock. They would stop all vehicles passing through, search them and frequently detain their drivers or passengers for questioning; many of the latter simply disappeared after such questioning, never to be seen again. This almost within earshot of the Army post.

San José is a village of some one thousand souls that, in early 1997, received a flood of displaced persons from more remote communities higher up in the mountains, forced out by paramilitary incursions from neighbouring Córdoba Province. In the space of week or so, its population more than doubled, though most of the newcomers were able to find lodging by squeezing into existing accommodations.

The population of San José now went through a process directly comparable to that which led to the creation of the Community of Peace of Saint Francis of Assisi. Meetings were held (endlessly, in the Colombian style), rules were established, and yet all the time the paras and the FARC – alternately – prowled around the outskirts of the little settlement, each periodically picking off individuals whom they suspected of giving succour to the other side. By the time I attended the first anniversary celebrations of the community, in March 1998, over sixty individuals had been killed; their names were listed on a banner that hung on the wall of the Parish House, on the main square.

Eighteen months later, at the thirty-month anniversary, the list had grown longer, albeit at a lower rate; among those killed in 1999 was a young man called Aníbal who had been in charge of the Community's Cultural Committee and whom I had met several times. We sat and watched a short video that he had only completed a few days before his death. Some young children, in the manner of children in less benighted

The return to La Unión

spots who might take you to show you their favourite tree or swimming spot, took me to the location a few hundred metres out of town where Aníbal's bullet-riddled corpse had been found.

In spite of these trials, and aided by the solidarity of the Catholic Church and a number of international development agencies, including OXFAM, the Community held firm: a number of "mini-returns" took place, starting in March 1998. The first such return from San José was to La Unión, a settlement of fifty houses two hours' ride into the mountains from San José. I attended the formal launch ceremonies, which, as at Pavarandó, were biblical in nature. After a morning of prayers, dances, and feasting, the inhabitants of La Unión assembled themselves in procession, with all of their farm animals, and were ceremonially escorted back into the hills by the entire population of San José, to pick up their lives where they had left them twelve months earlier. Embarrassingly, everyone else was on foot, but, as the guest of honour, I was assigned my own donkey, called Rosita; I felt a little as Christ must have when entering Jerusalem. But as we were leaving the village, a cloudburst began – lightning, thunder, and torrential rain. In that San José had been suffering from a drought, this was universally seen as a

The author on Bright Star of the Dawn

great omen. Unfortunately for me, Rosita would not cross the stream outside the village, which had in a few minutes risen to become a torrent. Regretfully, I was forced to let the procession move ahead, leaving me to wrestle Rosita back to San José.

In September 1999, I finally made it to La Unión. This time, the Sister in charge (the reader will have deduced correctly that wherever there is a community in trouble in Colombia, there always seems to be nun on hand to help out ...) had commandeered for me a proper horse, with the romantic name of Lucero del Alba, Bright Star of the Dawn.

I still felt guilty, because Bright Star's owner was obliged to keep up with me on foot – but not too guilty, because I soon began to suspect that the horse was probably none too intelligent. Heavy rains had in places eroded the already precipitous upwards path we took, but Bright Star would invariably insist on treading on the very edge, a dizzying height above the stream into which half the path had so recently vanished.

La Unión is a huddle of wooden shacks set in bright green cleared meadows about 6 km east and five hundred metres higher than San José; to the northwest, when it is clear, you can just make out the blue

Outside the community centre, La Unión

waters of the Gulf of Urabá, while behind you the track leads into higher mountains still. The village, like San José but on a smaller scale, is centered on the Parish House, which is home to the only telephone. Outside the House is a loudspeaker mounted on a tall pole; this is used for all village announcements and to summon persons lucky enough to receive a phone call.

In La Unión, it was evident that the concept of the Community of Peace worked, and worked well. This was partly because the place was small enough for regular village meetings not to be too onerous and for solidarity to be easily maintained. Every morning, the day's activities were planned communally. It might be decided today that the men would work a particular cacao patch, while most of the women would be assigned to working on the new vegetable garden, the remainder on running the creche. As with the Community of Peace of Saint Francis of Assisi, the rationale behind working in this fashion was only partly one of efficiency; the main reason was that there is security in numbers; if they were part of a larger group, individuals were much less likely to be picked off by one or more of the warring groups that still roamed the neighbourhood. But the effect, intended or otherwise, was touching: a peasant community, really working together for a better future. Again, although there was no overtly religious dimension to this Community or to that of Saint Francis, the Catholic Church facilitated, but Evangelicals and non-believers were also warmly welcomed as Community members – one had a sense here of witnessing the putting into practice of many a church sermon. Or, you could say, this was communism as it is meant to be. But did this in turn attract the instinctive suspicion of the paras and only feed their allegations that the Communities of Peace are hotbeds of guerrilla sympathy? I'm still not sure about that one.

Just after we arrived at La Unión, the phone rang. Community leaders in San José had received an order for fifteen kilos of Cachama (a kind of freshwater fish); could La Unión oblige, and deliver to San José by noon the next day? An announcement went out over the loudspeaker, and, within a few minutes, the men whose turn it was to mind the artificial fish-breeding pools appeared. We trudged out into the gloom, netted the requisite number of fish, and delivered them to the women's team whose responsibility it would be to clean them. A second call went out for a volunteer to ride down to San José next day.

We sat chatting for much of the night in the mud-floored Parish House. At ten the power went off, as it did every night, and candles were brought out. Tall and taciturn campesino men, cowboy-hatted and machetes at their waists, periodically wandered in, squatted for half an hour or an hour on their haunches, making the odd comment, then wandered off again into the night. The children played dominoes on the mud floor, whispering excitedly to each other, occasionally glancing up to sneak a look at the gringo. Then there were long periods of silence, interrupted only by the occasional slapping sound as one of the men flicked mosquitoes away with the little towel he wore over his shoulder.

We were about to go to bed when I heard it again: the same rolling thunder I remembered from Pavarandó. The Sister and I went to the door. There was no moon, but the sky was cloudless, the stars bright, the surrounding hills black. Behind one of the hills to the north, there would be a short white flash then, two or three seconds later, we would hear the thunder. Occasionally, more distant, there was a pop-pop-pop sound.

The children left their dominoes and came to stand with us. A four-year-old reached for my hand and, with his other hand, began sucking his thumb. After half an hour, it all stopped. We went to bed.

5 Returning to Darién

The Cuenca del Cacarica

WE ARE STILL IN URABÁ, but now we move up to its very northwestern corner, to an area known as the Cacarica Watershed. Cacarica, translated literally, means "Rich Shit." This region, which is more attractive than its name might indicate, is hard by the Panamanian border and in the heart of the Darién Gap. It was colonized by Afro-Colombians from Central and Southern Chocó Department in the late 1960s. Controversially, the area of their original colonization was reduced in the early 1970s, when they were forcibly ejected from what is now the Los Katíos National Park and from a number of territories that were simultaneously decreed as reserves for the Katío Indians, part of the Embera ethnic group.

It is a spectacularly beautiful area of dense jungle, rising from lowlands and mangrove swamps around the Atrato and Cacarica Rivers to the peaks that form the border with Panama and from which, according to legend, Balboa (Cortés in Keats's well-known poem) first glimpsed the Pacific. It is rich in wildlife – red and howler monkeys, sloths, caymans, tapirs, and jaguars – and the small clearings made by the colonists around their wooden stilt-borne shanties provide a good living. The waterway of the Cacarica is also the nearest thing there is to a road between South and Central America, and as such is a major route for contraband, illegal arms, drugs, and guerrillas on the run. It is also thought that, as and when that missing link in the Panamerican Highway is built, it will parallel the Cacarica – indeed the twenty-shack village at the junction of the Cacarica and the Atrato is known as Puente América, on the (optimistic?) supposition that this will someday be the site of a great suspension bridge that will join the Americas together.

On account of the obvious strategic opportunities it affords – in particular, control of trafficking routes of all sorts between the two continents and the proximity of a safe haven in Panama should the going get too hot – this territory has long been a stronghold of the FARC (57th Front). Over the years since their arrival, the Afro-Colombians learned to coexist with the guerrillas: a number, it must be supposed, co-operated with them actively. However, for the same reasons that it was an attractive base for the FARC, so the Cacarica became, in the 1990s, an appealing target for the paramilitary movement, whose national base was in the neighbouring department (to the east) of Córdoba. In moving into the Cacarica, it must be supposed that the paras were interested principally in wresting away from the FARC its stranglehold on key narco and arms-smuggling routes; it is said they also received some support in this enterprise from land speculators eyeing the dotted red line that shows the projected route of the Panamerican Highway or (this was more probable) from cocaine producers being squeezed in the South and looking for new, rich land conveniently closer to the drug markets than Guaviare or Putumayo Departments.

Whatever the motivation, the upshot was a ruthless, well-planned north-south sweep by paras through the twenty or so scattered and remote settlements of the Cacarica in February 1997. There were a number of exemplary murders. One man I met had seen a fifteen-year-old boy decapitated, another had witnessed a simultaneous murder and castration. Villagers were given three days to leave. The vast majority did, in a panic-stricken rush down jungle paths and waterways, many of them finally reaching the distant port of Turbo on makeshift bamboo rafts, with no possessions whatsoever. A smaller group, finding its way to the Atrato River blocked by paras, had to trudge north, across the border into Panama. This odyssey, about which I was later to hear first hand, led to an international incident.

In total, five thousand persons were displaced from this region over a period of a few weeks, the vast majority ending up in hot and filthy Turbo. Here, based in a crumbling concrete basketball stadium, the community gradually began to reorganize.

I became involved with the Turbo displaced at the invitation of a Bogotá-based human rights non-governmental organization called Justicia y Paz. This organization decided to take the group under its wing and, in a novel initiative, convoked a multi-agency Verification Commission. The idea of the Commission was (and is) to bring together all the governmental agencies that nominally have some responsibility in addressing the displacement phenomenon, along with key UN agencies, international development agencies, and – in an observer capacity – foreign embassies. The Commission, working closely with the leaders of the community itself, seeks to create the various conditions necessary for a safe return – in this case, to the Cacarica – recognizing that safety is a relative concept in Colombia. The Verification Commission's first initiative was a fact-finding visit to Turbo and the Cacarica Watershed in May 1998.

As I was introduced by candlelight to the several hundred displaced who turned out on a velvety night to meet the Verification Commission, I noticed on the wooden wall behind me the names of the seventy or so from the Cacarica who had been killed during or since the displacement (some dragged forcibly from the stadium), many with Polaroid pictures pinned underneath; on scraps from notebooks or on the back of official forms, also pinned up, children and old women had laboriously transcribed in pencil descriptions of the moment the paras arrived, or of the days they had spent drifting hopelessly downstream to Turbo. A Vallenato group performed for us a song specially composed for the occasion: I had the sense that our humble Commission was already entering into the mythology of the displaced of Turbo. The ceremonies ended with a rousing rendition of a song I was to hear many times over the next few days – "*No nos moverán*," a homegrown version of "We Shall Not Be Moved."

But already we had bad news for the community. Entire branches of government, written commitments to the contrary, had failed to show up for our visit. The key Office of the Presidential Counsellor for the Internally Displaced made available only the head of its Turbo-based logistical office. Such government agencies that were represented were at a middle to low level. All next day, community leaders argued back and

Children at Bocas del Atrato

forth as to whether, in these insulting circumstances, the Commission should indeed proceed; finally, it was reluctantly recognized that, with the federal government's term of office rapidly drawing to close (it was May, and we were in the dying months of the administration of President Samper), the only alternative to proceeding now was to wait until September, a prospect that few of the displaced were prepared to accept.

The second disappointment was not entirely unexpected. After a bumpy one-hour east-west crossing of the Gulf of Turbo, we entered the maze of waterways and mangroves where the Atrato River debouches into the Atlantic. Speeding upstream, a further two hours brought us to the waterfront settlement of Puente América, where the Cacarica joins the Atrato. Two of the fifteen displaced who were with us were originally from Puente América. Of the settlement's two dozen one-storey wooden shacks on stilts, half had been burned to the ground; all that remained were sheets of brittle and rusting corrugated iron already half lost in the undergrowth. On the front of one of the remaining houses was a carefully painted slogan: "*A/C. Muerte a la Guerrilla. Muerte a sapos*" ("A/C" stands for Autodefensas de Córdoba – the main paramilitary group on a national scale; "Sapo" is a term that usually means "guerrilla collaborator"). Other houses were daubed more crudely with skulls and crossbones and slogans such as "*Muerte a la subversión.*" Passing the first moonless night on the floor of one of these hornet-infested cabins, as howler monkeys growled from the nearby treetops, was unnerving.

Barely a mile up the Cacarica, on a hilltop that commands the river junction with the Atrato and that has a spectacular view over half of Darién, there was worse. A dilapidated building that had seen better days as a National Parks station was now an occasional paramilitary base. It was covered from wall to wall with graffiti that went from the satanic to the obscene – death's heads wearing military berets, stylized AK-47s doubling as phalli, everywhere the taunting word "paramilitares." The ground outside was littered with used cartridge cases, among which was the occasional live bullet. The most recent date on the graffiti was one month previous to our visit.

As if there was any doubt that the paras were still around, we were faced with more direct evidence when part of the Commission called in on the only civilization in the area, the HQ of the National Park, to make a radio call back to Turbo. Lounging around the dock by their high-speed launch were fifteen to twenty camouflage-wearing and heavily armed men – with no shoulder insignia. They began by asking the Commission members for their ID cards, but backed off when they realized there were government officials present. In the course of the subsequent conversation, they admitted openly that they were "Autodefensas," "on a routine patrol," under the command of one Comandante Javier. Their principal base, they indicated, was on the other bank of the Atrato, a few miles away, by the lagoon known as the Ciénaga de Tumaradó; there were a further 170 men at the base, they said. Tumaradó is approximately 40 km, as the helicopter flies, from the headquarters of the Army's XVII Brigade in Carepa, where only the previous day my old friend General Carreño had apologetically told me that he had no information regarding any armed groups on the

Paramilitary graffiti at the old National Park station

Cacarica region, and that he would be most grateful for any news we could bring him.

A timid young man who had been living a lonely gypsy-like existence in the ruins of Puente América for a month later took me on one side. Every few days, he said, the paras passed up and down the Atrato in their launches. They made no threats. Both the Army and the guerrillas had also been here; before "the trouble," he said, the Army and the paras often came together. Now it was "*cada uno por su lado*," each group on its own, never together, never at the same time. "Should the desplazados return?" I asked. "Maybe. But not those who've got problems."

From Puente América we moved up the Cacarica and spent the next three days exploring the possible sites for resettlement. The displaced recognized that, if and when the decision to return was made, there would still exist the threat of another forced movement. Accordingly, instead of returning to the original twenty-three settlements, the idea was to concentrate the population in only two, with particularly good escape routes. The two chosen villages were unsurprisingly dilapidated and overgrown, the houses completely empty of the possessions the displaced had abandoned; there was no sign of the hundreds of ani-

Don Pipo contemplates the ruins of his home

mals (pigs, cows, mules) they also left behind, presumably slaughtered or carried off by the paras.

Standing in the ruins of his burned home, one man, Don Pipo, insisted that the paras had support from the Army in the February 1997 pogrom: pointing to the treetops, he described how five helicopters had come in low only minutes before the paras' arrival. Only the Katío Indians stayed put, he said. Colombian legislation allows the country's aboriginal people considerable latitude in enforcement of the law, and – this conforming to a pattern I had observed elsewhere – the paras let them remain on the condition that they immediately deal with, "in their own way," any individuals whom the paras might choose to finger as guerrilla collaborators.

Singing coplas in the chalupa

As the Commission moved from one site to another in the forty-degree sun, we concluded that – security considerations apart – resettlement was possible, but that there would need to be much reconstruction and, what would be more costly, there would need to be a dredging program of a number of currently silted rivers if indeed the communities were to have viable escape routes. Occasionally, someone would tug at my sleeve and take me wordlessly to the piles of ashes where their house once stood; one man had heard where the bones of his child might be buried and pleaded with other displaced to help him search; firmly but kindly they told him there was no time for this now.

But, in spite of everything, spirits remained high: the women (this was to be a men-only mission until it was belatedly remembered that the Commission would have to eat) led raucous, sometimes ribald singsongs when the dugouts got stuck in the weeds, as they did repeatedly. There was great joy when the first Guacuco fish was caught; this repulsive-looking leftover from the age of the dinosaurs is a black, oleaginous bottom-feeder unique to the Atrato system and is famous for its aphrodisiac powers; this of course provoked further ribaldry. One of the women, a fat, squat Black woman called Doña Rosalba, adopted me: every night, to the amusement of all, she would fuss over my mosquito netting to make sure it was properly tucked in.

As the days passed, an ever-lengthening ballad was composed, verse by verse, or copla by copla: it began with a satirical account of the visit by the displaced committee to the president in Bogotá (complete with sarcastic references to Samper's electoral slogan, "*El Gobierno de la Gente,*" i.e., "The Government of the People") and, last I heard, concluded with our return to the dock at Turbo, where the community band had been awaiting us all morning and preparing a tumultuous reception. It even included a reference, charitable as far as I could tell, to the *Embajada del Canadá*.

There were two problems the desplazados had not mentioned to us when this mission began, but that would nevertheless have to be factored into any eventual decision regarding the viability of a return. One was the proximity of the Los Katíos National Park to the planned return sites. This was no ordinary national park: it was a rare and as yet untouched depository of biodiversity and deserving of the UNESCO "Heritage of Humanity" designation, which the Colombian government was seeking for it; and yet its presence astride such rich lands and adjoining the Cacarica River was seen as an obstacle by the displaced to their own development plans. And then there were the Katío Indians themselves.

We met with thirty Katíos in an abandoned village known as La Virginia. As the physically dominant Black displaced leaders lectured the Indians, documents and plans in hand, regarding complicated bilateral land disputes that they wished to resolve prior to a return, the Katíos – their women painted in a uniform dark-blue body paint, fingering their brightly coloured beads in silence – listened nervously. I had the sense of two irreconcilable worlds clashing. As is apparently their style, the Katíos would commit to nothing at this meeting and sloped back into the jungle with scarcely a word exchanged, but I had the sense that they had been ambushed by the highly organized, articulate, and angry displaced, and that they would get the worst of any deal that was struck.

Over the coming months, the Verification Commission met repeatedly in Bogotá, addressing these and a multitude of other problems, with occasional further forays into the field. Progress was frustratingly slow. There was, for example, a hiatus of several months following the elec-

Katío Indian woman and children, La Virginia

tion of the Pastrana government: much of the Commission's work was lost and much energy was expended simply on bringing all the new government officials into the picture. But, somewhat to my surprise, the patience of the Turbo community leaders held solid, and, indeed, in some ways the entire project gained momentum.

One symptom of this was the development of an integrated survival strategy with a view to the eventual return. This strategy, as it had evolved by early 2000, was in many ways comparable to that adopted by the Communities of Peace, but, for reasons to do with inter NGO and even intra-Church politics, the Turbo displaced avoided this term and instead described their threefold objective as self-determination, life, and dignity, their five ruling principles (to each of which a colour was assigned) as truth, freedom, justice, solidarity, and fraternity. Another was the decision by the community to bring into the process those several hundred persons who, at the time of the original displacement in February 1997, had fled not to Turbo but into Panama.

This group – men, women, and a few domestic animals, and whatever possessions could be carried – had trudged northwards from the

Hacienda El Cacique, Cupica

Cacarica for fourteen days and into an international incident. In a rushed operation in which the UN High Commission for Refugees (UNHCR) was not consulted and in which a variety of international instruments were violated, the Governments of Panama and Colombia worked together to forcibly repatriate these displaced by helicopter almost immediately to a small but apparently peaceful plot of land on Colombia's Pacific Coast, about 150 km southwest of the Darién. Here they had lived ever since, housed in self-constructed palm shacks in a meadow known as Hacienda El Cacique, near the small coastal settlement of Bahía Cupica.

In many ways the setting was idyllic: spectacular rainforest-clad hills sloped down dramatically to the sea, the beaches were vast and empty, toucans and macaws flitted through the treetops. Dolphins calved in the bay, and, at certain times of year, humpback whales migrated past. David Suzuki once made a documentary here and described the area as one of the great forgotten paradises of the world.

But there were problems in paradise, as I found out in the course of a Verification Commission site visit in February 1999. In the first place, for a displaced persons' camp this location was remote and supplying food and other essentials was time-consuming, expensive, and occasionally dangerous. The nearest road to Bahía Cupica and the Hacienda was 100 km away and completely inaccessible overland. All supplies had to be flown in first from Medellín, by tree-clipping Twin Otter, to the little settlement of Bahía Solano, 150 km south; they had then to come by boat across an expanse of open Pacific and be landed through the surf. As I found out, this operation could be hazardous: our high-speed launch sprung a major leak 10 km from land, which the passengers were only able to plug by stuffing their T-shirts and other clothing into the hole, then bailing constantly; this was capped by a damp beach landing through four-foot rollers.

More seriously, the camp was right on a key smuggling route – and had long been so; in fact the meadow itself and the small ranch house around which the camp was built were once the property of Pablo Escobar and the ranch's name, El Cacique, means "The Boss." Only five days before our arrival here, a Navy patrol chanced upon a launch with engine trouble just off the bay and found it to be carrying a large shipment of AK-47s, M-16 rifles and grenade launchers bound for Carlos Castaño, the greatly feared and near-mythical leader of the paramilitary movement; the shipment had originated in Colón, Panama. (How did the Navy know the arms were bound for Castaño? Simple – on the blue plastic barrels containing the weapons, there were large address labels with his name ...)

The paras, here led by an individual known as El Cepillo (The Comb), were widely thought to be involved in cultivating coca locally, receiving arms, and shipping out illicit cargo from elsewhere in Colombia: several sources told me of routine nighttime movements through the area of unlit light planes and fast boats – "and they surely weren't carrying coconuts or tourists." At the time of my visit, there had as yet been no major incursions into the camp, but there had been threat after threat and the paras seemed to be getting ever more bold in circling the camp. Members of the community told us that they had recently seen uniformed paramilitaries on the beach only a few hundred metres away; one day a tall Black man had even wandered drunk into the camp and openly boasted that he was the boat driver for the paras. More seriously, three days before our visit, a man on the beach had offered to a member of the displaced the equivalent of one thousand Canadian dollars if he would "bring to him" certain leaders of the community – an inducement, it has to be presumed, to participate in an execution. Our launch driver told us that he had been intercepted by paras three times on food runs.

Inexplicably to an innocent observer, in view of the widely acknowledged presence of this illegal armed group, the National Department of Civil Aviation had recently certified (i.e., authorized) the use of several local airstrips that, as recently as three years ago, the Army had bombed so as to interdict to narcotraffickers. Inexplicably as well, just after making their spectacular arms seizure, Navy commanders announced that they were henceforth suspending most of their patrols in the region due to diminished resources. A cynical observer might have suggested that these developments were an indication of official collusion with the paras.

The 57th Front of the rebel FARC, "in groups of ten to twenty" also routinely passed through the area; on 21 December 1998, a couple of months before my visit, they had robbed a cargo boat at Bellavista, a few miles to the north. But most of the people with whom I spoke, with the exception of the police and Army, downplayed the FARC threat, blithely commenting, "They like to come here on their holidays."

The police, sensitive to the continuing vulnerability of the community, had assigned a detachment of eight men to protect the encampment. They were rotated through every month or so, but often assignments stretched to two or three months; both police launches in Bahía Solano were out of action when I visited and the police commander had to rely on the Navy to move his men back and forth.

The detachment was a sorry sight. Contrary to explicit regulations, none of its members were in uniform; they explained to us innocently that, in the event of an attack on the camp, their plan was simply to melt among the displaced and hopefully avoid detection. They had six twenty-five-year-old carbines between them and, when we spoke to them, had not had radio contact with HQ for several days, there being no gas to run the generator and charge their batteries. Also for this reason, there was often no illumination here other than candlelight. The police did not have any cooking implements and had to rely on the goodwill of the displaced to feed them; this left the displaced in a difficult situation. The young corporal in charge of the detachment said to us "We're displaced persons, just like they are," while one of the men joked grimly, in a reference to upcoming talks between the government and the FARC aimed at securing the release of three hundred police and

Army and to their own lack of heavy weapons, that "We're in training to take over from the prisoners the FARC have." The good news here was that we were able to verify from several accounts that a succession of corporals, rotating through the Hacienda, had firmly rejected overtures from the paras to help out in identifying possible guerrilla sympathizers in the camp and had indeed strongly warned the paras against any incursions.

There was a further disadvantage to the camp's location at the Hacienda El Cacique that did not become apparent until late 1999. Following torrential rains throughout Chocó Department, the small river that debouches into Cupica Bay suddenly swelled to catastrophic locations, sweeping away in a matter of minutes the nearby village of Cupica itself. Suddenly, this camp for two hundred displaced was home to nearly two thousand.

The civic authorities in Bahía Solano, in whose jurisdiction the camp falls, were careful to express to me their sympathy for the displaced, but it was clear that they were a major headache that the municipality would much rather do without. Municipal programs in support of the camp had steadily been cut – for example, while the mayor originally supplied the periodic use of his township's launch, gas, and the services of its driver for free, the displaced now had to pay for this by digging into the credit for food that was transferred on an irregular basis to the grocery store by various governmental and non-governmental agencies. It was out of the question for the township to supply a teacher for the nearly one hundred children in the camp. At the hospital, the story was a similar one; wringing his hands, the director said that he would continue to treat members of the community for free, but that he could no longer supply drugs nor could he transport sick persons from the camp to the hospital – in justification he brandished bills that showed his institution to be US$20,000 in the red. Meanwhile, as the director freely admitted, 95 percent of the community at Hacienda El Cacique suffered from malaria. Central government had also been cutting back on assistance: one year ago, food shipments to a value of US$2,000 were being despatched every fifteen days, but now the flow was down to US$1,200 of food once a month.

In spite of undeniable budget constraints, careful triangulation of accounts from different sources led me to the conclusion that the mayor and other municipal employees were actively "squeezing" the displaced here; certainly I had the impression that at times, in the course of our meetings with officials, our own Commission was being manipulated, with a view to our recommending an immediate return of the community to their place of origin. We even suspected that the mayor was not above exaggerating certain elements of the security situation here: while there was no denying the threat faced by this community from paras and other armed actors, he went over the top by trying to persuade us that there also existed an explosive situation with the local community – a manifest exaggeration – and gave himself away by repeatedly and darkly blackmailing us, saying, "When there's a massacre, don't say I didn't warn you." The mayor was noticeably uninterested in hearing about still-existing conditions of grave insecurity back in the Cacarica area: he just wanted the displaced off his turf.

Meanwhile, as in Pavarandó and as in their sister community located in Turbo, the displaced of Hacienda El Cacique (who totalled 198, in fifty-seven families) were highly organized and articulate in their positions. The settlement was clean, with neat paths laid out, centering on a makeshift schoolhouse and chapel. A European NGO had installed latrines and drinking-water tanks. As at Pavarandó, the community was organized into various committees (health, food, culture, sports, security), each with its representative on a central committee. The cultural committee was particularly active, and we were treated to a welcoming performance of traditional songs and dances, the highlight being an intricate dance/song entitled "We Are the Children of Chocó." The community had controversially turned down a number of proposals for small productive projects at the Hacienda, their fear (perhaps not unfounded) being that, were such projects to be successfully implemented, the government would use this to evade its responsibility of ensuring their safe return to their communities of origin. The displaced had also refused temporary relocation in smaller groups to other areas, reasoning that – divided – they would lose what little bargaining power they had thus far gained. At the same time, community leaders expressed to me in passionate terms their growing shame at being seen as freeloaders, spongers. Maintaining one's dignity in a situation such as this is a challenge indeed.

As I was about to leave the El Cacique camp (and face 150 km of increasingly rough open Pacific Ocean in our now less-than-seaworthy craft ...) one of the community leaders asked if I would take with me two displaced persons whom the community judged to be in grave danger of their lives. I did so. The individuals asked, still afraid even in

Welcoming songs, Cupica

the town, to share my large hotel room in Bahía Solano, and, next day, I accompanied one of the two on the plane to Bogotá. He travelled with a single small bag. He had left his wife and three-year-old boy behind at the Hacienda. It was his first time in the capital, but he walked with touching faith and blitheness over to the NGO member who had come to meet him in the hurly burly of El Dorado airport and take him to a safe house. He had told me on the flight that he thought he could never go back.

By the end of 1999, the Verification Commission had reached a turning point. Almost three years had gone by since the original displacement from the Cacarica and the situation was critical in both Turbo and the much smaller El Cacique: humanitarian relief was drying up, and, although both communities had held up remarkably well under the circumstances, some groups were drifting away from the process. Notably Adán, one of the leaders whom I had got to know quite well, had – much to the disgust of his fellow displaced – cut a deal with a company engaged in illegal logging in the Cacarica and had taken with him, back to the region, an important faction of the community. The government was meanwhile twisting and turning: while on the one hand it was seeking to portray this as a model return process, its unconscionable delays in actually delivering on its commitments were making a mockery of that claim. The displaced of Turbo and El Cacique, now working together, decided to play one of their final cards: a group of about eighty would launch a forty-five-day "Exploratory" or "Preparatory" return in the dual hope of rallying internal solidarity and of shaming the government into action.

I was asked to accompany the planned final days of this Exploratory Return, and in early December 1999 I found myself again bumping across the Gulf of Turbo and into the mouths of the Atrato River. On the way upriver, as part of a discussion about fishing, I learned in passing that one of the more important rules in these parts is not to retrieve floating human bodies out of the river – persons who do so risk the same fate, I was earnestly told. Paras and guerrillas used the river as a kind of constantly moving billboard to spread their message of terror to communities along the riverside. Something to bear in mind in the course of my future travels here. More pleasantly, with dusk falling, we nosed our way by dugout into ever-narrower river channels that looked quite different from my previous visit – which had taken place when the river was at least ten feet lower. The evening sky was flecked with flocks of parrots and colourful macaws returning home; howlers began their evening chorus, and – an unforgettable moment – a jaguar lazily contemplated us from a branch high above the river, yawned, and then crept off into the gloom.

In the course of the exercise, the community leaders had planted twenty-eight hectares of assorted crops, cleared body-high undergrowth from the two small settlements that they hoped would be the centre of their new community, and – like the members of the Community of Peace of San José de Apartadó – had posted large signs indicating to all the "actors" their neutrality. But as we gathered under the straw roof of the community roundhouse, with mosquitoes swarming in clouds and a throbbing generator providing uncertain light to three forty-watt bulbs, I sensed the mood was a sombre one. In spite of all the community's efforts and their trust in agreements already initialled by the government, they had during the course of their forty-five-day exploration been badly let down. The government would still not sign the critical papers, would still not disburse the long-promised funds;

the president's visit had been postponed *sine die*. In consequence, the community leaders had determined to go back to Turbo, to the squalid refugee shelters and the overcrowded and unsanitary basketball arena that had been their home for the past thirty-three months. There they would simply wait once more – for God knew how long.

The last of the speakers, a Black man some eighty years old, provoked hilarity when he began his "short history of the community" with the words "In 1492, Cristóbal Colón set sail from Cadiz ..."; but by the time he had completed his long saga of trials and tribulations, he had his audience spellbound. When he concluded, no-one said a word. I momentarily remembered being forced to learn, as a child, John Keats's famous (if historically inaccurate) poem:

> ... like some watcher of the skies
> When a new planet swims into his ken;
> Or like stout Cortez when with eagle eyes
> He star'd at the Pacific – and all his men
> Look'd at each other with a wild surmise -
> Silent, upon a peak in Darien.

The return to Turbo began at 1:00 AM, by starlight, as dugouts shuttled families, dogs, and roosters down the narrow, tree-overhung channels to where the community's chalupa (small open cargo freighter) waited; the chalupa was optimistically dubbed "La Nueva Esperanza" (New Hope) and was painted in the five bright colours of the community. Yet again, I felt I was reliving some episode from the Old Testament as we made our way back to Turbo, with the patriarchs leading the entire boat in songs of their own composition as well as some Evangelical hymns. More prosaically, there was a near disaster when it was decided to transfer a large 125-HP engine from one dugout to another, this in midstream with a strong wind blowing: in the course of the subsequent chaotic manoeuvres, a number of people fell into the river but were rescued quite promptly.

Meanwhile, I found time to accompany representatives of the federal Office of the Procurator General on a side trip up the Cirilo, a tributary of the Cacarica River. Here, in spite of a recent law to the contrary (of which I was shown the text), logging was proceeding on a massive scale – huge and valuable Cativa tree trunks blocked many of the river channels, and the buzz of chainsaws could be heard every-

"New Hope" en route to the Cacarica

where. Darién is in fact one of the most biodiverse regions in the world, a direct extension of the forests of Chocó that have been declared a Heritage of Humanity. When would something actually be done to stop this? I asked. The couple from the Procuraduría shrugged; "It's very complicated" was all they would say, after taking a few photographs. To me it looked remarkably simple.

Back in Bogotá, developments took a further twist. Days after our return to Turbo, the government finally did deliver the long-awaited land titles, albeit not from the hands of the president, as he had promised; a diplomatic but still plainly worded letter to the powers that be, from the Canadian Embassy, may have contributed in a small way to this positive development. And yet more "definitive" promises were made ... With many misgivings, the Return was on again, its first wave set for 28 February 2000.

Was this really it? I was beginning to think that, however shabbily the Cacarica displaced might have been treated, they were probably now best advised to cut their losses, take the little that was on offer and return. The prospect of another year or more in the Babylon of the Turbo sports stadium was now surely worse than any dangers or hardships they might face back in the Cacarica.

On Saturday 26 February 2000, the entire membership of the Mixed Verification Commission assembled near Turbo for a final preparatory meeting and to discuss with the XVII Brigade arrangements for the return that would begin the following Monday. While this meeting of the Commission was in many ways depressingly typical – after no less than two years of negotiation, the dredge promised by the Ministry of Transport was still not available, and the Ministry of Health could lend a doctor but no medical supplies – the mood was nevertheless one of cautious optimism. There were several moments that hovered between farce and tragedy: General Vargas, for example, actually suggested NGOs pay for the gasoline that would be needed for his men to run escort duties (a proposal angrily rejected by the NGOs) while an official for the Red de Solidaridad, crestfallen, announced that after she had spent the last week fighting to obtain gasoline for the Turbo Hospital launch that would accompany the return, she had now learned that the hospital had no such launch.

On the late evening of 27 February, at the basketball arena, the community began the ceremonies that would jointly mark three years of displacement and the first phase of the return. While everyone held candles that flickered in the hot breeze, the 250 who had been selected for the first wave were ceremonially named, presented, and exhorted to uphold the principles of the Territory of Life. Persons accompanying the return, including myself, were given tiny replicas of the community's bright five-coloured flag and solemnly asked to watch over the journey. A memorial to the community's dead was unveiled, and the elder women led the crowd in a dirge.

A motley procession then formed. At its head: forty widows wearing the white kerchief of mourning that is traditional to Colombia's Afro-Colombian community, with three donkey-drawn floats following them. Behind came all the children, each carrying huge cardboard placards with letters making up the words "Life," "Dignity," "Truth," "Self-Determination," "Solidarity," and "Justice"; by night's end, "Self-Determination" had become incomprehensibly jumbled. On one of the floats functioned the community's own fledgling radio station: its power drawn from a car battery borrowed from Justicia y Paz's jeep, it consisted of one elderly man (known as a "Patriarch") carefully car-

Children at the return ceremonies, Turbo, February 2000

rying an antenna on a long and bendy pole, while another tweaked an amplifier in a tent on the float and a third – tethered by his cable to the float – walked alongside, describing into a microphone the scene as the procession wound through Turbo. Fifty metres behind walked another man with a transistor at his ear; he would occasionally rush up to the radio float to report on reception quality. Every so often, as the procession moved from the pool of light cast by one street lamp into the darkness preceding the next, transmission would cease as the reporter struggled to read his notes.

Meanwhile, all through the night, the four massive chalupas that would form the heart of our flotilla were being loaded up at the harbour. The pigs, chickens, and fourteen mules were left to last. At 9:00 AM (only three hours after schedule), the chalupas finally pulled out, to a rousing wharfside send-off. Along with the members of Justicia y Paz and Peace Brigades International, I rode shotgun in one of the three faster launches that would simultaneously serve as sheepdogs and advance scouts.

Loading the chalupas at Turbo, February 2000

With all the predictable mishaps (dead outboard engines necessitating delicate mid-ocean operations, seasick children, a mule breaking loose, an anxious pig jumping overboard) the fleet headed out, first into the windy and rough Gulf of Urabá, then into the mouths of the Atrato. Nearing the turn-off to the Cacarica, we caught up with the Navy patrol – four fast and heavily armed gunboats (piranhas) and a mother ship. There was much huddling among the men of the community and shouted suggestions from boat to boat: the escort was finally asked to move way ahead, out of sight. The last thing anyone wanted was to be seen by the guerrillas to be returning home in the company of the Navy.

Motoring up the Peranchito river as dusk falls

With late afternoon coming on, we moved up the ever-narrowing Cacarica and into its even smaller tributaries, the Perancho and Peranchito. At one point we "internationals" sped ahead to string an enormous welcome banner across the river and forty feet up, a complex operation that predictably led to three people falling in. As the four chalupas, led by the Diós Sabrá ("God will provide" or "God Knows"), punted their way slowly under the banner in the twilight, a silence fell over everyone, broken only by the far-off and haunting cries of the howlers. It was, I sensed, a moment both of fear and of rejoicing by the community: while they had waited three years to reach this point, few could forget the terrible events of 28 February 1997 and the dead they had left behind; few were under any illusions that the months ahead would be easy.

Over the subsequent days, dining off rice and river fish and sleeping in the hornet- and mosquito-infested ruins of the two settlements that would form the nuclei of the Territory of Life, we helped to set up the Ondas del Cacarica radio station and sat in on long meetings on the riverbank at which the priorities for the next few months were end-

At the landing place, Cacarica

lessly debated. Every meeting began with a rousing rendition of the gospel-like "Oyeme Chocó," an anthem of the community's own devising that recounts its history and its hopes. There are many reasons to despair of Colombia, but the stoicism, endurance, and spirit of these people are not among them.

On our return to Bogotá, I received a fax from members of the community still holed up in Turbo, waiting their turn to go home. It was full of spelling mistakes and many of the signatures were mere Xs. It read, in part: "We wish to thank you for your presence on our return ... We hope that your support for us will help bring people together, so that nobody else will ever have to endure what we have endured, here or anywhere else in the world."

6 Quibdó, the Medio Atrato, and the Pacific Coast

CHOCÓ IS COLOMBIA'S forgotten department. Fringing the Pacific from Panama almost to Ecuador, it is a land of lush green jungles and mountains that come right to the water's edge; there is great beauty and grinding poverty.

The capital of Chocó is Quibdó. This oppressive, filthy, and ramshackle riverside city of sixty thousand people could come straight out of Conrad's *Nostromo*: with only the most tenuous of links to the outside world, it feels cut off both geographically and in time from the rest of Colombia. Its small airport is capable of handling propeller planes, and there is a precipitous and usually muddy dirt road to Medellín, but otherwise the main artery of transport is the River Atrato – it is 500 km downstream to Turbo, in the Gulf of Darién, 700 km to Cartagena. There is not a single kilometre of paved road in the department; even the electricity comes over the mountains and frequently fails. Grandiose plans to route the Panamerican Highway through the department and link remote coastal settlements by road with the interior remain only at the initial stage, in the face of budget constraints and opposition

The waterfront, Quibdó

from environmental and indigenous groups. As in Urabá to the north, the department is plagued by paramilitary activity.

In Quibdó the paras (in plain clothes) maintain effective control over the strategic fuel dock, where all vessels plying the Atrato must sooner or later call; in nearby Istmina, they do so in uniform. Sailing downstream from Quibdó by leaky dugout on my first visit in 1997, I passed by the poetically named village of Luna de Belén (Bethlehem Moon) that had been "cleared" by paras six months previously, while at Tanguí, further downriver, the village elders told me that uniformed paras had camped on the edge of town for several weeks. The paras were even at Bahía Solano, the coastal village that is the closest Chocó comes to having a tourist resort, even though there had never been a guerrilla presence here.

Most significantly, the paras control all the river traffic on the Atrato and its tributaries, that is to say 90 percent of all movement in the department. This is effected by means of blockades at narrow points on the river, or, more usually, campesinos are required to have a written authorization from a para leader before buying gas for their outboard or before making purchases in the department's few commercial centres.

I visited the town's ramshackle covered basketball stadium, where there were 512 persons camping on the court; a city official estimated a further four thousand to five thousand people were dispersed in city slums. Assistance to these individuals was minimal to nonexistent. The city ombudsman's office (staffed by a startling twelve persons, plus secretarial staff) told me flatly that they had no resources.

The displaced had no running water: drinking water was brought in every two to three days by a police tanker. There were three toilets, all out of order and/or overflowing into the nearby barrio. Once a fortnight, the Office of the Presidential Counsellor for the Displaced delivered food packages designed to last three days; the slack was haphazardly taken up by the local Red Cross and the Catholic Church. Although there were 150 children of school age here, only a dozen or so had been able to find places in local schools. In an effort to provide some modest form of employment, the Church was funding a small business producing mops and brooms – run out of the stadium's locker room. Cooking was on wood fires set up on the (fortunately concrete) bleachers; as a result, the whole building was perpetually clouded by woodsmoke, and the interior, with fires glowing eerily and dozens of families going about their chores on the bleachers, had a Dantesque feel. The community was relatively well organized: I was received by their committee, in its office close to the rafters.

Every individual, of course, had tragic stories: one of the committee members here calmly narrated the story of seven decapitations in his home village of Carepa and added that the paras had held a game of football with one head. Only about half the Quibdó displaced persons actually wanted to go back to their villages of origin: the other half either felt that the authorities would never be able to guarantee their security or – commonly – they were "jornaleros," dayworkers without even a notional title to any piece of land.

In rural Chocó, meanwhile, people were not starving – the land was too fertile for that – but there were the telltale pot-bellies that indicate infant malnutrition, and, more worryingly, dengue, cholera, and malaria were reaching epidemic proportions. In the river village of Las Mercedes – a community of about one thousand and where I stopped – four children had died of malaria and two of cholera in the past three months. Indigenous leaders earlier told me of eighty dead of malaria in jungle communities under their influence and complained that, although a recent program had trained many native health promoters, the investment had been wasted because there were no medical supplies available. The Las Mercedes village nurse was sick, having been diagnosed with stress, while in Tanguí, the health clinic – which anyway had no medicine – had been closed since late last year: the nurse, it was thought, was in Quibdó, attempting to claim several months of back salary owed her.

It had been years since the last governmental malaria eradication campaign in Chocó, and no new one was planned; anti-malarial prescriptions, even for those who had the money, could not be had in Quibdó. Although most villages now had access to a radio-telephone, there was nobody people could summon (in case of emergency) who would come to deliver medical care, except for a steep fee.

In schooling, the situation was no better. In rural communities there might be two teachers for three hundred children; others were supposedly served by teachers based in Quibdó, maybe an hour or two away by launch – elders at Baudo Bajo told me that they were lucky if the teacher showed up one day a week. At Tanguí, the school roof blew off the previous October and had still to be replaced; school was meanwhile impossible. Then there was the question of matriculation fees and uniforms; although education was nominally free in this country, both were in fact obligatory and often out of the financial reach of families that were hardly in the money economy. For all of Chocó's indigenous communities (pop. forty thousand), there were only ten teachers capable of speaking the indigenous languages. The bottom line: hardly anyone in rural Quibdó received a meaningful education or the most basic of health services.

Grassroots community groups had moved to fill the gap left by government and were doing a remarkably good job under the circumstances. The two most important of these were an umbrella grouping of the department's indigenous peoples, known as OREWA, and a similar grouping of Black communities, ACIA.

OREWA (Organización Regional Embera y Wounaan) – a sophisticated organization that had a fourfold mission: to promote the unity of the indigenous people of Chocó, to maintain their territorial integrity, to defend their different cultures, and to insist on autonomy – brought together the Katío, Embera, Chamí, Wounaan, and Tule peoples of Chocó. OREWA leaders have well-articulated views on autonomy in particular – as such, they have in the past been in touch with James Bay Cree, Mohawk, and Inuit groups. Meanwhile, ACIA (Asociación Campesina Integral del Atrato) is an umbrella organization for the rural Black communities (which, descending from "Maroons" or escaped slaves, are considered to be culturally homogeneous and distinct from the Caribbean Blacks) of central Chocó; it claims about 175,000 members in 120 communities.

Both groups have been successful in attracting local and international NGO support for a wide range of small developmental and environmental projects. Most remarkably, both have worked together over the past several years on a massive land claim settlement of over 800,000 hectares – remarkable because these two communities had so often been in conflict, the Black population having in historical times forced the Indians into ever more remote mountain territory, away from the rivers and the coast.

The land settlement, which gave collective title to hundreds of communities, was a landmark one for Colombia and was exemplary not just for the way in which ACIA and OREWA worked together but also for their joint cooperation with the United Nations Development Programme, INCORA (the National Agrarian Reform Institute), the Catholic Church, and a leading German NGO, often in spite of the overt opposition of armed groups throughout the department. It was hoped that one of the immediate benefits of the settlement would be to brake paramilitary-inspired expulsions. On account, on the one hand, of their efforts to have land titled and, on the other, of their refusal to deal with the guerrillas, leaders of both ACIA and OREWA had been targeted by both the paramilitaries and the guerrillas. Two ACIA leaders were shot dead outside their Quibdó HQ in August 1997, while OREWA handed me a list of six community leaders killed and four more disappeared.

Two years later, in January 2000, I was in Chocó again, this time at the request of the National Human Rights Ombudsman, who had invited me to participate in a multi-agency commission to investigate a recent catastrophe that had befallen the remote and exotically located Pacific town of Juradó. Juradó, which lies approximately 15 km south of Colombia's frontier with Panama and 50 km north of Bahía Cupica, was until 12 December 1999 a backwater; it could only be reached by trudging over 100 km through the trackless jungles of the Darién isthmus or via a four-hour fast launch trip from Bahía Solano, itself only accessible by sea or air. But on 12 December – not coincidentally on the very day that the USA was formally handing over the Panama canal – the idyll was shattered. At 1:00 AM, the rebel FARC threw six hundred men against the small hilltop base, manned by Marines, to the north of the town.

Townspeople, it seems, had warned both the Marines and the police that an attack was imminent: when many campesinos had failed to return from the fields on the evening of 11 December, people had guessed that they might be being held by the FARC in the run up to an attack. The eighteen-man police garrison at the south end of town took the warnings seriously and prepared for a siege, but the Marines commander in the north laughed off the warning as a false alarm. Many of his men were drunk when the attack began; others were still carousing in town. By dawn the rebels had overrun the base, killing twenty-six Marines (many of the sentries had their throats cut) and capturing most of the rest. They then moved on to the police station, where – amazingly – the police were able to hold out against constant machine-gun fire and homemade mortar attacks until 7:00 PM, at which point aerial relief finally arrived. Throughout this attack a Colombian navy corvette, the 1944-vintage ARC Sebastián Belalcázar, stood about 6 km offshore, apparently unaware that anything was going on. An estimated forty FARC were also killed in the attack.

When the rebels withdrew, all but a few hundred of the townspeople also left, many to Bahía Solano, others to Buenaventura, and about a thousand to the Panamanian town of Jaque. The surviving police and Marines pulled out, as did all the town authorities, the teachers, and the nurse. The townspeople said they would not come back unless and until the Marines and police issued formal guarantees of their safety.

It was into this situation that our humanitarian mission arrived. It had taken us the best part of a day to charter a fast launch in Bahía Solano, and our trip north had been a rough one.

At Juradó, we met with the remaining townsfolk on the beach. The corvette was parked offshore, just visible on the horizon; this was supposed to reassure the town, but, as the locals pointed out to us, its presence did them little good during the attack (what they didn't know,

Ruins of the police station at Juradó

moreover, was that the Belalcázar didn't even have a ship's launch, having lent it to a sister ship on Colombia's other ocean). In a word, the Juradeños had been abandoned to their fate.

But they were not taking this lying down: in a deft public-relations ploy, the families remaining in the town had recently hoisted the Panamanian flag and announced that, as Colombia appeared not to want them, they were inviting their neighbour to take them over. And the message to our commission was strident and unanimous: "It is the duty of the Armed Forces to protect us, their obligation is to return, and on this issue there can be no negotiation."

The dynamic was an interesting one, but neither typical nor transparent. The "typical" displacement is, in the first place, provoked by paramilitary incursions rather than guerrilla attacks; the guerrillas are

Remains of the Marine base, Juradó

marginally more socially responsible in this respect. And in this case, although the Marine and police bases were completely flattened, I observed that the guerrillas indeed seemed to have taken care not to damage civilian structures or housing. It was no doubt distressing for the townsfolk to be bystanders to a bloody battle, but they themselves were not directly affected.

It looked as though what had happened was that the guerrillas had attacked, but the paras had then encouraged the population to leave and in turn then pressure the military to reinforce the garrison at Juradó – thus providing a shield for a renewed para presence. Our delegation had to be careful not to get caught up in this game.

The remains of the police station were an awesome sight. For one hundred metres all around, the dirt was pitted by ten-foot craters left by the launching of the FARC's now trademark propane canister mortars. The frame of the three-storey reinforced concrete building was more or less standing, but all the walls had been blown in and there were a hundred or more machine-gun bullet impacts on each wall of the tiny tower that topped the building; the building would have fitted perfectly on the set of *Saving Private Ryan*. It defied understanding how eighteen men were able to hold off six hundred from a mere pile of rubble. In the wreckage, fluttering in the sea breeze, I found the station's duty rosters and daily log, with the routine events of the days leading up to the attack painstakingly recorded in a childish hand.

At the Marine base, the scene was even grimmer. Discarded uniforms and boots, some of them bloodstained, littered the ground. Inside battered ammunition boxes, there were mangled piles of metal – bullets that spontaneously fired in the conflagration. You could work out which were the last holdouts by piles of used rocket-propelled grenade cartridges. A bar-football machine in the other ranks' mess was riddled with bullet holes.

All this, of course, in that South Seas location. We boarded the Belalcázar at midnight for a ride back to Bahía Solano; the stars were so bright you could almost read by them, and the dolphins left phosphorescent trails as they dived under and around our bows. Another day in paradise.

My last trip in Chocó began again in Quibdó, this time at the request of the Catholic Diocese. The electricity had been off for three days, and the fan was dead in the windowless room of the waterfront hotel where I was staying. As dawn was coming up, I sipped a strong black coffee and then wandered for an hour on the waterfront, which was already coming to life and which was as pungent as I remembered from my first visit. Huge dugouts were unloading bananas, while double-decker wooden cargo boats were taking on mahogany beams; bales of dried fish stood piled up in the puddles on the quayside, as wizened Black men hobbled past with huge loads on their backs. At 8:00 AM, I started my rounds, with a view to getting an assessment of the security situation.

The Army's XVII Brigade, based 500 km downstream at the mouth of the river, had a Marine battalion that consisted of a mothership and four fast piranhas, but General Vargas (now commanding in Urabá, in place of General Carreño) had already told me earlier that he did not have enough gasoline to send his vessels as far upriver as the Middle Atrato. And now Colonel Perdomo of the Quibdó-based Manosalvo Battalion, which comprised seven hundred men, said he'd love to be able to patrol the zone, but he had neither boats nor access to a helicopter. I asked him, "So why are you here?" He replied: "Good question."

That left just two static police detachments who faced each other across the river at Bellavista (West Bank) and Vigía del Fuerte (East Bank) to cover the huge stretch of river between Quibdó and the mouth that was infested by illegal armed groups. The police detachments did not even have a launch to communicate with each other across the river.

The Catholic diocese of Quibdó, in the person of one Padre Albeiro, assisted by German missionaries Sister Ursula and Padre Uli, did their best to tend to the civilian population of the region; they received support from the German charity Misereor and the Spanish charity Pan Para el Tercer Mundo (PTM). On the one hand, they ran a monthly *African Queen*-type launch (the Doña María) that delivered basic supplies to beleaguered communities downriver; there was a tacit agreement by the armed actors that they would let pass this launch, which was always accompanied by Church personnel and which flew a white flag, even though all other traffic was subject to searches, ransacking, and harassment of those on board. On the other, they lobbied with the authorities (civilian and military) to warn of imminent displacements of the civilian population and to ensure minimal conditions of survival for communities already displaced. The Diocese also tried to engineer the return of displaced communities whenever and wherever possible.

Along with Alice, a young British human rights worker seconded to the UN High Commission for Human Rights in Bogotá, I was to accompany the Doña María on a mission that doubled as a supply run and a "return" – in this case of the one-hundred-strong community of Mesopotamia. Our role was, in essence, to serve as human shields, deterrents to guerrilla or para attacks.

Our journey was uneventful, apart from repeated breakdowns that left us drifting downstream in slow circles; flying a large UN flag was probably helpful in deterring potentially hostile actors. But the river was rarely this quiet. On 19 November 1999, Spanish aid worker Iñigo Eguiluz and local priest Jorge Luis Mazo were killed here when their launch was rammed at high speed by another launch laden with paramilitaries. We passed the wreckage of the launch. Padre Uli made the sign of the cross but said nothing.

At Bellavista ("The Capital of Paradise," according to a large billboard at the wharf), 200 km downriver from Quibdó, we landed. Alice and I met with the young Afro-Colombian officer who led a fifteen-person police detachment here. He commented that the last time he had seen the Marines was early November 1999 (several months ear-

The Bellavista waterfront

lier). We raised with him a rumour that the mayor's personal launch had been manned by paramilitaries in the course of a recent displacement; he sounded unsurprised but said he would investigate. When we raised the same issue with the mayor himself, there was a pregnant pause, after which the mayor said only that he was out of town on the day in question.

Across the river at Vigía del Fuerte, we held a long, confidential interview with young Lieutenant Peña, in command of the twenty-one-man police detachment on the East Bank. Peña had only been seconded to Vigía two months previously, but he had been keeping busy. Notably, on 2 February 2000, a routine police patrol reported back to him that they had detected a large group of paramilitaries (one hundred or more) encamped in the primary school at one end of the 1,500-person settlement. Peña immediately launched an attack on the paras and, over the course of a four-hour firefight, drove them out. The paras returned that night and laid siege to the police station; there was some damage to neighbouring houses, but the affair ended in a stalemate. The paras withdrew and were now, so Peña said, located at Villa Nueva and San Alejandro, about 3 km downstream. Their commander, Peña said, was known as "Paticas" (Sideburns) and was from the Caribbean coast. Meanwhile, the FARC were upstream, Peña told us, in probably larger numbers. To sum up: "*bastante delicado*" (a little delicate).

It was most rare (and accordingly praiseworthy) for elements of the Colombian Armed Forces, whether police or Army, to actively engage large paramilitary units. The action of Teniente Peña in confronting this unit had been a very brave one, the more so in that it immediately brought down upon him the wrath of the local authorities: enraged at Peña and his men for having expelled from their town "our friends," the mayor of Vigía had cut off power and water to the police station and was, when we spoke, doing his utmost to have Peña reassigned. Peña told us that he had received several death threats since February and that at times he feared being fragged by his own men.

Lieutenant Peña was not completely alone in Vigía. We met with the local judge, who trembled visibly as he addressed us in a whisper so low as to be almost inaudible. Vigía, he said, had for the past several years been under de facto siege by the FARC, so that when the paramilitaries appeared on the scene a year ago and began recruiting within the local community, they were warmly welcomed. The judge expressed his admiration for Peña, but suggested that he was hopelessly idealistic: the townspeople would in the end get the better of him.

Back in Bogotá, a few days later, I received a call from Alice. Three hundred members of the 34th and 57th fronts of the FARC had launched an all-out seventeen-hour attack on Vigía, with gas-canister mortars. Peña and his twenty men had been wiped out; their bodies were mutilated with machetes. Eight civilians, including the mayor and two small children (three and four years old), had also been killed. The mayor's body was doused in gasoline and set alight. By the time the Army was able to mount a relief mission it was too late. Over the river at Bellavista, two police were killed and a further nine were missing. I had started writing a letter to Police Commander General Serrano commending twenty-one-year-old Teniente Peña; now I redrafted it as one of condolence.

7 In the Fields of the Drug Lords

AROUND THE WORLD, Medellín, Colombia's second-largest city, is synonymous with one thing – cocaine. Ten years after the death of Pablo Escobar, it remains known as one of the most violent cities on Earth, with a murder rate of 186 per 100,000 – exactly one hundred times that of Canada.

Medellín is also known as the City of Flowers or the City of Eternal Spring, and most Colombians will boast proudly of its ultra-modern and clean metro – a contrast to the chaotic and dirty public transport system of Bogotá, where a metro has been dreamed of for decades. It is beautifully set in a high and steep-sided mountain bowl. My first visit to Medellín, I spent looking at projects supported by our small Canada Fund for Local Initiatives.

Barrio Popular Número Uno (which, unsurprisingly, is adjacent to Barrio Popular Número Dos) is a slum settlement high on the mountainside to the northeast of Medellín proper. This area was invaded by squatters about thirty years ago, but the local community has, over the years, forced the authorities to lay on basic services (water, electricity, paved streets), so that the area is no longer as rough as it used to be. But in the late 1980s and early 90s, this barrio of some thirty thousand people was effectively ruled by the "sicarios" (paid killers) of Escobar and the other drug lords of the Medellín cartel. Fourteen-year-old children were at that time regularly claiming bounties for each police officer or soldier they killed, and uniformed authorities still did not venture anywhere near this part of town. Street gangs remained prevalent and "forasteros" (outsiders) who did not have a good reason to be here were likely to receive a summary welcome. Unfortunately, the reputation of the barrio remained such that young men who grew up here and sought a job elsewhere in Medellín were likely to be turned down the moment they mentioned where their home was. My taxi driver needed a little persuasion (i.e., financial inducement over what the meter showed) to venture here.

The project Canada had supported in Barrio Popular Número Uno was part of a wider operation run by the Fundación para el Fomento de la Educación Popular y la Pequeña Industria (FEPI – Foundation for the Development of Popular Education and Micro-Industry), which operated only here. The Fundación ran a small but well-patronized library for children (the local school had no library) and, from its modest but clean set of offices on the third floor of a three-storey building, offered adult education classes, health clinics for the elderly, cultural events, and so on. The physical plant of FEPI was built largely thanks to a donation by the Embassy of Holland.

The most innovative area of FEPI's activities was its program to create small community-run businesses that both generated income and provided training for FEPI members. FEPI thus ran three or four small corner stores, which were manned by FEPI members who received a small wage (just above the legal minimum wage) and on-the-job training. The particular project we had supported (to the tune of US$12,000) was the stocking and establishment of a "ferretería" (ironmongers'), known unoriginally as *Numero 42* (after the street number).

Two young women and a man ran the ferretería on a day-to-day basis. It was open twelve hours a day, six days a week. The shop was small but very clean, well-stocked, and well patronized. It had only been up and running two or three months. Turnover was between US $5,000 and US$10,000 per month, mainly in the form of plumbing materials (plastic piping, etc.), paint, cement, and hardware fittings; the break-even threshold was about US$4,700, so the ferretería was work-

The staff at *Número 42*

ing within projected parameters at this time. The accounts were meticulously kept and the two young women were also currently attending night school at FEPI to learn about inventory control. I noticed pinned to the wall what was obviously an internal FEPI document listing the strengths and weaknesses of this particular operation – this was a professional, realistic assessment, and, talking to the two women, it was evident to me that steps were being taken to address the various problems that had inevitably shown up after the launch of the shop.

The unremarkable and helpful young man who helped part-time at the shop introduced me to a friend. The friend, so he told me with candour, worked for Pablo Escobar as part of a two-man (or two-boy) motorbike team. Together, they had performed numerous hits. He described the routine. After a brief early morning visit to the streetside shrine of the Virgin Mary, where they would pray for success in their upcoming assignment, they would locate the home of their assigned quarry and wait for him to emerge. Once he stepped out and into his car, they would don their helmets (to avoid possible identification) and follow him until a good straight stretch of street came up. They would then pull up past the driver's door, the pillion rider would pour in a few rounds of his automatic pistol, and they would ride on, dump the bike in a side street, and make off on foot. For this they would be paid between US$50 and US$100, maybe more if the target was a police officer. Not once had they come close to being caught.

"And what did you think of Escobar?" I asked. He shrugged and looked a little embarrassed – he knew that he was expected to condemn him. But he would not. "He was not a bad man, you know. He did many things for us. He built our stadium. He built houses. He put in electricity and water. We loved him. The government has done nothing like that."

He told me I should visit Escobar's grave before I left Medellín. When I finally did (on another visit), I was not that surprised to find it strewn and garlanded with fresh flowers; on its marble top were sad written prayers.

Drugs pervade all of Colombian society. On the surface, just as the young man in Medellín had assured me, their effect is not all negative. The industry pumps billions of dollars into the Colombian economy and, as it has alternately waxed and waned, has generated employment booms and building frenzies; most of the plush homes in Medellín's ritzy Envigado district were built when the cartel was at its apogee and were financed directly or indirectly by the proceeds of cocaine. So substantial an industry is this that the international accountants have now decided pragmatically to include it in calculations of Colombia's GDP. But the long-lasting effects of the drug trade are devastating.

In the first place, the need to launder huge amounts of money in a rapid manner means that businesses are built up artificially, forcing more legitimate enterprises out of the market. A case in point was a chain of pizza houses that, at the time of my arrival in Colombia, was cornering the market in pizza delivery with an incredible incentive – buy a twelve-inch Hawaiian, get a coupon for another larger one. This was too good to be true: in fact, it was a money-laundering operation. The owners did not care that the business was losing money hand over fist as long as they could process their drug proceeds through it in an on-going manner at a cost of "only" 10 percent or so. Eventually the business was shut down when the proprietors were investigated; but in the meantime dozens of perfectly legitimate and competitive businesses had been forced to close.

Even more corrosive are the effects of the drug industry on political life and on the democratic process in Colombia. The cartels, their money, and the loyalties and terror campaigns that the money could buy cowed President César Gaviria to the point at which, in spite of intense pressure to the contrary from the USA, he amended the Constitution of Colombia, so as to eliminate the possibility of extradition.

The allegation (believed by almost everyone) that Gaviria's successor, Ernesto Samper took US$6 million of Cali cartel money to finance his successful 1994 presidential campaign dogged his entire tenure. The perception that the president was dirty meant that for four years Colombia's relationship with the USA was a battlefield; it brought with it not only international opprobrium for the country but economic sanctions by the USA.

But when Samper, in his last year in office, launched an attempt to rehabilitate himself and restore the option of extradition, Western countries leapt in to encourage him and his cabinet: by doing so, the Government of Colombia would not only be conforming once again with international impunity standards but also be making an important statement to the narcotraffickers.

Canada had a particular interest in having extradition restored: one of the Orejuela brothers, the imprisoned capos of the Cali cartel, was wanted not just in the USA but also for crimes committed on Canadian soil. We were instructed in late 1997 to lobby Foreign Minister María Emma Mejía, as the time of the vote drew near.

Mejía, who remains active in Colombian politics and who ran later as Horacio Serpa's vice-presidential candidate, was one of the few bright lights of the Samper administration. From Medellín, where she had as a young woman worked as a volunteer in barrios such as the one I knew, she was drop-dead good looking, with integrity and intelligence to match. We met in one of the beautiful and ornate high-ceilinged old rooms of Simón Bolívar's old residence – now the Foreign Ministry.

Gently fingering a string of pearls over her Dior blouse, she heard me out. There was a long pause.

"Let me tell you how it works," she eventually started in her husky voice. "You're elected a Member of Congress or, maybe – like me – you're called up to join the cabinet. You're full of ideals. You want to change the world. You're not going to make much money, but you knew that when you signed up." She paused for a moment. "Then one day you find in your bank account that there's an extra $10,000. You ask the bank manager, but he doesn't know where it's from. You wonder what to do, but decide in the end it's probably a mistake and they'll catch up with it sooner or later. A month later you bump into a distant acquaintance, a businessman, at a party. You chat inconsequentially, and then he lets slip that he's so glad to have been able to make a contribution to your successful election campaign." She paused again and looked up at me with her trademark and much-caricatured flutter of the eyelashes. "It's too late to reject the money. A few weeks later, a few months later, there's a vote coming up – like this one, perhaps. He calls you and just says that he and all his friends are counting on you to do the right thing for the country ..."

Sometimes, she went on, it was done a lot more crudely. "*Plata o plomo*" – "Silver or lead." "Not everyone gives in," Mejía said. And she named several Congressmen who had been killed, just within the life of the present legislature.

Moving to business, she gave me her estimate of how the voting might go. A third would vote against extradition because they genuinely believed they were doing the right thing – out of nationalism, out of distrust of the USA. A third would vote in favour because they agreed with the government line – that international law and international justice demand that country A be able to extradite criminals from country B for crimes committed in country A. "And a third will vote against extradition because they have been bought."

We left Bogotá's darkened El Dorado airport at 5:00 AM in a green and white Twin Otter belonging to the Colombian National Police, and, an hour later, with dawn coming up over the Eastern Cordillera, we landed at the National Anti-Narcotics Base at Neiva, Huila Department. As we climbed down from the plane, we felt the wind from the rotors of the four twin-engined Bell 212s in which we would soon be flying. The choppers' red and green navigation lights burned brightly in the light morning mist. There was an air of great purposefulness: one of the helicopters was still fuelling; fatigue-clad gunners were ducking under the rotors and loading bandoleers of fifty-millimetre machine-gun ammunition into the other three; around the perimeter of the helibase, soldiers stood guard.

Anti-narco police helicopters warming up at Neiva

Over a hurried coffee in the briefing room, Colonel Barragán, wearing the trademark wide brimmed camouflage-green hat of his elite force, with one side pinned up, pointed at the large red blobs on the map of central Colombia. These, he explained, were his units' current targets: large expanses of prime heroin poppies, growing on the eastern slopes of the Cordillera, on the very edge of the FARC-controlled "demilitarized" zone.

The poppy fields, which are typically in jungle clearings on steep hillsides between two thousand metres and three thousand metres high, are a relatively new development on the Colombian drug scene, but so rich has the local soil proved to be that Colombian heroin producers, over the space of the past three to four years, have now cornered the market on the East Coast of the USA; rival Asian drug lords are reported to rue the day that they ever agreed to send over their own teams of advisers to help their South American colleagues diversify from cocaine.

The day's targets had been identified by a combination of satellite imagery and aerial reconnaissance undertaken in the course of the last few days. It was hoped that the operation would be a surprise to the

Turbo-Thrush crop sprayer used to eradicate poppies and coca plants

growers, but the Colonel spread his hands apologetically: due to a rumoured heavy FARC presence in the area we would not be able to land to inspect the results of our spraying.

Of the four Bells parked out on the tarmac, two would serve as armed escorts, one would be a high-altitude spotter on the watch for possible ground fire, and the fourth was for eventual search and rescue; we Canadians were split between three of the helicopters, escorting three clumsy-looking Turbo-Thrush crop-duster planes, painted in the grey and maroon colours of DynCorp, the civilian-staffed USA State Department contractor that does all of the actual fumigation in Colombia, using mainly ex-USAF pilots. The complement of the chopper I boarded included a young green-overalled National Police pilot with a bright Colombian flag flash on his arm; his even younger co-pilot; a Black gunner who would man the strut-mounted light machine gun on the rear port side; another gunner who climbed in clutching his machine gun as best he could, eventually propping it up on the floor; an observer who sat on top of the first-aid box; and we two Canadian passengers wedged tightly into the webbing seats by the starboard door.

Flying anti-narco escort duties

The racket was unbelievable – the only communication for the next ninety minutes would be the occasional shout and a few unintelligible hand signals. We lifted off in formation, one after the other; I could see the Turbo-Thrushes lining up on the runway to follow us.

For nearly forty minutes we clattered northeast, first over the badlands of the Tatacoa Desert, then into the more lush foothills of the Eastern Cordillera. The pilot mutely pointed out, four thousand feet below us, the neat grid pattern of a tiny town called Colombia, with its central square and a white colonial church. Ten minutes on, and we were into the target zone. We were barely below the cloud ceiling, and wisps of cloud still clung to the deep green hillsides that rose all around us. Brilliant near-horizontal rays of sun briefly broke through, but, with the cabin doors wide open, it was cold. I could make out a number of brighter green clearings, with trees felled on their edges, and there were two or three tin-roofed shacks on the edges. Parts of the clearings had a purplish red tinge: opium poppies.

It seems to me that we were rather low, but suddenly one of the Turbo-Thrushes was down there, far beneath us, swooping over the treetops. There was a puff of what looked like smoke or a contrail. The pilot soared to avoid the fast-looming hillside, and the cloud he had left behind lingered, ever so slowly drifting down to settle on an irregular bright green patch. The five-second burst of glysophate appeared perfectly placed, although it was invisible by the time it hit the ground. Later, Colonel Barragán explained that the exact duration of every burst was automatically timed and the geographical coordinates of the beginning and end of the burst were plotted by GPS: from the readouts at the end of every mission, it was possible to calculate the exact number of hectares sprayed.

For the next forty minutes we circled, covering the Turbo-Thrushes; our side doors were wide open, the rear gunner had his thumbs resting on the outside of his twin trigger guards. Later I asked him how, over the racket, he could even know if anyone was firing at us: he looks for muzzle flashes and, of course, a tinkling noise on the fuselage is another giveaway. The acrobatics of the Turbo-Thrushes were strangely artistic: the way they placed their whitish-blue clouds so exactly and gracefully, then swept silently up and away to look for the next tiny rectangle of bright green clearing. Our own pilots muttered into the tiny microphones of their jet-fighter helmets – inaudibly over the din of the rotors and the cold wind blowing through the cabin – and periodically tweaked one of the hundreds of switches on the battered consoles of our machine, causing perplexing changes in the frequency of our rattling. Finally, the Turbo-Thrushes finished their task; we pitched forward and, in procession, began the journey back to base. As we hovered down to the tarmac, our observer leaned out of the door to guide the pilot down onto on the large yellow H, our landing pad: when I got out I saw that the skids were no more than half an inch off centre.

The Bells and Turbo-Thrushes began refuelling for their second mission of the day. As we walked back to the briefing room, Barragán explained that they try to squeeze in two missions before 9:30 every morning, because after that the clouds usually come in or – failing that – bright sunshine can have the effect of atomizing the glysophate before it reaches the ground. Barragán was ebullient. "Give us the equipment," he said, "and we could do this job in two years." By this he meant the wiping out of all of Colombia's coca and poppy plantations.

What precisely would that take? According to him, another sixty helicopters on top of the forty on which (on a good day) the National Police can lay their hands – and another dozen or so Turbo-Thrushes or OV-10 Bronco sprayers. By spraying every known site in the country once every four months (the approximate replanting cycles of both coca and poppies) for this period, Barragán estimated that his men could force both the growers and the processors into bankruptcy. But therein lies the rub – as the Colonel frankly admitted. Wipe out the business at that speed and you have a full-blown employment and social crisis on your hands. And there is no political stomach for that.

There are also, of course, serious environmental questions associated with the crop-spraying programs, to which Barragán did not refer. For all the skill of the Turbo-Thrush pilots, some glysophate does end up in the neighbouring forest canopy and a good amount leeches through the soil into the water table. Scientists are making considerable progress in developing a coca-eating virus that could eventually replace the chemical approach, but no similar solution is in sight for poppies.

There are also those safety issues. Three months previously, one of the Bell 212s we had flown in had taken eleven bullet impacts to its fuselage. Kevlar armour on the cabin floor and around the pilots' seats had averted a disaster on that occasion. But the Bell's twin jet engines are not armoured: forced landings following catastrophic engine failure have become something at which Colombian pilots are now the world's experts. And there have been Turbo-Thrush crashes too, usually very underpublicized, as no-one wants to draw attention to American fatalities – even of civilians – in Colombia's drug wars. The latest spice in the life of these pilots was the rumour that the FARC now had SAMs – given credence by two incidents in January 2000 – and that they may also have acquired as many as three armed helicopters; another intriguing rumour had it that one of the latter was lost in December 1999 when the rebels were trying to ship it by barge across a river.

Before returning to Bogotá, we made a stop at Larandia base, near Florencia, in the hot jungles of southeastern Colombia. The anti-narco police's new forward base was not as yet fully operational; from there they planned to attack the coca fields of Putumayo and Caquetá, at present out of range from Neiva. It partially replaced the Miraflores base that was razed by the FARC, with heavy loss of life, over one year ago. But this time the police did not intend to be taken unawares: at the time of my visit, this base – which was in FARC-dominated territory, just to the south of the demilitarized zone, and located on an island in the middle of a swamp – was protected by no less than four Army battalions. Plans called for the fully operational base to have sixty anti-

Huey gunship, Larandia anti-narco base

narco police personnel stationed there, housed in (presumably rather steamy) converted shipping containers parked around the runway.

As at Neiva, the crop-spraying at Larandia is done by DynCorp pilots, here flying a squadron of six dark blue OV-10 or "Bronco" planes, a model originally designed as a tank-buster, the same model I had witnessed in action over Pavarandó. The OV-10 is less manoeuvrable than the Turbo-Thrush, but coca is grown in flat country, so acrobatics are not required; on the other hand, it is fully armoured on its underside and has a longer range than the Turbo-Thrush. The pilots – crewcut, sunburned, and beer-bellied Americans – have all given their planes personal names: Santa Ana, Lovely Rita, and (more dubiously) Speedball. Although DynCorp is nominally a civilian operation, it is run out of Patrick Air Force Base in the USA and a casual stroll around showed that its staff can do more than just fly and dump glysophate: next to the relatively innocent Avionics Shop (also located in a shipping container) is the Gunnery Shop.

Running interference for the OV-10s at Larandia are venerable UH-1H camouflage-painted "Huey"s of early 1960s vintage. They are fitted with internal flexible fuel tanks to allow them to cover all of Putumayo and have inaccurately named Mini-Guns capable of delivering 7,500 fifty-calibre machine-gun rounds in each port; they otherwise look like props for MASH, apparently as battered and war-stained as the day they last lifted off from Pusan or Saigon. Like the Bells, they have removable Kevlar floors, but these are often jettisoned: their weight significantly reduces the Huey's range. Fortunately, the terrain favoured by coca growers does not require the Hueys to fly so high as the Bells at Neiva: I had the feeling that these craft would not make it. The equipment every Colombian pilot would love to fly, of course, is the Sikorsky Blackhawk, a treasured few of which are now on Colombian soil but which, at US$18 million to US$20 million are four to five times more expensive than a Bell 212, ten times more than a reconditioned Huey.

Back to El Dorado. Here, and indeed at all of Colombia's air and sea ports, the fight on drugs is continued, although by this stage of the game it's a rearguard action.

At the international terminal, all your bags – including those going into the hold – are searched and sniffed. As you make your way to the gate, you go through check after check, and there are strategically placed posters warning would-be mules of the many further obstacles they will face before they can breathe safely in Miami.

And even the aircrew have special training. Cabin staff are warned to look out for passengers who sit abnormally still throughout the flight, who refuse the in-flight service and never go to the washroom, who sweat or look pale: it may well be that they have ingested – in little rubber capsules the size of grapes, coated with olive oil to ease swallowing – a couple of kilos of heroin or cocaine. Their seat number and description will be quietly noted and the information radioed ahead. As they disembark they will be scrutinized through two-way mirrors, and, if the profile still holds, they'll be X-rayed and directed to a special toilet.

The mules, of course, still get through. Their ruses are ingenious and numerous.

A favourite tactic is to send three or four mules on a single flight, then arrange for a discreet tip-off to the Miami police. On arrival, the unlucky one is immediately grabbed and searched, the drugs found; the others slip through in the general commotion.

Sometimes young children will be used, on the supposition that they will attract less suspicion. Or invalids. A German quadriplegic tourist used the tubes of his wheelchair to conceal a kilo or more of drugs, but was given away by his nervousness and is now serving a long sentence in Bogotá's La Picota jail. A middle-aged housewife had her buttocks cut open and packages of heroin inserted; but the surgery was botched and the ruse discovered when, suffering from septicaemia, she had no choice but to turn herself over to a doctor on arrival in the USA. Old men are often employed as mules: Colombian legislation prohibits persons over seventy from being sentenced to prison.

The airline crews are often in on the game. One clever plot had seen the crew of a well-known American airline stowing shipments aboard almost every Bogotá-leaving flight for months; the trick was not so much in where they hid the packages (in the gap between the cabin lining and the fuselage itself) but in the fact that they would not seek to extract them immediately upon arrival in Florida. Sometimes they would wait days or even weeks and then tip off colleagues at whichever regional airport – Minneapolis, St. Louis – the aircraft was visiting on that day, where security would be much lower and the recovery could be made without attracting suspicion.

A development in the late 1990s was the dyeing of cocaine: a technique was developed to turn it dark brown or black, which allowed mules to pass it off, without suspicion, as other substances. In one possibly apocryphal story, black cocaine was packaged as instant coffee and carried in the cabin on a commercial airline out of Colombia. The ploy was supposedly only discovered when an unwitting stewardess, short of supplies, decided one morning to break into the reserve stocks in the galley and actually served passengers with diluted cocaine.

Two of the most famous episodes of cocaine running in this period involved officialdom – on one side and on the other. The existence of a Blue Cartel, so dubbed on account of the uniforms of its Air Force members, had been suspected ever since, in 1996, three kilos of heroin were found aboard President Samper's official 707, immediately before he was to undertake a flight to the United Nations in New York (Samper was never given a visa to the USA proper). It was not seriously suspected that the president himself was running drugs on this occasion, but there were strong indications that his crew were – or that they were planning to tip off American authorities in New York and thus discredit the president.

This suspicion was confirmed when, on 9 November 1998, Drug Enforcement Agency (DEA) personnel made a routine search, with dogs, of a Colombian Air Force Hercules C-130 at Fort Lauderdale; the crew and aircraft were on a procurement mission to purchase spare parts for Air Force and police helicopters. Welded into the metal cargo pallets in the hold, the authorities found seven hundred packages of cocaine, weighing 450 kilos: a street value of US$15 million. From the ease of the operation, many guessed they had been tipped off.

The crew were promptly arrested and eventually flown back to Bogotá. For a while they professed their ignorance, even suggesting that, in the course of one of the plane's many missions to Putumayo, narcotraffickers had somehow obtained illegal access to the hold without their knowledge. But the story didn't wash: several senior officers were found guilty and sentenced to long terms. Air Force Commander General José Manuel Sandoval, although he had not been personally implicated, did the honourable thing and resigned. The affair became known as the "Narco-Hercules."

The highly embarrassed Colombian Armed Forces got their revenge a year later. At diplomatic cocktail parties and once or twice over working breakfasts at the Official Residence, I'd met the young head of the DEA in Colombia. He was personable, enthusiastic, every inch the committed professional. I never met his wife – rumour was that she enjoyed wilder parties than the diplomatic scene normally afforded. She had a job, I later learned, in the very busy diplomatic mail room of the huge, bunker-like American mission.

Like many of his colleagues, the DEA man – it seems – was a workaholic. His wife led a virtually independent life, but with the privileges of an armed chauffeur and diplomatic plates on her car. It was alleged in the course of the subsequent investigation that she had been having an affair with the chauffeur. Hardly unusual; in fact it was a running joke that the wives of all of the expatriate oilmen in Bogotá, heavily guarded against kidnappers by squadrons of young and good-looking bodyguards while their husbands spent weeks away in the field, would in their loneliness turn either to drink or to the bed of their bodyguard. In this case, said the prosecutors, it wasn't drink but cocaine – and also the bodyguard.

One day the bodyguard allegedly asked her to send a package through the diplomatic pouch, to an address in New York. She complied, later saying she never asked what was in it.

Over a period of several months, she mailed six or seven packages in this way. But then she and the driver got unlucky. In a routine inspection at the New York post office through which one of the packages was eventually processed, a mail clerk became suspicious; the package was opened and found to contain a kilo or so of cocaine. Incredibly, there was a return address – the USA Embassy in Bogotá – and the name of the sender.

The operation was quickly broken up, and all three of the principal parties were investigated, along with the addressee in the USA. Although the DEA man admitted that he had on occasion stored large amounts of cash in his office safe on behalf of his wife, he said he had never asked where the money came from.

She was given a suspended jail sentence in the USA; he was given a reprimand, but was not otherwise punished. The USA authorities demanded the extradition of the chauffeur.

This caused a huge outcry. The Colombian public had first followed this case with a kind of sardonic amusement. Tired of endlessly being castigated by USA drug tzar Barry McCaffrey and a host of USA personalities as the source of the greatest evil afflicting the streets of America, it was satisfying for Colombia to see Americans in the dock at last and to see them found guilty. But the public had expected a massive sentence. It was not uncommon for mules arrested in Miami to receive twenty-five years or more, with no chance of parole; if apprehended carrying especially large quantities or while engaging in organized narcotrafficking, they might get one of those ludicrous sentences of two hundred years or so. Wasn't that what Carlos Lehder was serving? The "punishment" delivered to the two Americans – the trial had included day after day of glowing character references – was seen as a grotesque slap in the face, and the extradition request for the chauffeur an added insult.

Especially bitter was General Rosso José Serrano, National Police commander and the boss of our Colonel Barragán. Endowed with near-mythical status by the public, in part on account of the many attempts on his life and in part for his no nonsense, gruff, and lead-from-the-front manner, Serrano had always been a great friend of the USA. The admiration had been mutual: he and his family were reputed to have been granted permanent resident status in the USA by a grateful nation, and he had recently been voted the world's top police officer. But for Serrano this was too much: in a totally uncharacteristic outburst on TV, he complained that the USA's handling of this case summed up everything that was wrong with the US approach to combatting narcotrafficking. And then he shut up.

Indeed, the decision of the New York court *did* highlight the fundamental failure of the USA, in its approach to Colombian-based drug trafficking, to accept any great share of responsibility for the problem. For it is the unbelievably lucrative market in the USA for cocaine and heroin (still by far the world's largest market) that drives impoverished Putumayo farmers, German quadriplegics, middle-aged Colombian housewives, and seventy-year-old men to risk all and try to smuggle a kilo or two of white powder into the USA. It is that market that allows Colombia's Marxist guerrilla movements and paramilitaries to hold all Colombia in thrall, when Marxism has long since disappeared from the rest of the world. And it is on account of that market that hundreds of Colombian pilots and other law-enforcement agents lose their lives every year, egged on by the USA.

Serrano said to me in private, shortly after this incident and just before his retirement: "How many American police die each year breaking up distribution networks in America? Why do we only ever hear about the Cali and Medellín cartels? Who do you imagine distributes our cocaine in the USA? Who do you imagine takes bribes to let it through? It's so much easier to point the finger at a bunch of Latin American generals and let them take the blame for American kids dying, than to actually get out on the streets and stop your kids buying the stuff in the first place."

8 Despatches from the Colombian Elections

July 1997 to August 1998

25 JULY 1997 – THE ELECTORAL YEAR AHEAD: NO MESSIAHS IN SIGHT

On 20 July 1997 President Samper presided over the formal opening of the final session of Congress that he will see as president. On 8 March 1998, voters go to the polls to renew the entire lower and upper chambers (163 representatives and 102 senators). The first round of presidential elections is then due on Sunday, 31 May 1998; there will be a second round on Sunday, 21 June (i.e., a run-off) if no candidate emerges with more than 50 percent of the vote. The new government will formally assume power on August 7th 1998.

In the presidential election, electors vote for a two-person slate (president and vice-president). The Liberal Party will select its slate on the basis of a poll of all Liberal supporters who are interested in participating in the process. The Conservative Party will hold a convention and choose its candidate by a vote of party members at that time. Ideologically, there is little if any difference between the Conservative and Liberal Parties; the labels are more tribal than political.

The most likely Liberal nominee for president is the former Interior Minister Horacio Serpa. Serpa is close to Samper, who has made no secret of his preference; he has the support of the party machine and of many important members in the new Congress, but, of all the "pre-candidates," he is the one most vulnerable to accusations (or insinuations) of corruption arising out of Samper's 1994 campaign (when the Cali cartel was shown to have given substantial financial support). Such accusations – many of which have resulted in convictions – continue to dominate the Colombian media three years after the event and have greatly weakened the credibility of Colombia's Congress as a whole. Opinion polls (notoriously unreliable) last week predicted that Serpa would win 30 percent of a first-round presidential vote.

The frontrunner for the Conservative nomination is Andrés Pastrana, who lost (by a very close margin) to Samper in 1994. Pastrana is the son of former President Misael Pastrana (1970–74); polls have him running at a very distant 11 percent.

Greatly complicating the picture for the official candidates of the two leading parties (Liberal and Conservative) will be a slate of independent candidates. A number of these are well-known figures who have cut their teeth in the ranks of the two established parties and who are choosing to run as independents for a variety of reasons: some perhaps believe, on the one hand, that Serpa and Pastrana already have their nominations sewn up and there is no point in running against them for the party's official nomination and, on the other, that it may make tactical sense to put some distance between themselves and their party at a time when both principal parties are perceived to be worn out and to have nothing new to offer.

The most prominent Liberal independent is Alfonso Valdivieso, the former attorney general, who could be capable of mounting a serious challenge to Serpa in the presidential race by taking away the traditional Liberal vote. Valdivieso, who led the prosecution on corruption charges of many members of his own government, is perceived as morally irreproachable. The most high-profile Conservative independent is Noemí Sanín, a woman who has served as a minister in the Conservative Government of President Betancur (1982–86) and as Foreign Minister for the Liberal President Gaviria. Sanín has had a stellar career in politics and is still only forty-two years old, but many doubt that Colombia is ready to vote for a woman president.

There are two further dark horses. The first – and most visible – is the former rector of the National University and mayor of Bogotá, Antanas Mockus. The colourful Mockus rose to fame (or notoriety) when he was dismissed as rector for mooning an inattentive university audience, but later won widespread support as mayor, shaking up the way Bogotá is run. Mockus has no machine and was for a while reduced to charging journalists for interviews; after effectively disappearing from the national stage for several months, he has now (reluctantly) been forced to admit that market forces will henceforth oblige him to grant free interviews. A recent poll had Mockus placing third in a first-round poll, at 15 percent (behind Serpa and Valdivieso, but ahead of Pastrana, the probable official candidate of the Conservatives).

The other (very) dark horse is the hardline but respected former head of the Armed Forces, Harold Bedoya; if Bedoya (who was fired only yesterday by Samper) should run, he will appeal to small "c" conservatives looking for a Fujimori-style crackdown on the guerrillas. Bedoya had said prior to his firing that, if the public of Colombia so wish, then he would consider putting himself forward. Bedoya supporters have recently been adorning the streets with the slogan "*Sin Bedoya, en la Olla*" (Without Bedoya, we're done for).

As talk of the elections begins to fill the papers, the existing Congress enters its final session with a severe credibility problem. It is widely thought that, in its original form, some 30 percent of this Congress was in the pay of drug cartels; revelations this week in a Miami courthouse by the former accountant of the Cali cartel are adding fuel to a fire that has refused to go out these past three years.

Key indicators or markers of the voters' intentions for the climactic May/June 1998 presidential election will be not only the March 1998 vote to renew this Congress but local elections on 26 October 1997. In October voters will elect, in each of the country's 32 departments, a governor, departmental representatives (i.e., MPs for departmental legislatures), mayors (in a total of 1,050 municipalities), concejales (i.e., regional councillors), and Juntas de Acción Local (local councils).

Meanwhile, there will be a novel element in the presidential elections in that small incentives are to be offered to encourage voters – particularly young people – to go to the polls (high abstentionism has been a problem for years: in the two rounds of presidential elections in 1994, abstention was 66 percent and 57 percent, the third highest rate in the

Americas). For example, those who have not yet done their military service will be offered a small reduction in the time they must serve; persons seeking admission to public universities will be moved to the top of waiting lists; persons who vote will be given preference on housing subsidies.

30 JULY 1997 – SAME OLD MOVIE, ENGLISH SOUNDTRACK

Chilean-born Guillermo Pallomari, the accountant for the Cali drug cartel from 1984–94, has for the past ten days been testifying for the prosecution (under a plea-bargain deal) at the Miami trial of two American lawyers and four alleged traffickers, all of whom are accused of being in the employ of the cartel. Pallomari began his testimony with fascinating glimpses into the workings of the Cali cartel, which, following the death of Pablo Escobar in 1993 and the collapse of the Medellín cartel, briefly became the most powerful drug cartel in the world. Pallomari estimated that in the final years of his tenure as accountant the cartel did US$50 billion dollars worth of business (a combination of drug sales and the income from the relatively legitimate businesses through which drug profits were laundered). The cartel, controlled by brothers Miguel and Gilberto Rodríguez Orejuela, José Santacruz Londoño, and Helmer Herrera, was subdivided into five arms:

NARCOTRAFFICKING controlled routes, sought out new routes, shipped in precursor chemicals, and managed processing labs;
MILITARY was responsible for security, for bribing police and military, and for "discipline" (read "executions");
POLITICAL developed contacts with members of Congress, the federal government, and local authorities;
FINANCIAL supervised money-laundering operations, bought businesses, and created "front" businesses;
LEGAL took care of contracting of American lawyers, anti-extradition lobbying, and the defence of arrested narcotraffickers.

Pallomari's description of the cartel's money-laundering operations was illustrated dramatically – and to the shame of most Colombians – even as he spoke. In the dying minutes of a crucial World Cup qualifying game in Barranquilla, watched by the entire cabinet and most of the country, Colombia scored a dramatic, match-winning goal. The scorer then publicly dedicated his goal to the Rodríguez Orejuela brothers, the unseen financiers of América de Cali, the football club that gave him his first break.

Conspiracy theorists claim that Pallomari is part of an all-out plot by the USA administration (or at least the DEA) to discredit definitively the president and either bring about his fall or pave the way for an eventual extradition request by the USA (or even for a Noriega-like extraction). This seems unlikely in the extreme: Samper is already down and hardly worth kicking, and – in any case – the offences of which he is accused, while grave, are hardly extraditable. Most likely, a good part of what Pallomari says is true. The effect of his testimony will be to render even more forlorn the hope that Samper can somehow get up off the floor and tally up substantial achievements in his last year. In particular, the longtime assertion of the guerrillas that this is an illegitimate, discredited government that has no mandate to negotiate peace finds now more rather than less resonance; accordingly, Samper's intention to ensure that substantial negotiations are under way by the time he leaves office looks like a non-starter. President Samper, of course, has meanwhile dismissed all the charges, saying that he has already answered to them in Colombia: "It's the same old movie, but with an English soundtrack."

12 AUGUST 1997 – ANOTHER DAY, ANOTHER ASSASSINATION

Senator Jorge Cristo Sahium and his professional bodyguard were shot dead in Cúcuta (Norte de Santander; Northeastern Colombia) on Friday morning as Cristo was about to enter his downtown office. The Ejército de Liberación Nacional (ELN) is widely blamed for the killings, which come upon the heels of threats the rebels had made in July against the "political class" of Norte de Santander Department and which should also be seen in the context of earlier ELN threats to do everything possible to disrupt the cycle of elections that begins with state-level elections this 26 October, culminating in the May 1998 presidential elections.

By early this week, however, a second theory was also circulating: that this was a direct attack, not necessarily by the guerrillas, on the presidential campaign of Liberal Horacio Serpa. Cristo was a close friend of Samper and had played a key role in the narco-tainted elections that brought Samper to power in 1994; he was also seen as the key to former Interior Minister Serpa's eventual success in this department. Five arrests have been made; accordingly, it seems likely that the motivation for the killings will be known sooner rather than later.

Between January and July this year, ten incumbent mayors have been assassinated, a further thirteen have been kidnapped, eight have fled, and twenty have resigned after receiving death threats. Although right-wing paramilitary groups may be responsible for some of these crimes, the majority are likely attributable to the ELN or the FARC, both of which have warned the population at large not to stand for elected office nor to participate in any way in the forthcoming electoral cycle.

The killings and harassment of incumbents and potential candidates for elected office are having two contradictory effects on the population at large. On the one hand conservative forces, now personified by General Harold Bedoya, are saying it is time for an all-out onslaught on the guerrillas, while others are saying that the guerrillas cannot be defeated militarily and that it is time for serious peace negotiations – and, if necessary, major concessions.

The effects of this wave of violence on candidates and Colombian democracy are more complex. Some districts (primarily in guerrilla-dominated territory) now face the prospect of no candidates whatsoever presenting themselves for the elections: the local would-be politicians are (understandably) simply cowed. The government has indicated that, where no candidates come forward, it will name military officers as mayor: in the eyes of many, this will be worse than having no mayor at all. Meanwhile, in other areas there is a massive over-subscription of candidates: for example, there are now sixteen persons running for the mayoralty of Bogotá.

Cristo had distinguished himself as a member of the Senate's Foreign Relations Committee (he was also father of the current Colombian ambassador in Greece), but, on account of his close association with the Samper campaign and later rumours that he might be involved in money-laundering, Cristo's reputation for probity was less than perfect. By Monday, the killing of Cristo had been relegated to page ten of the national newspapers, a depressing measure of the degree to which Colombia has become anaesthetized to atrocities of this kind.

26 AUGUST 1997 – OIL PROFITS OUTWEIGH BOMBINGS

In 1996, petroleum overtook coffee as Colombia's principal export, generating US$1.6 billion in government revenues. However, this year alone, the 480-mile Caño Limón pipeline that links the Arauca oilfields with the Caribbean port of Coveñas has so far been attacked by guerrilla forces forty-seven times (cf. forty-five attacks in all of 1996). Spills have totalled an estimated 1.5 million barrels and have created enormous environmental damage. A wave of three attacks in late July led Occidental Petroleum, the USA company that operates the Arauca fields in cooperation with Ecopetrol, Colombia's national oil company, to suspend extraction from 175 wells for a period of ten days. Lost revenues in this, the worst such stoppage ever, were estimated at US$3 million per day. Meanwhile, the rebel ELN army announced that all British Petroleum workers in the nearby Casanare fields would henceforth be targeted.

Industry executives with whom I spoke this week were relatively phlegmatic about the recent attacks. Their immediate effect on the industry has been to cause companies to dig in and state publicly that, in view of the government's evident inability to provide adequate security, they will not accept any increase in the $1 a barrel "war tax" they already pay in recognition of the protection afforded by the armed forces in areas of oil exploration.

23 SEPTEMBER 1997 – EXTRADITION: BETTER A COLOMBIAN GRAVE THAN A USA PRISON

In a stormy and chaotic late-night Congressional session at which three cabinet ministers spoke, the following language was finally approved by a margin of fifty-two to twenty-four votes: "Extradition may be requested, granted, or offered in accordance with public treaties or, failing this, legislation. The extradition of Colombians by birth will be granted in the case of crimes committed abroad that are considered as such in Colombian penal legislation. Extradition will not be granted in the case of political crimes. Extradition will not be granted in the case of crimes committed before the entry into force of this Article." (My translation.)

This development is not good news. In the first place, we were all hoping for retroactivity: only this would allow Canada to get our hands on the Rodríguez Orejuela brothers. In the second place, the decree appears to rule out the extradition from or to Colombia of non-nationals. It has been claimed that an immediate effect of this omission will be to turn Colombia into a haven for international criminals.

The reaction of the USA to this development has been immediate, loud, and negative, both from the State Department and from Janet

Reno. A State official was quoted as saying, "This will weigh heavily in the certification process ... it is a setback that will be taken into account." MFA Mejía called the current draft "as good as worthless."

26 SEPTEMBER 1997 – ELECTIONS UNDER FIRE

For several months now, the ELN and the larger FARC have been waging a campaign aimed at disrupting elections slated for 26 October. Only yesterday, a plot was frustrated that would have seen one of the principal candidates for mayor of Bogotá, Rudolf Hommes, kidnapped, apparently by the ELN. Eighteen offices of candidates have been bombed, including several in Bogotá.

The wave of attacks has led the Senate to purchase bulletproof jackets for all members, at state expense. The Chamber of Representatives (lower chamber) debated a similar move, but rejected it on the grounds that "this would only invite shots to the head." Elsewhere, the controversial and dynamic governor of embattled Antioquia Department, Alvaro Uribe Vélez (whom I met last week in Medellín), has been declared a military target by the ELN; everywhere he goes, he wears a bulletproof jacket. He has gone beyond President Samper's exhortations to candidates that they "be brave" (which were not well received) and has said that his department will insure the lives of all candidates for public office. Electoral authorities have announced that, to obviate the need for candidates under threat physically to take to the hustings, they will grant political candidates extra air time on radio and TV.

3 OCTOBER 1997 – BONETT SURVIVES ASSASSINATION ATTEMPT

General Manuel José Bonett, overall commander of the Colombian Armed Forces, yesterday survived an attempt on his life, apparently by the FARC. Bonett was travelling in an armoured BMW, in convoy, on the road between the Santa Marta airport and the city of Santa Marta (Caribbean coast). One of three large homemade Claymore-type mines buried in the road was detonated by means of a cable as his car was passing over it. Miraculously, the other two mines failed to detonate.

Driving on rims alone and with the car pouring smoke, the driver managed to drive a further kilometre before grinding to a halt. The general and others in the car were unhurt, although the driver of a car that was passing in the other direction was killed by the explosion. Radio intercepts subsequently indicated that the FARC was responsible for the attack. Bonett, who comes from the remote and swampy Santa

Marta hinterland that inspired Gabriel García Márquez's *One Hundred Years of Solitude* and who has sometimes been compared to its hero, the mythical and immortal Colonel Aureliano Buendía, attributed his survival to the skill of his driver, to his patron saints, and to German automobile technology.

7 OCTOBER 1997 – INTERNAL COMMOTION?

On 3 and 4 October, Colombia was shaken by two particularly violent and gruesome massacres. In the first, a large contingent of police and lawyers – who had just finished an inspection of a finca (ranch) in Meta Department that is to be confiscated by the state under new legislation allowing for the seizure of proceeds of crime – chanced upon a 350 kg shipment of cocaine under the protection of paramilitary forces. Three members of the paramilitary forces were killed and two captured, but several hours later the paras launched a counter-ambush and killed eleven police and legal officials. Quite apart from the killings, the indications that paramilitaries, in this area at least, appear to be involved in narcotrafficking on a big scale and that they are prepared to take on the government when their interests are threatened have given commentators much food for thought and have vindicated the many who have long doubted the wisdom of the Army's turning a blind eye to the activities of the paras.

The following day, in an unrelated incident near San Juan de Arama, also in Meta, a force of up to two hundred members of the FARC ambushed an Army patrol and killed seventeen soldiers, seriously wounding many others. The few who survived the massacre have recounted in dramatic detail how they saw their attackers deliver the coup de grace to their wounded comrades trapped in their jeeps. Most of the bodies were received at Bogotá airport yesterday, in an emotional ceremony, by the Minister of Defence and other senior officials. A timid editorial in a national newspaper today suggested that it was time the president considered declaring a state of "internal commotion."

24 OCTOBER 1997 – OAS OBSERVERS KIDNAPPED

Rebels from the Carlos Alirio Buitrago front of the ELN yesterday kidnapped Raúl Martínez (Chile) and Manfredo Marroquín (Guatemala), two of the thirty-six members of the Organization of American States (OAS) mission that is currently in Colombia to oversee this Sunday's departmental and municipal elections. Along with the two OAS representatives, a member of the Antioquia Departmental Government (with whom I happen to be acquainted) was also seized. There is little doubt regarding the authenticity of this kidnapping; the ELN has formally claimed responsibility. The ELN has also indicated it will release the hostages next Monday or Tuesday, once election day is past.

27 OCTOBER 1997 – MUNICIPAL ELECTIONS: GUERRILLAS GO DOWN TO DEFEAT

On muncipal election day – a brilliant windy and sunlit Sunday in Bogotá – Colombians collectively thumbed their noses at the guerrillas and (with notable local exceptions) turned out in numbers far higher than expected. Although participation levels were not consistent nationally and will likely turn out to have been around a modest-sounding 55 percent, this should be seen in the context of only 43 percent participation in the 1994 presidential elections and of a virtual shutdown of public transport in rural areas on account of guerrilla threats against bus operators.

The high turnout can be attributed to popular rejection of the guerrillas' stand against elections and to the growing momentum gained over the past two weeks by the Mandato Ciudadano por la Paz, la Vida y la Libertad (Citizen's Mandate for Peace, Life and Liberty). This NGO-based initiative had voters deposit, in special urns, symbolic pledges by which individuals committed themselves not to engage in acts of violence or kidnapping and not to bear arms and by which they called on all the players in Colombia's armed conflict to respect the norms of International Humanitarian Law and negotiate an end to the conflict. Approximately ten million voters participated in this exercise, including all the country's leading politicians except one (presidential candidate and retired General Harold Bedoya, who termed it "a foolish, utopian idea"). A considerable number of voters in fact turned out only to vote for the Mandato, leaving their votes for governor and mayor blank.

A group from the staff of the Canadian Embassy publicly supported the Mandato by voting at a location specially set up for Bogotá's foreign residents (the entire exercise was financed in small part by our Canada Fund for Local Initiatives). In moving ceremonies at the main military hospital, soldiers severely wounded in recent guerrilla attacks also showed their support by voting. Special urns for the Mandato were set up at Colombian Embassies all over the world; it was reported that 1,500 had voted in New York, 400 in Mexico City, and 2,100 in Lima.

On Saturday, Alvaro Uribe Vélez (governor of Antioquia) narrowly escaped an assassination attempt; a Catholic priest accompanying him at the time was shot dead. On Sunday, a number of electricity pylons were blown up, five bridges in César Department were dynamited, ambulances were hijacked in four separate departments, and there was a skirmish between the Army and the guerrillas in Meta Department. The guerrillas also installed roadblocks in a number of locations. All in all, a quiet day for Colombia; General Bonett, overall commander of the Armed Forces, beamed as he informed the media that not one soldier had been killed.

24 NOVEMBER 1997 – PARAS BECOMING MORE ADVENTUROUS

Early last week a group of uniformed paramilitaries struck in the community of Tenjo, a dormitory suburb of Bogotá. They killed the caretaker of a middle-class residential complex, leaving leaflets alleging that he was a guerrilla and threatening that there would be more killings unless everyone in the complex (some two hundred persons) left immediately; in the leaflets, the group identified itself as "Colsingue," short for "*Colombia sin Guerrilla,*" a small paramilitary group that has previously been involved in attacks in Cali. Residents complied with the demands of the group and have fled the complex. The attack is thought to stem from public statements in October by General Montenegro, director of the DAS (intelligence services), to the effect that this particular block of apartments was home to several close relatives of prominent members of the FARC.

In an unrelated incident at noon on Friday, fifteen uniformed and armed men killed fourteen civilians in the community of La Horqueta, 80 km to the southwest of Bogotá. Witnesses reported that the men arrived with a list of names and, after locating the individuals, who were presumably thought to be guerrilla sympathizers, shot them and a number of bystanders. One of the perpetrators was apparently killed in answering fire – the body of a young Black man, dressed in military uniform but with no badges, was found. Locals said he was a stranger and the colour of his skin has lent fuel to speculation that the killers were from the north of Colombia, the country's traditional paramilitary stronghold. Regional leaders of the rebel FARC have claimed that troops of the Army's XIII Brigade were responsible, but this theory has not been given wide credence.

On Monday news came through of another, smaller-scale massacre by paramilitaries, in the community of El Aro de Ituango, 200 km north of Medellín in Antioquia Department. The four (or more) killings took place on 15 November, but it was only this weekend that the first of seven hundred persons who have now fled the village reached civilization to tell the tale.

Meanwhile, painstaking investigations by a leading Colombian news magazine appear to indicate – as long rumoured – material collusion by the Army in July's horrific massacre in Mapiripán (Meta Department), in which between six and twenty-five local people were killed by paramilitaries (some of them decapitated) and following which the entire population of the town fled. The magazine has documentary evidence of two transport planes, immediately prior to the massacre, leaving a military base in Urabá, in northwestern Colombia, for Mapiripán; a civilian pilot has provided further details and has admitted his own participation; the Army is unable to explain the purpose of these flights, although it has promised a thorough investigation.

25 NOVEMBER 1997 – PRESIDENTIAL ELECTIONS: SIX MONTHS TO GO

A long-time Liberal insider and former Interior Minister, the extravagantly mustachioed Horacio Serpa maintains a good lead in all opinion polls, with six months to go until the May 1998 presidential elections. President Samper makes no bones of the fact that Serpa is his candidate, but it remains unclear whether Serpa will ultimately be the official candidate of the Liberal Party, or whether the party will indeed have a single official candidate (Serpa recently indicated his preference that the first round of the presidential elections be the de facto Liberal candidate selection process). Rumours that were aired in *Newsweek* and *Time* to the effect that Serpa, as a close confidant of Samper, may have in the past enjoyed the same undesirable friendships as Samper (i.e., with leaders of the Cali cartel) have not been greeted with great surprise here and do not appear to have dented Serpa's prospects; indeed, there is a constituency in Colombia that (until concrete proof emerges) is likely to see this as another dastardly gringo plot and will consequently be even more favourably inclined to Serpa than before.

Meanwhile, just as at the USA Embassy, the business community's refrain is also "anything but Serpa," but for different reasons: it is difficult to pin Serpa down ideologically. He is somewhere left of centre (indeed he makes no bones of earlier sympathies with the Colombian guerrillas, before they became corrupted). This could spell a slowdown in the economic apertura that President Gaviria (1990–94) began and which President Samper has allowed to continue.

Pastrana is conceded, by most, to be the frontrunning Conservative – with or without a large "c" – but, as a one-time loser, is perceived to be tired and uninspiring. Meanwhile Bedoya, until three months ago Samper's commander of the Armed Forces, is now daily biting the hand that fed him and is unashamedly pandering to the right-wing vote that would like to see a dramatic crackdown on the guerrillas (not that Bedoya was particularly successful, as commander-in-chief, in this regard). Alfonso Valdivieso, across the political divide and calling himself an Independent Liberal, is perceived as a decent chap who successfully prosecuted two of Samper's cabinet for election-related corruption but failed to follow through (i.e., to convict Samper himself). He is widely thought to be honest, but is unexciting and a poor public speaker.

Noemí Sanín trades with some success on her good looks and aura of sophistication (as does current Foreign Minister María Emma Mejía) and is creeping up in the polls, but is found by some to be rather brassy, more ambitious than a woman should be in Colombian society. And then there is Antanas Mockus. He has no chance of becoming president, but he will enliven the race and is riding even in the polls with Sanín at 9 percent.

The most novel feature of this campaign so far (Mockus's antics excepted) has been the evident keenness of all candidates to distance themselves from the two established political tribes (rather than parties) that have dominated Colombian politics for fifty years: Conservatives and Liberals – Blues and Reds. They have clearly detected in the electorate an understandable disillusionment with the two, which now appear to be taking Colombia back to *La Violencia* of the 1940s* from which the parties themselves emerged as the country's saviours, and every candidate now accordingly wishes to be a breath of fresh air. For a while it looked as though Serpa would be the only one to unashamedly embrace party colours, but even he joined the bandwagon two weeks ago when he declared that he would not take part in the party's internal candidate-selection process and would simply let

* *See page 197*

the party faithful use the first round of the presidentials for de facto selection.

Serpa is streets ahead in the polls. Electors at large seem unfazed by the fact that he may be corrupt and are evidently unconcerned by the fact that he is emphatically not the American choice (which would considerably complicate his presidency).

22 DECEMBER 1997 – FARC OVERRUN MILITARY BASE

At 2:00 AM on Sunday, some three hundred men of the rebel FARC's Southern Bloc stormed a remote mountaintop communications post of the Army, on the border between Putumayo and Nariño Departments in the Eastern Cordillera of the Andes. Contact with the post has been lost; as of noon on Monday, Army helicopters had been unable to reach it on account of bad weather. The post is/was manned by thirty-four personnel: heavy Army losses are feared. This post, called Patascoy, is about 50 km from an area I visited only last week.

Meanwhile, close to the displaced persons' camp of Pavarandó in the northern region of Urabá (Antioquia Department), clashes between the guerrillas and right-wing paramilitaries and attacks by both on the civilian population have led to an unknown number of deaths: the respected NGO CINEP has reports of the death of up to twenty-six campesinos. The fighting was apparently the result of incursions late last week into traditional guerrilla territory by some 150 members of the Autodefensas de Córdoba y Urabá, one of the country's principal paramilitary organizations.

On Monday morning, the Army lost four men in a firefight with the FARC. The skirmish took place 100 km north of Pavarandó, near Turbo.

22 DECEMBER 1997 – PRISON OVERCROWDING? JUST LET THEM OUT

Colombian jails hold forty-three thousand prisoners, 50 percent over their designed capacity. The most serious situation is in Bogotá: its two prisons hold 4,926 and 1,410 inmates respectively, having been designed for 1,020 and 700. Just as seriously, twenty-three thousand prisoners (i.e., more than half of the total) have not yet been charged, tried, or sentenced. Justice Minister Almabeatriz Rengifo two weeks ago presented to Congress, on behalf of the administration, draft legislation whose avowed intent was to ease prison overcrowding by easing parole requirements, i.e., letting half the prisoners out. It appears that neither the option of building new prisons nor that of speeding up the processing of the 50 percent of unsentenced prisoners, a good number of whom will likely be acquitted, were ever seriously considered.

The draft legislation, which caught most by surprise, had the effect of suddenly and dramatically raising the hopes of most of the prison population that they would be released early; a smiling but awkward looking Ms Rengifo was feted in some jails, while the inmates of others across the country held demonstrations and sit-ins (some of which turned violent; there were several deaths) with the aim of pressuring Congress to pass the legislation quickly.

Just as she mishandled the extradition debate, Ms Rengifo fluffed this one. Early versions of the legislation failed to exclude from the provisions a number of the country's most notorious criminals. The government said it had inadvertently overlooked this: not only guerrilla leaders but big-time narcotraffickers and a variety of once-prominent political personages being held for their part in the so-called Proceso 8000 (the ongoing scandal surrounding the financing with drug money of President Samper's 1994 presidential campaign, named after its file number) would have profited. A number of analysts suspected – perhaps not without reason – that the government had in fact overlooked nothing, that this legislation represented the government's final payoff to all its long-term benefactors.

3 FEBRUARY 1998 – COLOMBIA CERTIFIED, SORT OF

For several years the USA State Department, in response to a Congress ever more perturbed by the impact of drugs on American youth, has engaged in a process by which it unilaterally "certifies" certain countries (where illicit crops are grown) if they are seen as co-operating with the USA in the war on drugs – or alternatively "decertifies" them if it believes they are not doing enough to fight drug cultivation and narcotrafficking; decertification brings with it a raft of economic sanctions. Colombia breathed a collective sigh of relief when USA Secretary of State Madeleine Albright last week announced that, although Colombia would be formally decertified, the sanctions entailed in decertification would be waived "for national interests." Many had feared a third consecutive full decertification this year (and a likely campaign in the USA Congress to apply sanctions more severe than those hitherto applied), particularly on account of the Colombian Congress' failure last year to legislate for retroactive extradition and of recent stats indicating that Colombia has climbed to the top of the world table in the growing of coca, surpassing Peru and Bolivia.

No doubt partly in order to stave off full decertification, the National Police under General Rosso Serrano had for the past several weeks been engaged in an unprecedented campaign to destroy drug labs and confiscate precursor chemicals, especially in the south of the country, this on top of having eradicated more hectares of coca this year than any country has hitherto managed. Three days before State's announcement, the police also pulled in the highest-profile drug trafficker still at large in Colombia (the alleged number two of the Cali Cartel) and, on the day itself, not only arrested two Congressmen (one serving, one retired) for drug-related corruption but also moved to arrest Colombian Controller General David Turbay. The latter has long been suspected to have repeatedly taken money from the Cali Cartel. Turbay is the fourth controller in succession to face similar corruption charges (two of his predecessors are already serving jail sentences, a third is awaiting trial); his visa was long ago pulled by the USA, which has never made any secret of its suspicions.

12 FEBRUARY 1998 – SERPA ANOINTED

After much dithering and internal wrangling, Colombia's ruling party has finally chosen Horacio Serpa, President Samper's former Interior Minister and a one-time sympathizer of the Colombian guerrillas, as its candidate for the 31 May presidential elections. Serpa himself insisted throughout this wrangling that it was immaterial to him whether or not the Liberals chose him – he was going to run anyway, as an independent if necessary (a studied stance: with Samper so unpopular, the official Liberal endorsement is of doubtful value). A poll this week, asking whom voters intend to support in the first round, had Serpa at 35 percent, followed by Conservative Andrés Pastrana at 20 percent, retired General Harold Bedoya at 13 percent, and former Chief Prosecutor and once-leading candidate Alfonso Valdivieso fading at 10 percent.

Pastrana, pointedly alleging scant funds (a veiled reference to the US$6 million of Cali cartel money that is widely thought to have bought Samper his victory in 1994), waited until this week until formally launching his campaign. Like Serpa, he feigns indifference to whether or not his own Conservative Party will formally support him, and for similar reasons: there is widespread disillusionment with the two traditional parties and Pastrana, whose own father Misael was president, is most definitely from the Conservative establishment. With the Samper administration having done such a poor job in so many areas, it is not surprising that Pastrana has chosen as his campaign theme the need for a complete break: he characterizes Samper's regime as "one thousand days of shame"; his own slogan is "Change Is Now" ("*El Cambio es Ahora*").

I attended Pastrana's opening campaign rally, and it was easy to see where, for the moment at least, his support resides. Although his forty-minute inaugural speech was periodically interrupted with applause, what really brought the crowd to its feet was Pastrana's bitter denunciation of corruption within the present administration. With ever-greater vehemence, he listed one scandal after another, rhetorically asking the faithful, each time, "Is that what you want?" No doubt aware that he would be on shaky legal ground if he dared directly to accuse Serpa of such corruption, he nevertheless slipped in an arch reference to "the flame of reform that will burn the whiskers of some," an allusion to Serpa's extravagant moustache. Unfortunately for Pastrana, every other opposition candidate will be playing this exact same card in the weeks ahead; Pastrana has no monopoly on righteous indignation.

Perhaps the most interesting element of Pastrana's platform, as presented, is the domestic campaign against drug use. Pastrana explained first that Colombians have lost sight of the extent to which drugs are threatening the fabric of Colombian society, not just European and American. He stated his agreement with the long-held Colombian position that any approach to the drug problem must be an integral one, one that looks at both supply and demand, and then suggested, refreshingly, that there is no better way for Colombia to show how seriously it believes this than to launch its own drug-use prevention campaign in its inner cities and with young people (as mayor of Bogotá, one of Pastrana's most memorable achievements was indeed such a campaign in the nation's capital).

Serpa, by contrast, has yet to enunciate his platform as clearly as Pastrana. Essentially, it appears to be "more of the same," but, given the extremely low ebb to which the current administration has come, this is a proposition difficult to sell to the electorate: Serpa's challenge will be to separate the real achievements of the Samper regime from the many failures and capitalize accordingly.

General Harold Bedoya's message is a simple and hawkish one: corruption must be rooted out, the guerrillas crushed. His support (at 13 percent) looks solid for now and may be understated; many middle-class and upper-class Colombians may be ashamed to admit it to pollsters, but I suspect that his priorities are, for them, just what the doctor ordered.

Both Independent Liberal Alfonso Valdivieso and Independent Conservative Noemí Sanín are lagging in the polls. Sanín is long on style, short on substance. She recently requested the use of the Chamber of Representatives and filled its seats with life-sized stuffed monkeys, toads, crocodiles, dinosaurs, and elephants. Each of these animals has a place in the Colombian political lexicon, for example toads are tellers of tales, the elephant a symbol of the Cali cartel money about which Samper famously said, "If it was as much as they say, I would have seen it: it would be like having an elephant in your office." The stunt caused great hilarity but did little to enhance her as a serious candidate.

9 MARCH 1998 - CONGRESSIONAL ELECTIONS

With a participation rate of 43.7 percent (cf. 32.7 percent for the same round of elections in 1994), Colombians turned out in relatively high numbers on Sunday to elect a new Senate and Chamber of Representatives. This was approximately the same turnout as for the October 1997 municipal elections.

With 93 percent of votes counted, the ruling Liberal Party looked set to take fifty or fifty-one of the Senate's 102 seats, the Conservatives twenty-four, other parties twenty-four. Two seats are reserved for indigenous representatives, but in fact a third indigenous person also won a seat. This was not a major renewal of the Senate: half of those elected were already sitting as senators. Similarly, in the Chamber of Representatives, the Liberal Party continues to hold a considerable majority.

Big individual winners were former M-19 guerrilla and ex-presidential candidate Antonio Navarro Wolff, who was elected with an unusually large number of votes as a representative for Bogotá. Wolff has lately been held up as a living example of a successful transition from guerrilla to democrat: he was one month ago selected as one of the country's top three mayors. In the Senate, the thirty-seven-year-old Ingrid Betancourt, who heads her own movement, called Liberal Oxygen, was voted in with similarly impressive numbers: a Liberal by conviction, she has nevertheless been a tireless campaigner against corruption and is the author of a polemical book on President Samper, entitled

Yes, He Did Know (a reference to the Cali cartel money that Samper is alleged to have taken). Liberal presidential candidate Horacio Serpa will likely be moderately pleased with the results in both chambers: his candidates won in large numbers.

11 MARCH 1998 - EL CAQUETAZO

On Monday, 2 March, a small detachment of Colombia's elite 52nd Counter-Guerrilla Battalion was ambushed and annihilated on the Caguán River, near the tiny village of El Billar (Caquetá Department). As a general familiar with the terrain told me, the main force of the battalion then set off in hot pursuit of the units of the FARC's Southern Bloc believed to be responsible. But the FARC had cleverly laid a trail of discarded equipment that led the force into a steep-sided canyon. Over the next two days, an estimated four hundred to seven hundred FARC troops poured fire onto the encircled Colombian Army troops. A critical paucity of radio equipment and dead batteries meant that the Army troops were unable to signal their exact location (beneath the treetops) to support helicopters flying in already dangerous conditions of drizzle and low cloud cover. Three helicopters that attempted to land were hit by FARC gunfire and had to turn back, and armoured Bronco aircraft were similarly forced to retreat. During the day on Wednesday, 4 March, up to one thousand Army reinforcements were flown into the region, but they were able to locate only the battalion's commanding officer and six other men with him – who had the sole still-working radio.

Over the course of the subsequent several days, the Army has gradually recovered control of the killing zone and the grisly task has now begun of finding and identifying the dozens of bodies that litter the jungle. There are forty-seven confirmed Army survivors (out of a force of 154). Eighty-three soldiers are thought to have been killed, the remaining twenty or so either killed or captured by the FARC.

As funeral ceremonies began yesterday, in a reference to a killing in Spain's Basque country, the officiating priest commented: "While in another country a whole nation mobilized over the death of a city councillor, in Colombia we have become used to barbarism ..." Army Commander-in-Chief General Galán, in a bitter reference to allegations of incompetence, said: "It is painful to see that after forty years the sacrifices made by our soldiers are still not recognized ... It is sad to witness the citizenry of Colombia railing against those who are putting our lives on the line ..."

19 MARCH 1998 – ELECTORAL FIELD SLIMMING DOWN

Former Attorney General Alfonso Valdivieso, who had been describing himself as an Independent Liberal, has now quit the Colombian presidential race: unable to move far past 10 percent in the opinion polls and losing rather than gaining momentum, he announced his decision late last week. What is interesting about the move is the fact he has gone now to work not with former Cabinet colleague Horacio Serpa, the official Liberal candidate, but with Conservative candidate Andrés Pastrana; he is also encouraging his erstwhile supporters to move their allegiance to Pastrana. As every day passes, it is more and more clear what this race is about: "continuism," as embodied by Serpa, or "anything but continuism," embodied by Pastrana and others. Serpa himself sardonically describes this dynamic as "*El fenómeno Toconser*" – "Toconser" being a short form of "everyone against Serpa." It is Serpa's misfortune that, in spite of his protestations to the contrary, he is seen as Samper's heir – and Samper is the most reviled Colombian president in recent history.

Valdivieso's quitting and his move to Pastrana's camp has dealt a severe blow to plans that were developing for a number of the minor candidates to bunch together and provide a viable third option to Pastrana and Serpa. As it is, Noemí Sanín and maverick Antanas Mockus have agreed that one of the two will withdraw before the first round and support the other – the betting is that Mockus will be the one to go, leaving Sanín as the third candidate, after Serpa and Pastrana. Although Sanín's campaign is going quite well (her unofficial slogan is "*Noemí sí tiene cojones ...*" or "Noemí's got balls") she does not have a realistic chance of finishing ahead of either Pastrana or Serpa in the first round, which means that the speculation now is: "Where will her votes go in the second round?"

And then there is Harold Bedoya, soldiering on at 10 percent to 15 percent in the polls and determined to stay the course until the end. He will have been particularly disappointed in the results of the recent Congressional elections, where two former military men running under his colours failed to win seats and where the meagre number of votes they mustered casts into doubt the legal status of his Fuerza Colombia as a political party. It has long been common wisdom that the political incorrectness of Bedoya's views means that polls understate his support, but the Congressional vote indicates that there really isn't that much there, after all.

26 MARCH 1998 – MARÍA EMMA BACKS SERPA

Not unexpectedly, Foreign Minister María Emma Mejía yesterday handed in her resignation to President Samper. It is widely expected that she will shortly announce that she is joining the campaign of Liberal presidential candidate Horacio Serpa, likely as his vice-presidential running mate.

Mejía, the most capable cabinet minister of the entire Samper administration and highly regarded internationally, will provide Serpa's campaign with a needed boost at this moment when, for the first time, polls indicate that arch-rival Andrés Pastrana may be edging ahead of him. Although a loyal member of the Samper cabinet, it has never been suggested that Mejía was in any way involved with the various scandals that have brought down other ministers and that have constantly dogged Samper; she successfully projected, throughout her tenure as Foreign Minister, an image of irreproachable professionalism and, in particular, won plaudits from all sides for her competent handling of Colombia's difficult relationship with the USA. Conventional wisdom has it that she will bring a touch of respectability to the Serpa campaign (he is still dogged by vague allegations of corruption), will reinforce Serpa's insistence that he is his own (and not Samper's) man, and bring in the women's vote.

17 APRIL 1998 – DEATH OF A TURBULENT PRIEST

When in early April the rebel ELN kidnapped some eight national journalists, there was widespread mystification as to how this tactic might aid the ELN cause. In fact, the journalists were kidnapped for a very specific purpose: to witness a radio transmission by ELN leaders in which they announced that El Cura Pérez, de facto leader of the ELN since 1982, had died of hepatitis on 14 February. Immediately subsequent to this announcement, on 6 April, a journalist from the NTC News Chain witnessed Pérez's burial in the mountains of San Lucas, Southern Bolívar Department.

Photos of Pérez, supplied to journalists by the ELN, show him lying in state shortly after his death, apparently in a hospital room. Minute analysis of these photographs has generated rumours that Pérez in fact died in a hospital in Havana (Cuba) and that his embalmed body was brought back clandestinely, in an Evita-like saga, through Venezuela and into Colombia. Also seized upon with enthusiasm by the local conspiracy mill is the fact that the photos of Pérez, showing him clean shaven, bear little resemblance to the bespectacled Fidel-like figure to which TV viewers have become accustomed over the years: already there are those who are saying that this is a subterfuge, that Pérez lives on, that the coffin buried in San Lucas is full of bricks.

23 APRIL 1998 – PASTRANA EDGES AHEAD

Opinion polls last week gave, for the first time, a significant lead in the presidential race to Conservative candidate Andrés Pastrana (40 percent over Liberal candidate Horacio Serpa's 33 percent). Pastrana's surge may in part be due to a growing realization by the voting public that neither of the other presidential candidates, both of whom are right-of-centre, stand a realistic chance of winning the presidency: his advance is at the expense of Sanín and Bedoya rather than of the centre-left Serpa.

This poll comes shortly after all four top candidates had confirmed the identity of their vice-presidential running mates. This had been keeping the media guessing for some time, but in fact it is not clear, given the insubstantial nature of the vice-presidency in Colombia, whether the candidates' choice of running mate weighs greatly in the thinking of voters.

Horacio Serpa (president) and María Emma Mejía (vice-president) are running as the official candidates of the ruling party. Common wisdom has it that the telegenic Mejía will be a boon to Serpa's campaign because, in the first place, she is a woman and, in the second, she is very popular in the key Department of Antioquia, where the Liberals are otherwise weak; she is also perceived as making a Serpa presidency more palatable to the international community, especially the USA. However, Mejía has no experience in hustings politics and has already raised some establishment hackles by appearing to lay into the current absentee VP (Carlos Lemos, Colombia's ambassador to London). Her coming on board does not appear to have added even a percentage point to Serpa's numbers. (Numbers: 33 percent.)

Andrés Pastrana (president) and Gustavo Bell (vice-president) are the official candidates of the Conservative Party, although they are running under the banner of Gran Alianza por el Cambio (Grand Alliance for Change). The forty-one-year-old Bell is a former governor of Atlántico Department (i.e., Barranquilla) and, although he enjoys the public endorsement of Nobel Prizewinner Gabriel García Márquez, is a relative unknown. The common wisdom is that he brings youth and the coast vote to the Pastrana campaign. He has also traditionally been considered a Liberal and has in the past identified himself as such – he may thus bring over some Liberal Party faithful with him. But he has no experience in federal politics and no national profile. In that Pastrana evidently chose him only after former Chief Prosecutor Alfonso Valdivieso turned Pastrana down, he may also be perceived as a second choice. (Numbers: 40 percent.)

Noemí Sanín (president) and Antanas Mockus (vice-president) are running under the banners of "*Sí Colombia*" and "*Opción Vida*" (Option Life), although Sanín also sometimes describes herself as an Independent Conservative. In a novel procedure, Mockus and Sanín jointly commissioned an opinion poll to see which of the two should run on the presidential ticket and which as vice-president: Sanín was the preferred presidential candidate by a wide margin. Mockus is widely seen as incorruptible and politically independent; he is famous for his publicity stunts, but the public has lately been tiring of, for example, his throwing glasses of water in the face of opposing candidates just to make arcane points about the nature of provocation and peacemaking. Sanín has meanwhile received an important symbolic endorsement: that of the granddaughter of the great Liberal caudillo Jorge Eliécer Gaitán, whose assassination exactly fifty years ago led to days of bloody riots in Bogotá (the "Bogotazo") and plunged Colombia into virtual civil war. This endorsement will have caused much chagrin in Liberal ranks; comparisons are being made to the moment when, eight years ago, the family of another slain Liberal leader, Luis Carlos Galán, endorsed César Gaviria. The polls, which showed Sanín surging forward in February and March, now have her falling back slightly but still in third place, at 13 percent.

Retired General Harold Bedoya (president) and Jorge García Hurtado (vice-president) are running as Fuerza Colombia. Hurtado, who is in his sixties, is a former auditor general in the then-Department of the Treasury: he is perceived to have done an honest job in this position and thus represents the anti-corruption element of Bedoya's platform that calls for simultaneous crackdowns on the guerrillas and on corruption in government. However, García is grey (literally) and, to put it bluntly, old; he does not add much to the Bedoya ticket. While media continent-wise talk of a resurgence of military men in the Americas (cf. Venezuela and Paraguay), in this most wartorn of countries the former general is in fact fading: the fact is that it would require much more than a Fujimori to defeat the Colombian guerrillas, and this tired and battle-weary electorate does not have the stomach for more killing. Bedoya now sits at 7 percent.

With six weeks to round one, the money is slowly moving from Liberal anointee Serpa to Andrés Pastrana. However, there is plenty of time for scandals to shift the balance back or even to rule out one of the frontrunners. In a bizarre twist, a major risk faced by candidates this year is of known narcos contributing to their campaigns in the explicit hope that their cheques will be traced and the recipient candidate thus discredited; all candidates are taking extraordinary measures to ensure they are not blindsided in this way.

27 APRIL 1998 – BOMBS ROCK BOGOTÁ

In a development that does not bode well for the remainder of 1998, several bombs were detonated last night in Bogotá. Two attacks were made around 10:10 PM, close to campaign offices of presidential candidates Horacio Serpa and Harold Bedoya. A third detonation occurred at roughly the same time close to a Toyota dealership in the south of the city. The bombs caused material damage, but only one person was killed – apparently the person carrying the explosives, in the case of the Toyota dealership. Rumours of a fourth bomb had not yet been verified by Monday morning. It is presumed, from the timing of these attacks, that the prime objective was not to cause loss of life. Police estimated the charges used at about 4 kg.

21 MAY 1998 – THE EVIL THAT MEN DO

Colombia daily sinks deeper and deeper into violence. Not just the violence of wars between rival drug gangs, of pitched battles between the left-wing guerrillas and the army, or even of the selective massacres inflicted on the country's rural population by paramilitaries. Quite apart from all of this, Colombia still has the third-highest violent death rate in the world, with an average of over seventy murders a day.

A horrific recent incident illustrates how pervasive killing has become as a solution to relatively minor quarrels: an entire family of eleven (two adults and nine children) was "executed" in Southern Santander Department as a result of some obscure disagreement. Among those shot with bullets to the back of the head was an eight-month-old baby. Every Bogotano has similar, if less dramatic stories to tell: of a taxi driver shooting his passenger dead because he slammed the door, of muggings that take place in front of a crowd of two hundred that stands by impassively, of drivers pulling out Uzi light machine guns to resolve traffic jams. Why are Colombians like this? How has the country sunk this low?

It is easier to explain why Colombia finds itself unable to emerge from its nightmare than to say why it began in the first place. The violence has crept up so slowly and so insidiously that it has now become a way of life to which people have learned to adapt. Many of the guerrillas, for example, are now second or even third generation and killing, kidnapping, and extortion are the only ways of life they have ever known. A vivid metaphor that is sometimes used to explain Colombian tolerance of what would be totally intolerable almost anywhere else is that of the frog in the stewpot. If you want to cook a frog, don't just dump him into the boiling water: he'll leap out before you even scald him. Place him in the water when it's cold, then gradually bring it to the boil: he won't even notice, and he'll cook quite happily. Other Colombians see so much violence going on around them that they are literally afraid to take action, even action so modest as attending a demonstration.

The media pander to this surreal acceptance of the unacceptable. One day, a massacre of twenty-five campesinos will be headline news, but by the next it will be almost forgotten. A recent front page of the Bogotá daily *El Espectador* is a case in point. Given prominence are three photos of women's legs, under the jocular headline "Whose legs are these?" In smaller type, at the bottom of the page, another heading: "Paras and guerrillas in a death struggle in Meta Department."

The unshockability of Colombians is something of which they are alternately proud and ashamed, and it is indeed both a vice and a virtue. Candidates for political office accept quite philosophically that they may well be shot – what admirable stoicism! But were a candidate to be shot dead tomorrow, would Colombians be out on the streets to protest in their millions, as Spaniards did last year? Not a chance. Oil executives nonchalantly claim that you can do business here just like anywhere else in the world (and indeed you can), but their wives nevertheless need two bodyguards to go to the supermarket.

Another factor that helps explain the persistence of violence in Colombian society is the glaring gulf between rich and poor in this country. Colombia has one of the highest Gini coefficients on the continent – i.e., its considerable wealth is concentrated in fewer hands than in most of Latin America. Much is actually centered on just four prominent industrial groups, headed by "*Los cacaos*" (the big cheeses): their companies alone reported profits in 1997 totalling nearly US$2 billion. This inequitable distribution of wealth (translated in rural Colombia into inequitable land distribution) continues to fuel both the guerrilla insurgency and the paramilitary response to it by large landowners.

And then there are drugs and narcotrafficking. Colombia is the world's top grower of coca and number one producer of cocaine; it is rapidly developing, too, as one of the world's prime heroin producers; it has been a major marijuana exporter for as long as anyone can remember. The fact that this industry is an illegal one means that, for the narcos to survive, they must buy protection and influence throughout the political system and the judiciary of Colombia: once a judge, a senator, or a police officer on the corner accepts that first bribe, they are on a slippery slope that leads into a world where the only values are "*plomo o plata*" – lead or silver, a bullet or a payoff. At the level of the small rural communities of Putumayo or Guaviare, the mere fact of being involved in an illegal industry has a corrupting effect far beyond the crime itself: it places the campesino beyond the pale, subject to intimidation, extortion, and recruitment into all kinds of other criminal undertakings and highly disinclined to solve personal disputes through recourse to the law.

Then the enormous profits generated by narcotrafficking (a kilo of refined cocaine that sells for US$1,000 in Southern Colombia fetches nearly thirty times as much in Brooklyn) must be laundered: it has to be supposed that narco money has long since reached almost every sector of Colombian business, almost tangibly infecting hitherto honest business people as it goes, insidiously debasing morality and exposing anybody who handles it to the risk of blackmail. It is narco money, too, that gives the Colombian guerrillas an edge and an invulnerability that their Central American colleagues never had: by systematically taxing the industry, the guerrillas are effectively self-sufficient financially and under no pressure to move to the peace table. It has to be said (and *The Economist* recently did as much ...): the legalization of cocaine in the world's principal drug markets would at a stroke vastly improve Colombia's prospects in almost every sense.

"Example" also has much to do with Colombia's lawlessness. No sane and/or moderately knowledgeable Colombian doubts that President Samper knowingly accepted US$6 million from the Cali cartel during his 1994 electoral campaign and that the only reason he got off was that the Congress that absolved him had also been bought. The congressman who led the fight not to approve retroactive extradition for narcotraffickers last year was unable to attend the final vote on the issue because he had been arrested for taking payments from known narcotraffickers. Only two weeks ago, a senator was arrested on no less than nine murder charges.

There is little wrong with either Colombia's laws or with its Constitution (which was renewed in a remarkable and enlightened exercise in democracy in 1991). There are one or two areas I believe could be improved (e.g., extradition), and some would even say the Constitution is too detailed (leading to frequent confusing clashes between its provisions and the law), but those who believe the answer to Colombia's problems lie in yet again reforming it are barking up the wrong tree. As elsewhere in Latin America, it is not the laws that are the problem, but rather their lack of application.

A more subtle and possibly debatable explanation of the failure of Colombians to halt their own descent into darkness may be found in a phrase Interior Minister López said to me once and which remains with me: "Colombia, in spite of everything, remains a mountain fastness, cut off from the world ..." Geographically, this is the most varied of all the countries of South America, with its complicated and challenging topography making both internal and external communication relatively quite difficult – it was not for nothing that it was Colombia that founded the first civilian airline (Avianca) anywhere in the Americas. The country's internal topography has made the imposition of law on a national scale especially difficult, while difficulty of access from the outside, so some historians would have it, has meant that for decades Colombia has developed at a pace and rhythm quite independent from the rest of the hemisphere. Some claim that what we are witnessing today is nothing but a direct continuation of the violent Liberal/Conservative rivalry that was born in the wars of independence and that has flourished almost uninterrupted ever since, immune to external influence.

Others take a different tack, saying the feature of Colombian history that is most to blame for the country's problems today is not the interminable Liberal/Conservative rivalry but, rather, the one interruption in their rivalry, the so-called Frente Nacional, a fifteen-year postwar period during which the Liberals and Conservatives came to a very cosy but formal power-sharing arrangement. According to this reading, it was during this period that favour-trading became institutionalized in Colombian politics, and voter cynicism scaled to unparalleled heights, with Liberal and Conservative becoming literally (even legally) interchangeable (witness the current campaign, where Conservative candidate Pastrana has a Liberal VP running mate).

Gabriel García Marquez (who, significantly, lives most of the time in self-imposed exile in Mexico) is one who shares the vision of Colombia as an unhealthily inward-looking, isolated land; for him, the relations between the Liberals and Conservatives have always been and remain disastrous for the country, whether they are formally rivals or at peace with one another. Among the many striking features of *One Hundred Years of Solitude*, which is in part an allegory of twentieth-century Colombia, are senses of physical claustrophobia, of timelessness, of history endlessly repeating itself. Macondo is completely detached from the real world and an unending succession of tyrants, whose names are variations on Aureliano Buendía and who sport Liberal and Conservative colours indiscriminately, leave no lasting impact on the village other than randomly killing off large numbers of its inhabitants from time to time. When the two bands do sign peace, it is invariably short-lived and illusory. There are only very rarely any newcomers to Macondo to bring in refreshing ideas – just as there has been no significant immigration to Colombia since colonial times.

The other great Colombian literary masterpiece of this century, Eustasio Rivera's *La Vorágine* (The Vortex) even more explicitly endows the dramatic physical landscape of Colombia with a real malignancy. Its two anti-heroes disappear at the end of the novel, corrupted in every sense by their savage environment; they are simply sucked up into the jungle.

Colombia now enjoys, of course, CNN, the Spice Girls, and plentiful air links to the outside world – and yet, and yet ... On account of the country's fearsome reputation for crime, corruption, violence, and drugs, Colombia is still shunned by travellers, distinguished visitors, and entire governments. The lowland jungles that devoured the characters of *La Vorágine* are now inhabited by the guerrillas who kidnap unwary travellers at random; the cities and the political parties are still ruled Macondo-like by the same Lópezes and Pastranas that have held power for fifty or more years. Colombia indeed has a time and a geography all of its own.

Other explanations? Middle-aged Colombians tend to grumble – like parents everywhere – that things aren't what they used to be because the schools no longer teach values. As everywhere, this must here be taken with a pinch of salt, but there is literal truth to the theory: until the late 1950s and early 60s, religion and civic education were taught in Colombia and now they are not. Unlike in some other countries in Latin America, the Catholic Church has generally failed to provide sufficient compensatory moral leadership. What has been particularly pernicious in the Colombian context has been the fact that through the 1980s the role models of many young Colombians were criminals of the worst kind: the infamous narco capos personified by Pablo Escobar, with their fast cars, gold neck chains, football stars, and beautiful young women in tow. Escobar, in spite of his ignominious end, is still revered by many.

All of this goes some way towards explaining why Colombia's problems persist, but what is at the heart of the matter? The fundamental problem is that effective government in this country – with all of the properly functioning institutions that this implies – has only existed sporadically over the years and certainly does not exist today. For many citizens, there are (in spite of an astounding body of enlightened legislation) no reliable and honest institutions to which a person can turn when in need. Whole tracts of the country are devoid of effective health or education services, and the police and judiciary are probably about as effective now as they were in 1810 (that is to say, not at all). It is and always has been the law of the jungle in Colombia. If you suspect your neighbour of stealing your pig, you do not go to the village police officer – you shoot the neighbour dead and take the pig back. If you do any less, you risk retaliation, from which the state will protect you not at all; thus death becomes a devalued currency. The consequences of such extreme behaviour? Little need to worry here. Of those seventy murders a day in Colombia, sixty-nine go unpunished.

These same Colombians whom might so cavalierly commit murder at home behave, when they travel to a "civilized" country, in a perfectly "civilized" way (narcotraffickers excepted). Colombians returning from vacation in Canada, Western Europe, or (even!) the USA, marvel about the truly "civic" societies they find in these countries. They themselves will respectfully stop at traffic lights, approach police officers if in trouble, wait in line at the bank. But the moment they drive into the traffic, leaving El Dorado airport, they are back to their old ways – likely with a gun under their seat.

The outlook is inescapably gloomy. Although the pot is now simmering nicely, the frog that is the Colombian public is sitting equally nicely – contemplating its fate with relatively equanimity as it cooks. Short-term developments that might tempt the frog out of the pot would include (obviously) the successful negotiation of a peace accord between the government and insurgent forces, rather less obviously and more controversially the legalization of cocaine, and, also controversially, the emergence of a strong and charismatic leader. It is interesting to note that, although Harold Bedoya is running a distant fourth in the polls, Colombians seem to have accepted remarkably easily the prospect of a just-retired general running for the highest office in the land: were things to deteriorate significantly and were a particularly appealing military figure to emerge from the shadows, it is by no means a given that the public would rule him out. But in the final analysis, to save itself from its plight, Colombia has to develop strong, trustworthy institutions at all levels of society and engineer a change in the mindset of its people, such that the villager whose pig has been stolen now takes the matter to the police or his local magistrate, instead of just killing the thief. Some challenge.

28 MAY 1998 – THE LA NIÑA EFFECT

Conservative candidate Andrés Pastrana, with former Liberal Departmental Governor Gustavo Bell as his running mate, is now the favourite to finish first in the 31 May first round of Colombia's presidential elections. Pastrana has fought a safe, steady, but unspectacular campaign, coming from behind in the polls to push past his rivals. This week he successfully evaded various challenges to participate in a candidates' debate, judging that – as frontrunner – he had nothing to gain from this. He is also firm favourite to win an eventual second round, the theory being that – if his rival is Serpa – he would draw off more of the third and fourth place finishers' votes than Serpa. Pastrana comes over as suave, even slick (he has USA campaign advisers on his staff), with a ten-point platform that is somewhat weak on specifics but which nevertheless gives voters something to go by.

Horacio Serpa, who initially led Pastrana in the polls by as much as 20 percent, has struggled of late (vainly) to shrug off the perception that he is Samper's man, in a campaign where the one commonly held tenet is that things have to change. Lately, with polls (admittedly unreliable) showing him slipping behind Pastrana, he has shown a touch of desperation – his campaign publicity now consists largely of photographs of large crowds at his rallies, as he seeks to show that the polls are wrong. Serpa has also not been helped by the Liberal establishment: former President López (an icon of the Liberal Party) announced last week, to gasps from the media, that he would support Noemí Sanín in the first round, Serpa in the second, thus implying that Liberal support for Serpa is at best half-hearted (a more devious interpretation has him announcing support for Sanín only so as to draw off votes from Pastrana).

Sanín is meanwhile rallying (the "La Niña" effect) and looks to be within five or six percentage points of Serpa; she is particularly strong in the cities, including Bogotá. With a low turnout in rural Colombia (where Serpa is strong), it is just conceivable that she could catch Serpa, grab second, and thus achieve the biggest shakeup in Colombian politics in fifty years (i.e., the end of the traditional Conservative/Liberal duopoly). Who would be the winner in a second-round face-off against Pastrana is anyone's guess, but one suspects, sadly, that Latin American machismo would kick in here and sink Sanín. In a series of TV interviews, Sanín has proved herself to be combative and articulate, with specific ideas on a wide range of social and economic policies. Through adroit TV advertising that has Pastrana and Serpa railing bitterly at each other, she has been successful in presenting herself as the real candidate of change and conciliation.

Lying in a distant fourth is retired General Harold Bedoya, nearly out of sight now. Bedoya is dull, wooden and – by his own admission – economically illiterate. It is expected that 90 percent of the vote will be in and counted by about 7:30 PM (local time) on Sunday, 31 May.

1 JUNE 1998 – PASTRANA AND SERPA ADVANCE

With 98 percent of votes counted, the following are the results of the first round of Colombia's presidential elections, held on 31 May 1998:

first – Horacio Serpa (Liberal): 3,634,823 (34.5 percent);
second – Andrés Pastrana (Conservative): 3,607,945 (34.3 percent);
third – Noemí Sanín (ind.) 2,824,735 (26.8 percent);
fourth – Harold Bedoya (ind.) 191,981 (1.8 percent).

There were a further eight minor candidates.

Election day, 31 May 1998

Approximately 10.8 million Colombians voted, from a roll of twenty-one million (i.e., 51 percent participation rate.) This compares favourably with 46 percent and 43 percent participation respectively in 1986 and 1990 and with 34 percent and 43 percent respectively in the two rounds of the 1994 presidential elections. Interestingly, Pastrana gained in this round approximately the same number of votes (in numerical terms) as he did when he lost to Liberal Ernesto Samper in 1994, while Serpa gained approximately the same total as Samper in that year – very crudely, the nearly three million votes for Sanín are new votes, which pundits have hastened to interpret as punishment votes against the Liberal/Conservative duopoly that has dominated Colombian politics since the last century. What is certain is that no individual has ever come nearly as close as Sanín to breaking this duopoly.

The results of this round have confounded pollsters, who had Serpa trailing badly behind Pastrana. It appears likely that the opinion polls had severely underestimated both the strength of the Liberal machine on the day and the popularity of Serpa in rural Colombia, terrain that political analysts in this country always find difficult to interpret. However, in spite of finishing second in this round, Pastrana remains the favourite to win on 21 June. If the Sanín vote is primarily a vote of protest and disillusionment with recent governments, then it stands to reason that Pastrana, the opposition candidate, will now take more than 50 percent of those votes. However, it is also possible that a large number of Sanín supporters, having failed bravely, will now decide simply not to vote in the second round or will vote *en blanco* (i.e., none of the above) rather than support either of two establishment candidates. Sanín herself is refusing to endorse either of the two.

Serpa and VP candidate María Emma Mejía were unsurprisingly beaming following their squeaky victory, Pastrana rather less sure of himself. The happiest person in Colombia was undoubtedly the near-euphoric Sanín. The magnitude of her achievement cannot be overstated: with no party machinery whatsoever and following a very shaky start to her campaign, she swept Bogotá, Cali, and Medellín and gave both of the establishment candidates a very severe scare. It remains to be seen whether she can somehow build on this momentum and construct a meaningful Third Way. Her supporters are largely urban members of the middle classes, predominantly but by no means exclusively women, who appear to relate to her claim that it is time for Colombia to break out of the destructive Liberal/Conservative rivalry.

The day was not without violence. Early in the morning, in Barrancabermeja (home town of Serpa) a bomb killed three people and injured two others; in Santander Department, four campesinos were murdered by persons unknown; ballot papers and urns were seized and burned by rebel forces in a number of locations, and a total of nineteen electoral officials were kidnapped, thus disrupting activities at the polling stations to which they were assigned.

Embassy officials observed voting in two locations in rural Cundinamarca Department, both of which are in territory where there is a strong guerrilla presence. At Guasca there were a large number of police and Army on patrol, with light tanks guarding the approaches to the town; however, voting went off quietly. Radio Canada (TV) spent two hours filming here in the morning and briefly interviewed me. At Choachí, there was a degree of political propaganda that almost certainly exceeded acceptable norms, but electoral officials to whom we spoke said that the guerrillas, while they were present in the suburbs, had made no attempt to intimidate voters.

This was a well-run election, with sophisticated computer systems at the federal electoral headquarters in Bogotá reporting changing vote totals minute-by-minute. By 6:30 PM only two and a half hours after the polls had closed, over 90 percent of the votes had been tallied, and by 7:30 PM the figure was up to 98 percent.

Some of the more colourful graffiti we have collected over the past few weeks:

"Noemí is the man" (later expanded by rivals with "No, she's the transvestite");
"Noemí's got balls" (later expanded with "Yes – Gaviria's");
"I'm a Serpathizer" ("Serpatizante");
"*Yo amo a María Emma*" (with a heart for a background);
"Andrew for President. Signed: D.E.A." (this one in English!);
"*Sin Bedoya, en la Olla*" ("Without Bedoya, into the stewpot"), subsequently altered to "*Con o Sin Bedoya, en la Olla*" (With OR without Bedoya, into the stewpot).

This was a good news day. While a first- or second-place Sanín result would have given Colombian politics a huge and much-needed shake-up, her showing was still encouraging and even more encouraging was the fact that, in these dark days, no less than 51 percent of eligible voters collectively thumbed their noses at those who would subvert the democratic process: an important sign of the growing strength of civil society in Colombia.

5 JUNE 1998 – PARAS KILL ANOTHER TWENTY-FIVE

On 4 June, the government announced that it had received a short communiqué from the Autodefensas de Santander in which the organization stated that twenty-five persons it had kidnapped on 16 May in Barrancabermeja were "ELN and EPL subversives," that their testimony had been taken, that they had been executed, and that their bodies had been burned. The organization denies holding a further two persons, whose whereabouts are unknown. While the remains of the bodies have yet to be found, there appears to be little doubt concerning the authenticity of the communiqué.

The news has been greeted with weary resignation by the authorities and the media. The capacity for shock and grief on the part of most

Colombians is now at a very low ebb. National newscasts last night ran uncut footage, without commentary, of distraught, hysterical wives and mothers in Barrancabermeja, receiving the news. Fresh graffiti near the embassy in Bogotá reads: "An eye for an eye – soon all Colombia will be blind."

8 JUNE 1998 – FIRST PRESIDENTIAL DEBATE

The first of the planned two televised debates lasted one hour and attracted a large TV audience, but provided few fireworks. The populist Serpa, whose preferred style of campaigning is in shirt sleeves atop a soapbox, looked ill at ease in his dark suit and red tie and visibly held his tongue (remember, this is the man who once called USA Ambassador Frechette "the evil gringo"). Pastrana, who used to be a TV presenter, looked suave and elegant as always (excessively so, his critics argue); prior to the debate, he had it leaked that the tie he was wearing was the same one he wore when he was kidnapped, several years ago, by Pablo Escobar's men. Outside the location of the debate, supporters of each candidate chanted their slogans. While Pastrana supporters attacked Serpa by wearing masks with enormous noses and moustaches, chanting "Pinocchio," Serpa's fans retaliated with mock-plaintive cries of "Daddy, Horacio's bugging me ..." (a reference to Pastrana's father, who was also president, and to whom Andrés was often accused of owing his political career).

Pastrana dwelt throughout on the theme of his campaign: "Andrés is change." In a carefully worded appeal to the 2.8 million voters who supported Noemí Sanín in the first round of the elections, he insinuated that they had – above all – voted for change and that, as the candidate of opposition, he therefore now deserved their votes in the second round. However, Serpa's riposte was not long in coming. In the only heated exchange of the debate, part of which was lost when moderators cut off an angry Pastrana, Serpa listed a clutch of defectors from his own party to Pastrana, one of whom is currently the subject of a criminal investigation, and asked how this represented change. This was evidently a prepared manoeuvre: a full-page ad in today's papers, which must have been taken out prior to the debate, lists no less than eight of President Samper's former ambassadors who are now on the Pastrana team, along with four former Samper ministers and two deputy ministers.

Serpa also won a brief exchange regarding personal assets, claiming that he had had to sell his apartment in Barrancabermeja to finance his campaign. Pastrana found himself floundering as he admitted that his last job was a well-paid UN consultancy.

All opinion polls indicate that peace is the number one preoccupation of the voters. However, neither candidate was convincing on this subject. Both pledged to manage personally peace negotiations; but personal management is hardly the issue. Serpa insisted that he has been trying to negotiate peace for twenty years and is therefore the man for the job (a double-edged qualification). Pastrana lamely said that he would announce his peace policies "tomorrow." Both candidates evaded concrete questions as to what they will do to curb the activities of paramilitaries. Serpa used the time allotted for closing remarks to quote extensively from a Chinese poem that, he said, sums up his philosophy: "Only when weapons rust and ploughshares shine in the fields, only when the prisons are empty and the granaries full, only when grass begins to grow on the paths that lead to the courthouses, only when the steps that lead to the temples are worn – only then will there be peace, progress, and social justice."

Virtually tied after the first round of the elections, both candidates were predictably nervous, rigid, and very cautious in this debate; it was obvious that the prime objective of each was not to make any serious gaffes. It is difficult to see what new ground the next debate (Wednesday, 10 June) can cover; it is to be hoped at least, that the panel of questioners will be emboldened to probe more extensively into the candidates' peace and economic plans, thus far meagrely articulated.

16 JUNE 1998 - PRESIDENTIALS: TOO CLOSE TO CALL

Following an unexciting initial TV debate, things livened up considerably when Andrés Pastrana and Horacio Serpa squared off for a second time, on Wednesday, 10 June. Serpa took advantage of a revised format that allowed for more give and take, and scored over Pastrana with witty, sarcastic repartee; commentators agreed that this was much more the real Serpa than the stilted version we saw in the first round. Notably, Serpa left his rival speechless on the question of Value Added Tax (IVA), which Pastrana has vowed to reduce from 16 percent to 12 percent: when this topic was last debated in Congress, asked Serpa, had Pastrana not in fact voted for its increase? Serpa also scored with a decisive and convincing intervention on human rights and punctuated virtually every segment of the debate with the de facto slogan of his campaign: peace above all else. Finally, in a transparent sashay towards the supporters of Noemí Sanín, Serpa dwelt on the virtues of his VP running mate, indicating that every woman in Colombia would be proud to have such a capable and extraordinarily talented woman as María Emma Mejía for vice-president. Pastrana, by contrast, never mentioned his running mate.

An initially bizarre-sounding question allowed some significant differences between the candidates to emerge: "Do you speak English?" Serpa responded with an unashamed "No" and insisted fervently that it was a sorry state of affairs if command of English had become an important requirement for the holder of the highest office in the land. His meaning was unmistakeable: I will stand up to the gringos. Pastrana was equally forthright in answering "Yes," saying that Colombia must proudly take its place in the community of nations, it must welcome economic globalization, that young Colombians must make the learning of English a high priority. The exchange was a telling one, but it is difficult to know which answer will have pulled in more votes.

The last question of the debate was even more bizarre: "As president, would you respond positively to a USA request for the extradition of Ernesto Samper?" Now in fact such a request is most unlikely ever to materialize – to be extradited, Mr Samper would have to be accused of having committed crimes on USA soil or crimes directly affecting USA interests or citizens; as his USA visa was lifted at the very beginning of his administration, it is difficult to see how he would have managed the former except in the course of fleeting visits to the United Nations. But the question galvanized the TV audience of a hundred with whom I watched the debate. What would Serpa, the loyal friend of Samper and enemy of the gringos, reply? And Pastrana, who makes no secret of his visceral hatred of Samper?

Serpa's reply was cautious, measured, carefully worded – and surprising. He indicated that if, by the time he reached the presidency, Colombian law provided for retroactive extradition, if the requesting country followed due process, and if the Colombian courts indicated that extradition were justified "then I would have no choice but to extradite." An even greater surprise was still to come. Pastrana, pounding his lectern with one hand, pointing at the camera with the other, unhesitatingly began: "I say to the president of Colombia and to all Colombians the following: I would not extradite Ernesto Samper."

The subtext of this debate was the simultaneous attempted seduction, by both candidates, of Noemí Sanín and her supporters. The glamorous former Foreign Minister garnered 2.8 million votes in the first round and has since maintained a hermetic silence in spite of pleas for guidance from her now-drifting supporters. Commentators have been reduced to staking out expensive Bogotá watering holes and reporting breathlessly, for instance, that one of Sanín's senior team members was spotted having breakfast with Pastrana and that "they were seen to smile." Indeed, in that Sanín stood above all for change, one would normally expect that her votes would go to the remaining candidate of the opposition rather than to the individual explicitly anointed by the current regime. But in many ways Pastrana is more establishment than Serpa, and, moreover, it is an open secret that Sanín personally loathes him – hence her quandary.

Polls early this week show Serpa ahead by two or three percentage points – easily within the polls' declared margin of error. The relentless insistence of Serpa and Mejía on one theme – peace – may be having its effect; Pastrana's message, by contrast, is "Change." Given a choice, it would appear that the voters would be prepared to tolerate many of the vices of the current administration in exchange for that one great prize: an end to the bloody forty-year guerrilla insurgency. But we should place no great faith in the polls: the margin is narrow, and they have been wrong before. Who will be president on Sunday night is anybody's guess.

22 JUNE 1998 – IT'S PASTRANA

After a long campaign characterized by a strong but ultimately abortive challenge by independent Noemí Sanín to Colombia's traditional Conservative/Liberal hegemony and by the failure of the opinion polls to sense subtle mood shifts in the electorate, Andrés Pastrana was this Sunday elected president of Colombia.

It is clear that Pastrana had been effective over the past three weeks in appealing to the erstwhile Sanín supporters ("You said you wanted change: if it's between me and Serpa, I'm change ...") and in muscling in on at least a part of the high ground on peace that Serpa had effectively occupied in the early stages of the campaign. The numbers, with 98.6 percent of the vote counted:

Andrés Pastrana – Grand Alliance for Change – 6,082,912 votes (50.45 percent)
Horacio Serpa – Liberal – 5,609,580 votes (46.48 percent)

The level of voter participation, at approximately 58 percent, was the highest it has been in more than twenty years. Overall, voting went smoothly and the speed with which results were computed could put to shame any sophisticated Western democracy: by 6:30 PM, two and a half hours after the polls had closed, 95 percent of the votes had been counted, and the gradual progression towards 98 percent – some results from smaller rural areas would come later – was being shown in real time as further results trickled in.

Leading up to the elections, the guerrillas burned some thirty vehicles over a seventy-two-hour period in Antioquia and mounted a number of road blocks during election day. Vehicles were also burned on the main road from Bogotá to Villavicencio, barely six kilometres south of the city limits. In Huila Department, guerrilla forces shot down a helicopter and killed two police involved in election supervision. A total of six bombs were defused across Colombia. Approximately twenty electoral officials were kidnapped in various locations. Elections did not take place or were seriously disrupted by violence in ten of the country's one thousand municipalities. There were various Army/guerrilla confrontations in which several people were killed, but these appeared to be unconnected with the elections.

Pastrana made a statesman-like acceptance speech at 7:30 PM. He gracefully extended an olive branch to the vanquished Serpa and VP running mate María Emma Mejía, indicating that they would have an important role to play – should they so desire – in the country's search for peace. The only discordant moment of an otherwise triumphant evening was when, on the podium, Pastrana accepted the embrace of the polemical retired General Harold Bedoya, a defeated candidate from the first round whose positions are so far to the right that he earned a few scattered boos and hisses from the otherwise euphoric Pastrana crowd.

I observed voting and counting in four small rural locations in the Cordillera west of Bogotá: Tenjo, La Vega, San Francisco, and Villeta. There was a heavy armed presence in all four locations, and there were army road blocks on the main road leaving Bogotá. However, voting proceeded smoothly. Pastrana and Serpa supporters alike had organized efficient busing systems (quite legal) to bring in supporters from remote locations and were discreetly lobbying virtually all voters as they entered the roped-off voting areas. Because voting stations are assigned by age and sex, it was easy to see that those who were voting in massive numbers were mainly older people, especially women: participation rates at these tables were as high as 80 percent. Voters were given certificates which in theory entitle them to cheap student loans and (in the case of young men) a reduction in military service, but persons to whom we spoke were doubtful as to whether this was an effective incentive: persons told of simply being laughed at when they had tried to use their certificates following the October municipal and March Congressional elections. However, this was a very impressive exercise in grassroots democracy.

When the hands of the clock in the covered sports arena of Tenjo reached 4:00 PM and the National Anthem was played over the PA system as a signal that the voting stations were now closed, some of the officials who stood to attention had tears in their eyes. This was an important day for them in every sense.

6 AUGUST 1998 – MIRAFLORES DESTROYED

The worst fears of many, as news of the guerrilla attacks on the Miraflores antinarcotics base started to come in, have been realized. Banner headlines on today's papers read: "Desolation at Miraflores" and "Death invades the jungle." TV news last night ran footage of planeloads of corpses being met at Bogotá's airport by weeping widows and a visibly emotional Police Commander General Serrano.

In an attack that lasted twenty-six hours, eight hundred to one thousand FARC troops had laid siege to – and eventually overrun – the Miraflores base, which was defended by approximately 180 soldiers and police. The FARC arrived by river at dusk on the evening of Monday, 3 August, and apparently went undetected until they were already at the lightly defended perimeter. In the ensuing firefight, FARC troops used to great effect propane canisters with hand grenades attached: there is no longer a single building standing on the base. The final toll was thirty police and soldiers killed, fifty seriously wounded, one hundred captured.

Reading between the lines, there looks to have been major incompetence on the part of the military authorities. Miraflores was taken once before, several years ago, and as recently as one month ago the FARC had publicly stated its intention to attack the base once more. Particularly mystifying is the fact that there were apparently no sentries posted anywhere along the Río Vaupés, which is the obvious (indeed, the only) approach to the base. Reinforcements arrived by helicopter only after everything was over.

Meanwhile, intense fighting continued at the other end of the country, near the displaced persons' camp of Pavarandó, Antioquia. The guerrillas also used novel tactics here: using a kind of portable high-pressure pump, they sprayed Army troops with gasoline then set them alight with grenades. In a fast-moving battle, the Army's XVII Brigade admits to nine soldiers killed, twelve wounded, and twelve captured, but claims that the guerrillas have also suffered heavy losses.

Bogotá itself has not yet been affected, although bomb-disposal experts yesterday defused an 80 kg bomb/mortar in the southern part of the city. In spite of all of this devastating news, the populace at large and many media analysts seem to be taking things with equanimity.

8 AUGUST 1998 – A NEW PRESIDENT FOR COLOMBIA

At the tail end of a week of unprecedented violence, Andrés Pastrana formally took office as Colombia's new president on Saturday, 7 August, succeeding Ernesto Samper. No president of this country has taken office in such difficult circumstances. On the morning of the inauguration, a spokesperson for the rebel FARC announced that after four days of attacks in twenty of the country's thirty-two departments, it had inflicted upon the Army and police 143 dead, 123 severely wounded, and 129 captured (the latter in addition to the eighty Army and police already in FARC hands). The Miraflores antinarcotics base had been completely overrun and razed to the ground. Unusually, even Bogotá had been touched by guerrilla violence: the day before the inauguration a car bomb exploded (without loss of life) close to El Dorado International airport, another was defused safely in Southern Bogotá, and – on the very morning of the event – a third 150 kg bomb was defused on the road to La Calera, about twenty blocks from the Canadian Embassy.

At the inauguration, the setting was dramatic. The ceremonies were held on a sombre, grey afternoon in the city's austere Plaza Bolívar, military snipers clearly visible on all the rooftops, bomb-sniffing dogs patrolling up and down the rows of chairs; three thousand security personnel were deployed for the event. Pastrana spoke from the steps of Congress, facing the Palace of Justice, which has only just been restored following its 1985 seizure by the M-19 rebel movement and its disastrous storming (with the loss of almost every member of the Supreme Court) by Colombian Army tanks.

An impressive five-hundred-strong military band, in formation on the steps of the Palace of Justice, played stirring martial airs that boomed and echoed around the vast plaza, but it was hard to forget, watching their precise manoeuvering and the dozens of cymbals catching the odd fleeting sunbeam, that this same Army had over the past few days taken the severest drubbing of its history. Ironically, the Bolivarian legend over the great doorway of the Palace of Justice reads: "Arms gave you freedom ..."

The only splash of colour in the ceremonies came when a few raindrops fell and the large seated crowd briefly deployed the 3,500 umbrellas that had been thoughtfully supplied by the organizers, in a pattern that recreated the brilliant yellow, red, and blue of the Colombian flag. Scared by the sudden commotion, hundreds of pigeons flew into the air, a scene captured by a media corps hungry for a happy symbol on this day that seemed so grim and so portentous.

9 To the Llanos

Villavicencio, Puerto Inírida, and El Tuparro

COLOMBIA'S EASTERN LLANOS – or plains – represent the least-known and least-visited region of this country, and, with increasing guerrilla and paramilitary activity, they are becoming more remote by the year. Visitors who travelled here in the 1960s and 70s talk nostalgically of riding the bus for days on end across the rolling plains that stretch for nearly a thousand kilometres eastwards from the Cordillera of the Andes, where Villavicencio lies, to the banks of the Orinoco: flaming sunsets, the passengers helping out when the bus bogged down in deep mud wallows or lakes of fine dry sand, the hospitality of Colombia's gauchos. Now you can still take a once-a-week bus to Puerto Carreño, the tiny capital of Vichada Department, but you are certain to be detained at least briefly – and possibly for a long time – by one of the marauding bands of FARC or paras that roam unhindered across this enormous extent of land, while the tracks that lead to Puerto Inírida and Mitú (the equally minuscule capitals of Guainía and Vaupés) have long fallen into disuse, meaning these towns can now be reached only by river or air. This is one of those rare parts of the world that is becoming less, rather than more, accessible.

In late 1997, I came to Villavicencio, the large and bustling market town that looks out over 1,000 km of savannah, with the Eastern Cordillera at its back. Capital of Meta Department, it is scarcely 120 km from Bogotá, but air is the preferred means of access, for the winding mountain highway from the capital is credited as the place where "miraculous fishing" was invented: the now-common guerrilla strategy whereby up to a hundred vehicles are detained at impromptu road blocks and ransacked for victims; out of a few dozen cars and trucks, it invariably turns out that one or two contain somebody worth ransoming (one giveaway for the guerrillas, reputedly, is a cellphone: owners of these devices now take great pains to hide them from view when travelling in the country).

I was met, after a bumpy ride over the clouds in an Aires Dash-8, at the steamy Vanguardia Airport; my host was the T-shirted Father Omar García, who runs the social arm of the Catholic diocese of Villavicencio. Before spending any time in the capital, he wanted to take me out to Granada, some way to the south.

We passed through a kind of no man's land in Omar's 4-WD. The guerrilla hideouts were barely ten kilometres away to the west, in the foothills of the Andes, and every few days the FARC launched raids. Favourite targets were the three highway toll stations between Villavicencio and Granada: each had been blown up several times over the past two to three years, and a number of soldiers had been killed. Slit trenches and sandbag emplacements defended the posts. Other targets had been the police stations in small towns: every one we passed was bullet-pocked or in the process of rebuilding from the last attack. In some of the villages the police had simply packed up and gone; in others every house within fifty metres of the police station had been vacated, in anticipation of the next attack (this despite the fact that the police itself kept relocating, in a macabre game that had police seeking safety in the proximity of a kindergarten, rather than vice versa).

Granada itself seemed to me a quiet town of some five thousand persons, but it was not always so; last time Father Omar was here with a foreign visitor, his pickup had been caught in police/guerrilla crossfire and a grenade landed in the (empty) driver's seat. The insurance apparently paid up.

Of late, Omar told me, another force had arrived to dispute the de facto ownership of this territory by the guerrillas: the paras. They had long been present in various parts of Meta, for example to defend the properties of absentee landlords such as emerald tycoon Victor Carranza, reputedly one of the richest men in Colombia and a native of Meta. Recently, though, they had taken it upon themselves not just to defend, like private armies, the haciendas and fincas of the landed gentry but to actively seek out the guerrillas and destroy their base in the local population. They had made raids on villages on the road to Granada – their graffiti were visible everywhere, and, more subtly, their presence could be detected in the slogan of Acacias's candidate for mayor: "Let us defend what is ours." Granada was still guerrilla-owned, but it might not be for long: two days before our visit, the guerrillas called a meeting in the town square and announced they were imposing a 6:00 PM to 6:00 AM curfew. The unspoken aim: to detect any possible influx of paramilitaries after dark.

The paras in Meta were to be taken very seriously: they had of late been reinforced by veterans from Urabá. They were also responsible for Mapiripán, an atrocity that had recently left much of Meta Department quaking at the prospect of a paramilitary onslaught. I met with two groups of survivors of Mapiripán.

Mapiripán had been a community of about one thousand souls, located on the Guaviare River 600 km to the southeast of Villavicencio. It could only be reached by boat or by air. It was coca-growing territory: one way or another (although they were loath to admit it), most of the population was involved in supporting the business and many had marched openly the previous year in so-called Marchas Campesinas to protest the government's coca eradication campaigns. The local front of the FARC oversaw the production and local shipping of coca, providing protection in return for a cut of the profits (as it did with most legitimate businesses in this part of the world). There used to be a police station in Mapiripán, but the FARC had attacked it over a year earlier and the police had withdrawn.

The paras had arrived after dark on the night of 15 July 1997. Mr Sinai Blanco was owner of a number of launches and sold gas. His son, a teacher, told me how he had seen his father grabbed and his hands tied behind his back. He found the father's body three days later, the torso slit vertically; his father's head was found some fifty metres from the body. Another woman told me how her husband, who worked as a dispatcher at the airfield, was pulled out of their double bed and stabbed to death in front of her. He was also later decapitated; it fell to the woman's sixteen-year-old daughter (who stood silently by her mother as she spoke to me) to cover her father's headless body with a sheet. There were ten confirmed deaths, but villagers told me of other villagers whose bodies had not been found; they insisted that up to thirty villagers had been killed. Their alleged crimes: to have participated in the Marchas and to have collaborated with the guerrillas by selling them gas, running launches for them, looking the other way when coca shipments left by air.

Following the massacre, the vast majority of the population, assisted by the International Committee of the Red Cross (ICRC), fled to Villavicencio, swelling the ranks of the hundreds of thousands of desplazados in Colombia today. They were taken in by friends and relatives, given emergency assistance by the Red Cross, local and international. But in one month, the government had supplied each family with only two food parcels. The departmental governor, with whom I spoke, was frankly unsympathetic. He had ordered the community's schoolteachers (who included the son of Sinai Blanco) to return to Mapiripán or be fired – aggrieved teachers gave me a copy of his ultimatum. "You have to understand that it is all the fault of narcotrafficking," the governor insisted, implicitly condoning the actions of the paras; he went on to blame the international community for this scourge and smugly concluded that, "Everywhere in Colombia is violent; it's just like Algeria ... This is something we all have to live with." To my suggestion that the government had a responsibility to ensure the safety of its citizens, he assented but then insisted that this is the role of the Armed Forces, not of the departmental government.

General Bonett, Commander of the Colombian Armed Forces, had in fact paid a high profile visit to Mapiripán some ten days prior to my arrival in Meta, to reassure the local population that all was quiet and that it was safe to return. The following day, reporters in the village heard bombardments within a few kilometres and at night saw shells bursting; the governor shrugged and said he had yet to receive a written report on this incident. Following the televised visit of Bonett, at least one and possibly two more villagers unaccountably disappeared. As if this were not enough to sap the villagers' confidence, they further steadfastly believed the Army to have facilitated the arrival of the paramilitaries and to have provided air support for them on the occasion of a subsequent confrontation with the guerrillas.

True or false? Certainly possible. Father Omar, as we drove south, related an interesting incident. He had been hijacked in his pickup the previous week, late at night, by persons in military fatigues – he could not be sure if they were paramilitaries or guerrillas. He was ordered to drive along a particular remote country road. When an army truck appeared in the headlights ahead, he hurriedly warned his captors to get out, but they told him not to worry. A financial transaction then took place: boxes of supplies were loaded into the back of Father Omar's pickup while an envelope was handed to the driver of the army truck. Unfortunately, documented proof of such collusion is difficult to come by.

Mapiripán was only the latest in a saga of abuses of human rights and international humanitarian law in Meta. Those who protest or point fingers do not last long. In October 1996, Josué Giraldo of the Meta Human Rights Committee was gunned down outside his house in suburban Villavicencio in front of his wife and two children; Sister Nohemy Palencia of the same committee was repeatedly threatened with death and now lives in Bogotá. The committee folded.

I met with the lone member of another human rights NGO in Villavicencio: the Colombian Association for Social Assistance. On the wall behind the current director's desk were the photos of his two predecessors – one was murdered, the other forced to flee after numerous death threats. He told me with a wry smile that the organization's name used to include the phrase "human rights," but that he had thought it wise now to drop the two words. Only the Catholic Church in Villavicencio had managed to keep the flame alight: Father Omar and a young lay assistant by the name of William, whose own family had been expelled by paramilitaries from Puerto Gaitán several years ago, hid their human rights work under the guise of "assistance to displaced persons."

There were also dedicated individuals within the machinery of local government who led a precarious existence addressing human rights concerns. On the frontlines were the personeros, or municipal ombudsmen, with whom I held a roundtable meeting on our arrival in Granada. As might be expected, these individuals, who were named by their town councils, were of variable quality. However, on the whole they did sterling work in the face of great odds. The twenty-five-year-old Ms Lidia Castillo, of the municipality of El Castillo, came to her job two weeks after the town mayor was assassinated by paras; the mayor's successor met the same fate; Ms Castillo's own predecessor as personero had been recently shot dead too.

In a climate of generalized fear, the role of the personeros was mainly therapeutic: they were literally shoulders to cry on and actually received relatively few formal complaints (the risk of filing written denunciations being too high). Were they to document the stories they hear, my contacts indicated, the vast majority of cases would technically qualify as abuses of International Humanitarian Law, i.e., the alleged perpetrators are either the guerrillas or paramilitaries. In second place would be intrafamily disputes – but all the personeros commented that these were typically "looked after" by the guerrillas themselves, in what is known hereabouts as jungle justice. In third place would come complaints regarding the failure of the municipal authorities, including the police, to provide basic services. Occasionally, the guerrillas referred cases directly to the personeros, which did not endear the latter, in turn, to the Army.

The federal ombudsman (Defensor del Pueblo) was also represented by an office in Villavicencio. Like the municipal personeros, the current incumbent told me that her job was mainly therapeutic. She gave talks on International Humanitarian Law to anyone who would listen – the Army, the guerrillas, schoolchildren – and, as such, spent a great deal of time travelling to remote locations and attempting to open channels of communication with the guerrillas.

With a view to disrupting the 26 October 1997 local elections the FARC, as elsewhere, had been kidnapping and killing potential candidates – at the time of my visit, it looked as though would be no candidates in six out of this department's twenty municipalities. They had said they would continue this campaign right up to the elections, but, in Meta Department at least, they were meeting increasingly stiff resistance from paramilitaries as the latter began to cast themselves not just as private armies defending the rights of landowners but also as the righteous opponents of communism. In some areas, the paras appeared to be winning: in several communities, the guerrillas had called the population together and warned them that they could no longer expect guerrilla protection, i.e., the paras were coming. As a result, the population sometimes resorted to fleeing en masse – the cure being worse than the disease. In El Castillo, the local populace simply abandoned the village at night (when attacks usually took place) and slept rough in the jungle.

I asked everyone I met whether they saw any hope ahead. The representative of the ICRC (who at one moment wept as he described what he had witnessed in Mapiripán and elsewhere) could point only to the activities of individuals such as Father Omar and the personeros; he was bitter in denouncing the Army, the paramilitaries, and the guerrillas as totally devoid of morality. The representative of the Defensor del Pueblo was equally bleak in her assessment; when pressed, she admitted that one positive aspect of the paramilitary activity was that it weakened the guerrillas' hand and might force them to the negotiating table earlier rather than later.

It was difficult to know what Canada could do in the face of the spiralling cycle of violence in Meta (and other parts of Colombia). Our presence in the field, accompanying human rights workers, was at least of some comfort to Colombians and possibly offered some protection. But I had no doubt the killing would go on for the foreseeable future: to paraphrase García Márquez, these were deaths foretold.

Puerto Inírida is on the river of the same name, just before it joins the larger Guaviare, which in turn flows into the Orinoco. Although my wife Jenny and I had come here to get some respite from the tensions of Bogotá life and the invariably depressing national news, a feeling that the place was under siege took hold even before we landed, after the ninety-minute flight from Bogotá, via Villavicencio. There were sandbag installations circling the runway, and the cabin crew advised that we would be aiming for a maximum total turnaround time of ten minutes (this to minimize the risk of an armed attack on the Satena Fokker 27). As we disembarked, a man filmed all the passengers in close-up: he was wearing a DAS (Intelligence Police) flak jacket and we guessed that the precaution was due to fear of another airjacking of the kind perpetrated a few months before by the ELN between Bucaramanga and the capital.

We had to hang around for forty-five minutes in the small airport terminal because Oscar, the guide that Puerto Inírida's mayor had recommended to us over the phone, worked part-time with his wife running the terminal coffee shop (not a strenuous job, as there were only two flights a week). While we waited, we filled out several forms for an interested and grenade-festooned army lieutenant.

Once Oscar had closed up shop, we squeezed into the old red Renault 4 he had borrowed for the occasion (one of less than a dozen cars in the town) and set off down the empty tarmac road into Inírida, preceded by our friendly lieutenant on a bicycle. A kilometre down the road, we watched in surprised silence as the lieutenant drove directly into the back of one of Inírida's few other motor vehicles and took a spectacular tumble over his handlebars. We accelerated to the scene of the accident and found the lieutenant lying on the ground, conscious, but apparently in some pain; the van driver had picked up his automatic rifle and was standing over him, looking rather perplexed. Soon there was a crowd of bystanders, and a third vehicle – a good proportion of the town's motor pool was now here – arrived to take the lieutenant off to hospital; he was apparently suffering from a broken collarbone.

Oscar took us to meet the mayor at his home while, clutching the bundle of pesos we had given him, he went off to buy a cooking stove, food, and other vital supplies for the short expedition we were planning. We guessed that he had not quite believed we would show up and had accordingly decided not to waste time on preparations.

As we sat in wicker chairs on the mayor's terrace, sipping iced water, he lounged in a hammock and reassured us about the security situation in Puerto Inírida. "It's true that last year's attack on Mitú was a surprise and that a lot of people were killed," he said, "but we're better prepared here. We have a lot of troops in town, and the Marines are patrolling the rivers. Anyway, in a couple of months, the rainy season will be over and we'll be off the hook ..."

"How's that?"

"Well, when the rivers are high, half the territory is covered with water, and the guerrillas can move around pretty much as they wish, but when the water starts to fall again, they're confined to the main waterways, where they're much more likely to be picked up by one of the Marine patrols ..."

It was mid-afternoon by the time Oscar had completed his shopping, found an outboard engine for our launch, shepherded us through the filling out of various forms at the Port Captaincy, and located our other crew member – Miguel, the motorista (driver). Loading at the town's small floating wharf – by a colourful collection of barges that, in the wet, ply the Inírida, the Guaviare, and the Meta almost to the foot of

En route to the Cerros del Mavecurí; Miguel driving; Oscar's legs in the foreground

the Andes – took only a few minutes. Then we were off, setting up a bow wave that looked as though it nearly swamped a fifty-foot-long passenger-laden dugout that was coming in just as we were leaving.

A few minutes out – as we roared up the glassy and wide Inírida under a deep blue sky, the riverbanks low and uniformly covered by the jungle – Miguel suddenly swerved and, allowing us to settle down into the water, chugged more slowly over to the bank, where I could now see a small red flag poking out from the trees. Perfectly hidden in the undergrowth, there lurked a Piranha: a specially armoured, armed, and camouflage-painted Boston Whaler with two huge black 200 HP engines tipping its stern back into the water. Five or six young Marine recruits lounged nonchalantly behind the vessel's three light machine guns, chewing gum. A young captain politely asked us for our papers, looked a little quizzically at our diplomatic carnets. "Be careful," he finally said, "and you will let us know if you see anything going on ...?"

For another two hours we sped steadily upstream, the river wide but winding. Oscar lay flat in the sun and jammed his hat firmly down on his face. I took mine off and let the hot wind stream through my hair. Once or twice we saw monkeys high up in the branches of trees on the

The Cerros del Mavecurí

bank; pristine white egrets flapped slowly into the air as our bow wave disturbed their contemplation of the shallows.

It was nearly five and we had just come out of the far side of a short rain squall when we made out our destination, three large black monoliths of rock rising abruptly out of the otherwise completely flat landscape: the Cerros del Mavecurí. The river's course took us first to the left, then to the right, but ever closer. As we came nearer we could see what looked to be long vertical streaks running down the steep and otherwise opaquely black face of the largest of the three 350-metre-high rock mountains.

"The tears of Princess Inírida," Oscar explained, and indeed we could now see that the streaks were streams of water from the same rain squall that had just soaked us. Oscar told us the legend of Princess Inírida, as recounted by the local indigenous tribe, the Puinave. The young and beautiful Princess Inírida, heir to the throne of the Puinave, had dared to fall in love with a commoner from a neighbouring tribe. The king and queen had forbidden her to see the young man, but she had run away with him all the same. The king sent his men after them

Jenny and Oscar, Puerto Inírida

and brought them both back here. The young man he ordered killed, but Inírida was sentenced to be imprisoned forever in the great black rock that bears her name. The streams that splash down after a rainstorm are her tears, the other two great monoliths her impassive mother and father.

The Inírida River narrows here and, although there appears not to be another single unusual feature on the landscape for fifty kilometres around, heads straight for the group of three monoliths and through the centre of the triangle they form. The constriction here is shown on the map as a set of rapids, but there is no white water, just traces of foam and sudden, shifting upwellings.

In the gathering twilight, we pulled up to the gently sloping rock foot of one of the three monoliths. Packs on our backs, Jenny and I set off up the slope, heading for what looked like a good camping platform, maybe one third of the way up. But the rain had made the black and deep red granite deceptively slippery. After twenty minutes of ever more tenuous scrambling uphill, we were forced to look for a gentler incline and bore off into a gully of dense undergrowth. By now it was quite dark, there was no moon, and we could not make out our boat, even though we could occasionally hear Oscar and Miguel talking to each other.

Eventually, sweating profusely and scratched by the undergrowth and unseen cacti, we found a relatively level area of smooth flat rock and, feeling around carefully in the dark, pitched our small tent. Even though it had rained, the rock floor was warm, almost hot. We had left our water bottles back at the boat, and we spent a very uncomfortable, thirsty night.

The next two days we spent climbing the one monolith that does not require a technical ascent, learning the ins and outs of yucca from a farmer at the nearby Puinave village (one variety is poisonous unless its juice is laboriously squeezed out prior to cooking), swimming with Orinoco River dolphins, and sampling Oscar's speciality, moquiao. This is smoked river fish; in fact its name is derived from *esmoquiado*, which in turn probably comes from the English "smoked"; I have no idea why this word is known and used in this remote part of Orinoquía and nowhere else.

On our way out to Inírida, we checked in again with the Piranha, which by now was hidden under a different but nearby riverine bush. One night at 3:00 AM we had heard a low-flying light plane near the Cerros. We reported this to the captain, who seem unsurprised: "Yes, probably narcotraffickers. We think they have a couple of clandestine strips up there."

Back in Bogotá, we had to explain laboriously to many of our Colombian friends exactly where Inírida was and why we had gone there. But barely six weeks later, it was briefly on the lips of every Colombian. Here is an excerpt from my report back to Ottawa one day in October 1999:

> Almost exactly a year after storming Mitú, FARC forces yesterday launched another surprise attack on a remote Llanos capital: Puerto Inírida. A force of up to 1,500 rebels was reported to have clashed first with a Navy patrol (one sailor killed) then, from a flotilla of launches, to have entered the town. Late last night, it was reported that street fighting was continuing but that the

authorities were still in control of key locations. There are an estimated one hundred police and three hundred Navy personnel in the immediate area. OV-10 Bronco aircraft were despatched from Villavicencio (800 km to the west) to support government troops, and it was reported that they had sunk at least one barge with twenty-five guerrillas on board (and with the presumed loss of life of the twenty-five).

The attack on Inírida was timed to coincide with offensives in other regions of the country. A total of thirteen towns were attacked ... According to a military spokesperson, the FARC troops participating in the wave of attacks were all based in the demilitarized zone of Southeastern Colombia. Commander-in-Chief General Tapias commented bitterly: "This is their response to the president's cease-fire proposal." The Army claims up to ninety guerrillas dead, with ten police and one Navy officer so far killed. Six small towns are in ruins.

In spite of what had happened to Puerto Inírida (the FARC eventually withdrew, rather bloodied), the dramatic landscape of the region had left its mark on us and in April 2000 we found a few days to explore another region of the faraway Eastern Llanos: El Tuparro National Park and the Maypures rapids of the Orinoco. Accompanying Jenny and me this time was a young Canadian intern from the embassy, Kathleen.

The 250,000 km^2 of El Tuparro are Colombian territory, on the west bank of the Orinoco, but getting there involves first a ninety-minute flight (again by Satena) to the tiny town of Puerto Carreño, a short river crossing to the Venezuelan five-shack settlement of El Burro ("The Donkey"), and an overland ride south on the Orinoco's east bank past the Atures Rapids to a place called Canturama, from where you must summon a launch, by radio, to take you back into Colombia and the National Park. If you are lucky, you can do all this in a day.

We were not lucky. As far as El Burro we obeyed all the rules – getting outward passport stamps from a bad-tempered DAS official in Puerto Carreño, checking in with the Venezuelan Navy at a shack on a bakingly hot mud bank apparently known as Puerto Páez, then checking in again with a police corporal at El Burro. But by now it was getting late: we decided to ignore the police's admonition that we should simultaneously check in and out with Venezuela's version of the DAS (the DIEX) down the road at Puerto Ayacucho; instead, we negotiated a taxi that would take us 120 km south, all the way to Canturama.

Taxi driver and taxi, en route to El Tuparro

At Canturama, which is a rather rundown fishing resort hotel located in woods on the smooth rock banks of the river and which was tonight full of sunburned Venezuelan families at the end of their Easter Week holidays, there was unsurprisingly no sign of the launch that was supposed to pick us up and take us to El Tuparro. But we had virtually no bolivars and were not in a position to pay the steep fees charged by the Canturama for overnight accommodation (and anyway the only room was one cabin "under restoration"). So we slung hammocks under the straw roof of the resort bar and enjoyed a bug-free night.

Next day, Carlos the park guide and Elvis, his sidekick motorista, finally appeared. Carlos was looking very bleary-eyed (we would later found out why) and in a state of disorganization unusual even in this part of the world. There was no food at the park, he announced, which meant that we would now have to find transport to take us all the way back to Puerto Ayacucho to buy supplies. But it was Good Friday; there was some doubt as to whether anything would be open. "Well," said Carlos, "even if we can't buy anything in Ayacucho, we should be able to catch some fish ..."

The Orinoco, El Tuparro National Park

We had by now been joined by three Spaniards also resident in Colombia and looking for a quiet weekend in El Tuparro. They were rather disgruntled by this chaotic state of affairs but, after huddling together, reluctantly agreed to join us in renting a small truck to go back to Ayacucho and see what we could rustle up. Fortunately, there was a shop open; by noon we were finally under way.

The Orinoco here is about one kilometre wide, flowing sluggishly to the north, and the landscape is similar to that around Inírida: utterly flat except for the occasional abrupt outcrop of steep black rock, rising to maybe 300 metres above the savannah. There is little human habitation. Of course, it's very hot. In the ninety-minute high-speed river run south to the park HQ, we passed only one structure: a large out-of-place-looking concrete building with, on the rock bank, an enormous Stalinesque concrete bust of Simón Bolívar, his hair strangely blown horizontal. This, Carlos explained, was a rehabilitation camp for young street children and underage offenders from Bogotá; it was run by an Italian priest. There were a number of children sitting idly at the water's edge, but when I waved no-one waved back.

The park hotel, a large wooden building consisting of five or six rooms and a spacious lounge area incongruously furnished with deep leather armchairs, was located on a rocky outcrop where the two-kilometre-long Maypures rapids of the Orinoco fan out into wider, quieter waters, to be joined by the green Tuparro River coming in from the east. Our earlier forebodings of disorganization were confirmed when Carlos shamefacedly explained that, in spite of the park's supposedly foolproof reservation system based in Bogotá – and in spite of its rigid no-refund policy – there was no room at the inn. We would be spread around in various locations until the large group currently in occupation (an appropriate term: radios were playing loudly, alcohol was flowing, and unsupervised children were running around creating general havoc) departed tomorrow. Moreover, we would have to eat our food in the staff's own quarters (exactly what the other group of thirty was eating, given that there was supposedly no food left at the hotel, was not made clear). Our Spanish companions began grumbling again.

The days passed quietly. Early one morning, to avoid the midday heat, we went exploring in the savannah about 15 km west of the park HQ. Here, in a dense copse under a huge sky and by a creek, almost completely strangled by the undergrowth, we found the remains of what had apparently once been a thriving little port. A hundred years and more ago, rubber had been shipped from the Amazon and Río Negro headwaters down the Orinoco to the top of the Maypures rapids. There the cargo was transferred to a short narrow-gauge railway that bypassed the rapids and, at this point, again met an Orinoco tributary, but below the rapids. When the rubber (the black gold of its day) started to run out, its place was taken by real gold: over the years the copse in which we stood had been dug over a score of times by treasure hunters.

But here there were not just ghosts of rubber barons and gold miners. The local indigenous people who were recruited to run the little port and the railway were held in conditions of the cruellest indenture – it was in fact slavery of the worst kind, and it had lasted well into the early twentieth century.

One day the slaves here rose up and massacred their white masters, leaving no-one alive. They walked off into the savannah and were never seen again. The little port and a small steel river freighter were abandoned overnight. The freighter is now disappearing under the white sand of the riverbank, and unidentifiable chunks of machinery in the

Rusting hulk, El Tuparro National Park

undergrowth will soon rust away completely. You can never get very far from death and violence in Colombia.

Another day we climbed the steep black granite outcrop across the river from the park HQ. It was five o'clock in the evening. Far to the south, great thunderheads were building, lightning flashing. You could see maybe 100 km all around: to the south, upstream from the rapids, the glassy waters of the Orinoco; to the west, an immense flat plain broken only by the occasional dramatic outcrop like the one on which we stood; to the east, hillier country and the maze of rivers and backwaters of the Casiquiare, that unique phenomenon of a river that actually joins the Amazon and the Orinoco. But Carlos and Elvis were calling from down below: we must get back before dark, they said.

The night before leaving, we learned a couple of things that explained Carlos's evident and ongoing nervousness and some furtive whispering between him and Elvis. In the first place, it seemed that the park was not quite so immune from guerrilla activity as we had been led to believe; the reason we had to get off the river by dark was that the army had imposed a curfew and had indicated that it would strafe any craft on the water after six. And in fact the guerrillas had been into the park HQ on the very morning we had arrived. They had found Carlos asleep and snoring in a hammock, recovering from what had evidently been a long bender.

Irately they had woken him up. "You are a disgrace to the National Parks Service and to Colombia," they had shouted. "What do you think the tourists who have come all this way to visit Colombia will think of us if they find you drunk?" If it ever happened again, they said, they would shoot him. "For the guerrillas, you see," said Carlos to us with a straight face as Elvis nodded seriously, "are very patriotic, very ecological, even."

10 The Royal Ways, the Nevados, and Armero

COLOMBIA IS ONE OF the most geographically varied countries in the world. The Andes, which run in a single unbroken chain northwards from Cape Horn, though Chile and Peru, start to divide into two parallel cordilleras in Ecuador, then three by the time they reach Colombia. This means that if you are travelling east to west – or vice versa – for any great distance, you face repeated steep ascents and descents. The three ranges reach as high as 5,700 metres and, although Southern Colombia is close to the equator, some peaks are perpetually snowcapped.

This makes for wonderful, if strenuous, hiking. The snag, of course, is that the FARC, the ELN and the paras also like to live in remote areas and do not always welcome intruders. Planning a few days' walking usually involves playing off scenic beauty against the risk of being kidnapped or worse.

For weekend sallies from Bogotá, the answer is to go with one of the surprisingly numerous informal walking clubs that function on weekends. It is one of the many paradoxes of Colombia that in this exceedingly violent land, and in a city that sometimes feels under siege, there are more active hikers than in any other country in the region.

The oldest and most popular of these clubs is Salsipuedes ("Get out if you can"), which began years ago when a group of young parents got together and started to organize walks in the countryside, each month exploring new routes and rediscovering the ancient Caminos Reales, the Royal Ways that were used in colonial days to bring up gold and supplies from Peru or from the Magdalena River to the highland centres such as Bogotá.

The patriarch of Salsipuedes is Alfonso, now in his early seventies, but as energetic and mad as ever. On both Saturday and Sunday of every weekend, year in, year out, he leads one of five or six organized walks in the environs of Bogotá; as often as not, his nephew Segundo serves as rastrillo (back marker). The walks are graded by difficulty and length, using the musical scale. *Do* walks are typically on level ground and may only last a few hours; they are suitable for grandmas and small children. But a *La* may be a strenuous 30 km affair with two thousand metres or more of ascent, often finishing at or after dark; you need to be fit on these.

On a typical Saturday, Alfonso, Segundo, and maybe fifteen others will assemble at the bus stop at El Campín football stadium near the city centre, at around 6:30 AM. Friday nights in Bogotá are boisterous, and at dawn on Saturday the city is invariably silent, litter-blown, and smelling faintly of old beer and piss. It can be difficult to find a taxi at this hour: more than once Jenny and I arrived ten or fifteen minutes late to find the group had already gone (quite uncharacteristically, Salispuedes is a Colombian organization that runs on time).

At the bus stop, there's always the same cheery man serving coffee – tintos – out of large silver thermoses: he has the pitch to himself and does good business. Alfonso is usually there first, with his Alpine-style walking stick and his trademark orange neckerchief, checking his lists. After you've been with Salsipuedes a few times, he learns your name and greets you heartily, as "*don Nicolás, el canadiense* ..."

One day in spring, as usual, we boarded our chartered green and white bus. There was a slightly forced joviality as Alfonso (who is deaf in one ear) rather loudly and in slow Spanish called on each person, one by one, to introduce themselves. The three or four foreigners on board attracted a warm welcome. The locals were especially gratified that foreigners had overcome the paranoia that sometimes seems to rule the expatriate community in Bogotá and were making an effort to get out and see the beauty of the country. Most of the walkers were unmistakeably middle-class: teachers, graduate students, doctors. When I introduced myself as working at the Canadian Embassy, there was a slight awakening of interest – most embassies would forbid their staff to take part in activities like this – but I had to add, only half jokingly, that I didn't work in the visa section; otherwise I knew I would spend half the day fending off earnest but not entirely innocent overtures.

We headed out west, over one of the crests of the cordillera, then down steeply hairpinning bends towards Villeta – only 60 km away as the condor flies, but almost two thousand metres lower down and hence much hotter. We stopped for a second breakfast at a little roadside joint and sat out in the still cool sunshine as heavy trucks and buses rumbled past at alarming speeds. Jenny and I ordered our usual huevos pericos – a local version of scrambled eggs – and hot chocolate, but our fellow Bogotanos stoked up more seriously, with pescuezo – stuffed chicken neck, served complete with head, red crest and unnervingly beady black eyes – and the even less appetizing *cuchuco de espinazo*: pig spine soup.

At about 9:00 AM, we were at our starting point, the picturesque main square of a small lowland town. The locals were starting to emerge, and from their park benches they observed with polite interest as Alfonso – a kind of latter-day Jane Fonda – orchestrated our warm-up exercises, as he always did. We earnestly rotated our necks first one way, then the other, then did the same with our ankles; we stretched our thigh muscles and rotated our arms like windmills. And then we sang the Salsipuedes song, a slightly cheesy little ditty invoking the virtues of fresh air and exhorting us all to leave no litter that everyone nevertheless took seriously.

Today's walk began by wending through narrow country lanes, with small bougainvillea-festooned and whitewashed farmhouses on either side. Alfonso sensed the neighbourhood to be a little iffy so, as he always did in these circumstances, he greeted every onlooker with a little explanation – "*somos caminantes* ..." – and he described where we were going. This was just in case anyone got the wrong idea and spread the word that the guerrillas had just passed this way.

All year round, the flowers are spectacular, the sheer greenness of the mountainsides overwhelming, and that day was no different. After an hour or so, the path steepened, the vegetation became a little darker

On the Royal Roads with Salsipuedes

and denser. As usual, the walk progressed ever upwards, never down. It drizzled for a few minutes, but we were sweating so much by then that the coolness was welcome. Once an hour there was a reintegración – a short rest – but as the day advanced the group spread out over a kilometre or so. We all looked for a grassy meadow: a spot to have lunch, eat our sandwiches, and doze in the intermittent sunshine for an hour.

An hour out from La Vega, we came across what looked like a pile of builders' sand on the path, protected from the rain by a sheet of corrugated iron. I trudged past, hardly looking, but then out of the corner of my eye I saw what was unmistakeably a hand protruding out from under the corrugated iron.

I walked on a few steps, absorbing this. I turned around and saw that the little group behind me had stopped and lifted the sheet of corrugated iron a few inches. There was a dead body lying there, blood on its chest. An old farmer looked on expressionless from behind a wall.

My fellow hikers looked at each other, said nothing, and shrugged slightly. They carefully replaced the covering and we walked on in silence.

Later I wondered if we should have done something. "No," said Alfonso. "He was clearly dead. What could we have done? Better not to get mixed up in anything."

One day we were on a long hike in the green hills to the northwest of Bogotá that conceal dozens of small family-run coal mines. Coming down the track towards us, we made out a man running at a strange rhythm – short rapid steps, his hands out before him as if he were holding some invisible divining rod, and swerving from side to side. As he got closer we could hear him making a "vroom vroom" noise, with an occasional simulated squeal of brakes as he took a particularly sharp bend. Spluttering and juddering, he came to a halt in front of us, pretended to park his invisible motorbike, and then proceeded to hold a perfectly normal and civil conversation. Nobody batted an eyelid when, with a polite "*Hasta la próxima,*" he revved up again, put his nonexistent Harley into gear, and roared on down the hill. One of our fellow walkers explained that he was a well-known character in the neighbourhood, known simply as *el motociclista* – harmless but quite mad.

Another morning we started a walk from a spot about 60 km to the southeast of Bogotá, known FARC territory – but things had been reported quiet for a while. Pierre, a hearty long-time Swiss resident of Bogotá teaching at the University of La Sabana, was our guide for the day. He decided the risk was a reasonable one. He had been asked to lead this walk because it began at a finca called La Bella Suiza.

Barely had we left the main road when we encountered, coming the other way, a long column of maybe a hundred Colombian Army troops. They were laden down with uncomfortable-looking old backpacks, many of them festooned with large plastic Pepsi bottles for water. They were all carrying automatic weapons. Bandoleers of shiny bullets dragged in the dust. They looked exhausted, their camouflage paint running in their sweat. Nobody even looked at us.

We wound our way up to the top of the treeline and by early afternoon we were emerging onto cold, windswept páramo: high altitude moorland at 3,500 metres or higher that derives its moisture from the clouds and that is characterized by frailejones – strange prehistoric-looking plants with down-covered leaves and trunks like stunted palm trees. There were few landmarks, and we periodically wandered off in the wrong direction, only to regroup when Pierre or one of the other veterans called us over by whistling.

Then abruptly, barely ten metres in front of us, there appeared from nowhere a platoon of ten or a dozen soldiers, armed to the teeth, looking ferocious and with their weapons pointed straight at us. They were nervous, visibly trembling, and their leader shouted at us in what sounded like near-hysteria.

It turned out that we had stumbled into the Army's frontline trenches. We were coming right from the middle of a small area where the Army thought they had a FARC unit bottled up. Dressed in our bright blue and red rainjackets (a few hardy ones in shorts), toting cameras and walking sticks, we didn't exactly look like guerrilleros in mufti. But the lieutenant took some convincing, all the same; he was particularly anxious to know if anyone had joined our group in the past hour or so. He told us we were lucky we weren't all shot.

By the time he let us go, it was dusk and the scene on the moors looked like the old black and white version of *The Hound of the Baskervilles*. It was a real relief when the lights of our bus started to shine through the swirling mist.

Usually on these trips the rule was to be back in Bogotá by dark, which was always around 6:00 PM. But, even if everything went according to plan, there was the Saturday and Sunday evening traffic to cope with. Coming in on the main highway from the north, you could easily spend two hours inching your way in through the suburbs and back to El Campín. If the day had been a hard one, most of us slept. But sometimes the Salsipuedes songbook was passed around. As we neared our terminus, one by one people asked to be dropped off – they got down with a cheery wave and a "*Hasta la semana que entra!*"

One long weekend Jenny and I decided to be a little more ambitious. Staying with us at home was Sebastian, a young Dutchman whom we'd met by chance a few months earlier on the Amazon and whom we'd invited to look us up if he was in need of a free bed in Bogotá for a few days. He was game for a bit of adventure, so we loaded up our little Toyota Tercel with camping gear and food, and early one Saturday morning set off west.

We wound our way down the mountainside along a familiar road to Tena, La Mesa, and – in time for lunch – Honda, a small colonial town perched on the west bank of the fast, wide, and muddy Magdalena

River. Honda ("Deep") is the most southerly navigable point on the Magdalena. Until the late 1970s you could – like Geo Lengerke, hero of *The Tiger's Other Stripe* – take sternwheelers all the way from Barranquilla, but the old town is now gently decaying away.

Up over a high pass to Guaduas and then down once more to steaming Mariquita. This is another town that has seen more glorious days: in the early years of the twentieth century, Mariquita was the eastern terminus of *El Cable*, the longest commercial ropeway in the world. Built and maintained by British railway engineers, it carried goods (and the odd railway engineer or honoured guest) 100 km west to Manizales and back. A few pylons still stand, incongruous on the mountainsides, but *El Cable* long ago lost an unequal battle with trucks.

Climbing for the third time today, we edged past several mudslides that had all but cut the road and up to moorland and a left-hand turn down a dirt road into Los Nevados national park. Dominating Los Nevados is the massif of the 5,325-metre Nevado del Ruiz – although today the clouds were too low to see anything. At the National Park entrance, a warden told us that Ruiz was currently active and hence out of bounds and that we'd need an authorized guide to climb any of the other peaks.

No problem. We attached ourselves to a friendly group of climbers who, in their two high-clearance jeeps, had just arrived from Manizales with the intention of climbing Santa Isabel, a little further southwards down the cordillera. Transferring all our gear and piling in, we bumped off almost immediately across grey lava slopes and up a laborious series of hairpin bends. Every so often, the track became so steep that, in the thin air, even our powerful jeep couldn't cope; we would have to get out for the driver to turn the vehicle around and then carry on up the hill in reverse gear.

On our right we passed the steep-sided Olleta crater, whose rim was out of sight in the mist, and then on the left there was a sign announcing the Ruiz Hostel – at 4,700 metres, long ago ruined by a too-close lava flow. Then we went down again, out of the clouds, and across a steep-sloping hillside to the lonely farmstead of El Cisne (The Swan), its white walls and red-tiled roof visible from miles away.

It was bitterly cold at El Cisne, and the only flat place to pitch our tent looked already waterlogged. As darkness fell we cranked up our ancient Bolivian-purchased Primus stove, but it had forgotten how to work at high altitudes such as this, and we had to beg ashamedly the use of a butane gas stove from our new friends.

After we'd eaten, on our feet, a hurried instant meal, the gruff farmer and his wife invited us all into the farmhouse for a cup of hot *Agua de Panela* – sugar-cane tea. By candlelight we warmed our hands on the cracked old porcelain mugs he served us, and we squatted on piles of smelly sheepskins. The couple's three runny-nosed and red-faced children had long ago been put to bed. "Where do they go to school?" I asked. The farmer waved down the valley; it was a two-day walk to a tiny one-room schoolhouse, "And you never know when the teacher will come."

With three of us crammed into our tiny mountain tent, the night was uncomfortable but warm – and anyway we needed to be up at 3:30 AM to have a chance of reaching the summit of Santa Isabel before the clouds came in.

I always have severe problems with high altitudes and early-morning starts, and next morning was no exception. Within minutes of starting to edge up the valley, picking our way through tufted grass and frailejones by torchlight, with a clear but moonless sky above, I was feeling alternately hot and queasy. It would only get worse, I knew, but years of bitter experience had taught me that having once thrown up, I would be re-energized for half an hour or so.

By 6:30 AM, we were resting on the fringes of a small tarn, bordered by yellow sage grass. Far below, occasionally visible as the clouds swirled in and out, was the brilliant vermilion surface of Laguna Verde, while directly opposite must have been the Nevado del Ruiz itself.

In a few minutes the clouds started to clear. Over towards the east – and Bogotá – the sun crept an inch or so above the horizon. Ruiz, we could now see, was a vast, almost flat, snowfield, with a few jagged pitons of black-brown rock thrusting upwards; exactly where the highest point might be was not clear. Behind, from what we could see at this steep angle, Santa Isabel seemed to be a softly rounded white dome. And just around the eastern slopes of Santa Isabel, the perfect white cone of the Nevado del Tolima – 20 km to the south – looked a tempting climb at 5,215 metres.

At the snowline, those of us who had crampons put them on, while the lesser equipped – including Sebastian in his thin running shoes and his almost equally thin sweater – interspersed themselves on the rope between us. Soon we were inching up a fifty-degree slope, kicking in our toes hard and stopping every ten steps to get our breath; the altitude was starting to kick in.

As the incline lessened – we must have been at 4,800 metres by then – the mist (annoyingly) came in again. By 8:00 AM we were standing rather forlornly on a flat and smooth snowfield but in thick cloud: there was nothing at all to differentiate where snow met cloud and nothing to indicate direction or orientation. We must have reached the top. I had only been sick twice, but, there being no view, the achievement was not entirely satisfying.

Next time I was in the vicinity of the Nevados was on 13 November 1998. Like many countries in Latin America, Colombia's best-remembered dates are to do with battles – usually victories of Bolívar in the war of independence from Spain. There has also been a good sprinkling of political assassinations, and there were the terrible years starting in 1948, known simply but appropriately as *La Violencia*, when perhaps 300,000 people lost their lives in an internecine bloodbath.

But, as if this were not enough, the country has had more than its share of natural disasters. On 12 November 1985, the Nevado del Ruiz began to go into eruption. This was no spectacle of spewing lava and flames, for the crater was capped by ice. But the heat and gasses generated beneath the ice created in the space of a few hours a vast cauldron of mud, rocks, and boiling water.

The deadly mixture sought the path of least resistance – a dry canyon flowing down to the east – and, at about 3:00 AM on 13 November 1985, a great wall of mud thundered down the mountainside, bringing with it rocks the size of houses. It travelled almost as fast as the roar it generated, so that the sleeping population of the prosperous market town of Armero, which lay directly in its path, had only a few seconds' warning. In the space of five minutes, twenty thousand lives were lost and Armero entered the vocabulary of the Colombian people: every adult Colombian alive today can remember where they were on 13 November 1985.

One tragedy among the thousands caught the imagination of the public, and indeed of the world, and may go some way to account for why Armero is still remembered so intensely. A little girl of five or six, trapped up to her neck in a sea of mud and heavy debris, was kept alive for days by desperate rescue crews who held her head above water, fed her, and comforted her constantly; TV cameras covered every minute. She hardly cried at all, indeed she was lucid and calm for most of her ordeal; but finally she died from exposure and exhaustion, and millions of TV viewers watched her body slide under the mud again.

There was a vast international rescue effort for Armero, with crews and equipment being flown in from all over the world. Much of the equipment and the funds donated were, it later transpired, spirited away by corrupt officials, but the grateful people of Armero nevertheless remember and every year they invite representatives of the countries that helped – including Canada – to the commemoration ceremonies.

Armero today is eerie. The main north-south road is lined for about a hundred metres, on the west side, by nondescript single-storey concrete buildings painted white, with the names of businesses and brands of pop faded but still clearly visible. You have to be told that what you are looking at is in fact the third storey of these buildings – you are now literally driving over Armero, the streets of which lie five metres or so below the rich black earth. In the hotel at nearby Ambalema are aerial photographs of Armero before and after: it looks as though the lab technician has taken a rag and wiped it across the neat geometric pattern of pre-1985 Armero, talking care not to leave a single indication that humanity had ever passed this way.

A vast and not very tasteful concrete arch marks what used to be the town square; bizarrely, some of the palm trees that grow in rows here are original, somehow surviving – even thriving – on the mud slide. Scattered around several square kilometres of now-lush green undergrowth and shrubs are single gravestones, or groups of two or three, tended each year by the survivors of Armero – known today with some pride as Armeritos. Incredibly, a few smallholders have started farming again, gambling against the chances of there occurring two eruptions in one place in a single lifetime.

The local Bishop said mass, and dignitaries presented the foreign visitors with leather scrolls in recognition of their countries' contribution to the relief of Armero thirteen years earlier. There were the usual long speeches. A children's choir sang. And a National Police helicopter clattered overhead. From it, and into the upturned faces of the crowd, there fluttered down a vast cloud of purple and white bougainvillea petals.

It was another scene worthy of García Márquez. There was not a dry eye to be found.

At Easter 2000, with only a few months left in Colombia, we made our last trip to the Central Cordillera, this time to the Fuji-shaped peak that had tempted us from the slopes of Santa Isabel: the Nevado del Tolima. After work early on a Wednesday, Jenny and I picked up Kathleen and her Colombian boyfriend, Hernán, and, with the four of us plus all our camping and climbing gear uncomfortably squeezed into the Toyota Tercel, set off through the suburbs and down the familiar winding roads to the hot country.

We approached Tolima from the south, via the provincial capital of Ibagué. The river crossing this time was at the Bogotanos' favourite resort, Girardot. Past that point, we embarked on a hot evening drive across the plains and to the cloud-shrouded massif of Tolima, in whose shadow lies the city.

Ibagué is frankly undistinguished. I knew of it only because once or twice a month a rather nervous Canadian mining executive, with his office here and a mine nearby, used to call me up to ask for my latest advice on security. He had been severely shaken up by the highly publicized kidnapping of another Canadian miner, near Bucaramanga, but not sufficiently to take me at my word and leave before he lived to regret it.

At 7:00 AM next day we were driving around in the northern suburbs of the quiet city, looking for the road up into the hills – "It's the only one, you can't miss it ..." Well of course we could, and it was nearly an hour before we were finally on our way. After a few kilometres the tarmac gave out, and we were in an ever-narrowing and -steepening valley, floored with bright green pastures and at whose head could occasionally be glimpsed through the clouds, far away and high up, a snowfield that could have passed for the Swiss Alps.

The road ran out at a small and isolated finca known appropriately as El Silencio. I was a little perturbed to see "FARC" daubed on one wall in letters a metre high, but the eldest son of the family – who seemed a little simple – said that everything was quiet and we were welcome to leave our car in his cow field.

We unpacked the car and loaded up our backpacks. The first hour of our walk was pleasantly bucolic – a path meandered through meadows, crossing the Río Combeima twice, climbing maybe a hundred metres. Where the path of the stream started to steepen we came to the last habitation, El Rancho – and to the hot springs that every weekend

El Silencio

attract a few trippers from Ibagué. But it's impossible to get away from human tragedy. A year previously, a large rock pinnacle just behind the main house had without warning and in the middle of the night collapsed on the house. Half the family was killed; primitive wooden crosses marked their supposed graves, and the survivors had moved the new house a hundred metres away.

We began climbing steeply up the right-hand side of the valley: a narrow, zigzagging, and slippery path in dense undergrowth, which disappeared at times, leaving us to scramble on all fours up steep earthy and rocky slopes, with our packs jamming awkwardly in low branches. After two hours, there was a welcome respite at a beautiful thread-like waterfall some eighty metres high, but then it was back into the undergrowth and an even steeper climb.

By early afternoon, the vegetation was thinning out, the air cooling. I knew from my many weekends of hiking around Bogotá that we must by now be above 3,500 metres and ready to emerge into open páramo, which we did half an hour later, although, disappointingly, the clouds were low and there was no sign of the Nevado itself, which must lie ahead.

The favoured camping spot here was a large rock overhang, known as *La Cueva*, but it was so dank and litter-infested that we chose instead to squeeze our two tents on the only flat ground in the vicinity. Worryingly, the stream at *La Cueva* contained only a sulphurous, creamy-coloured drip, and annoyingly the mosquitoes were out in full force; we went to bed early.

Next day we continued to wind our way upwards, over steeply sloping moorland, through yellow-brown tussock-grass and groves of the biggest frailejones I'd yet seen – up to four metres. Where we crossed a contouring path, there was a good flat space that had evidently been used recently as a camping spot; Kathleen picked up a scrap of camouflage fatigues, and we speculated as to just who might have been staying here recently.

Our destination that second day was a rocky ledge at the top of the páramo and the beginning of the rubble and lava slopes that lead up to the snowline. At 4,450 metres, it was marked by a large steel cross, visible for most of the day. We arrived in good time and went exploring, packless, further up. In the mist I twice heard a strange whooshing sound. On the third pass I saw them: a pair of Andean condors flying wingtip to wingtip, barely five metres away from me, their white collars precise and delineated as they craned their heads one way then the other. I don't think they saw me. I had been lucky, for there are only twenty pairs known to inhabit the Central Cordillera.

We were having a water problem. The only water available was the same unwholesome-looking trickle we'd shied away from at *La Cueva*. But you're supposed to drink as much water as you can at altitude; we found that by filling our water bottles and then letting them settle for an hour, the top few inches didn't seem too bad.

In the evening, at last, the clouds briefly cleared above us. The route to the summit snowfield looked frighteningly steep – even impossible – from this angle. The setting sun dyed the final couloir a golden yellow, with the steep rock pinnacles on either side of it darkening as we watched. Far, far below us in the darkening valley we could see a tiny, solitary light from El Silencio and, beyond, the loom of Ibagué. We heard a cow bell, ever so distant. We were probably as high up as anyone in the northern half of South America, and it felt both lonely and exhilarating. For once, the ongoing tragedies of this benighted land seemed far away – now it was the same cold and the same timeless beauty of the Rockies, the Himalayas, or Patagonia, and there was that familiar twinge of slight apprehension at what we knew would be a tough day ahead.

Kathleen rather spoiled the sense of isolation by trying to see if her cellphone (*Siempre en Contacto*, said the Comcel slogan) would work from here. It did, so she called friends who were at that time carousing in a Bogotá bar, it being Friday night. She lost the connection. Subsequently, we learned that they thought we had suddenly been swept away by an avalanche; they spent the rest of that weekend worrying.

Up at one, and, as usual, I was feeling sick. Tonight there was no moon, and the stars were only intermittent. Flashlight in one hand, ice axe in the other, we stumbled our way upwards on rubble and the occasional patch of dirty ice for what seemed like hours, with no sense of whether we were making progress or not. When we stopped, no-one spoke; it's at times like these, with the queasiness and a headache coming on, when I wonder what I'm doing at such high altitude.

By 5:30 AM we were on ground that was gradually levelling off – as we could now see in the grey light of dawn – before it abruptly rose again to form vertical ice cliffs, hung with beautiful yet menacing thirty-foot icicles. I wondered if the foul smell that was turning my stomach was some function of my altitude sickness before I realized that we were actually picking our way around small fumaroles that were letting out clouds of steam into the sub-zero morning air: this volcano might not be active, but it was certainly not extinct (in fact it had last erupted in the 1940s.)

Up to our right was a smooth patch of snow, maybe some sixty metres high before it curved away from us and out of sight. It looked to be about eighty degrees inclination, but on closer inspection turned out to be sixty – just about manageable for us non-technical climbers as long as we were careful kicking in with our crampons and roping up.

Coming up the crest, the sun burst gloriously over the clouds and everything went from pink to gold to white in just a few minutes. As we made our way up the now-decreasing slope, the snow crisp and squeaky under us, every crystal glistening, we could see our own shadows, even that of the rope linking us, cast on the opposite slope, far away on the other side of the couloir. Suddenly it was all worth it.

The views were, of course, magnificent: from the huge and rounded summit field to the north, we could see Santa Isabel and the Nevado del Ruiz, where we had stayed over a year before, while far to the south was the Nevado del Huila, at 5,700 metres, the highest of this range

Climbing the Nevado del Tolima

(and the most difficult to climb). At the highest point itself was, bizarre in this otherwise pristine setting, a small mountain tent; we trudged over and roused the two surprised lads who must have thought that, here at least, they would be able to have a lie in. I reflected that last evening, after all, we had not been the highest people in South America, but they made up for my disappointment by making us all a mug of tea.

In the middle of the snowfield is the crater itself: a steep-sided inverted cone maybe a hundred metres wide and deep, with huge icicles lining its lower parts and a cloud of steam obscuring the bottom. It was impressive and frightening for its very whiteness and cleanness. I could see how it might be easy to fall in, as it was tempting to edge just a couple of metres further down to see if you could actually see the bottom.

We made it back down to the valley at an agonizing and knee-wrecking speed, only to find our dreams of getting to Ibagué and a cold beer frustrated. The battery of the car was completely flat; it seemed we had inadvertently left one door partially open and the interior light had stayed on, draining all the power away. I wondered if this was the solitary light we had seen from atop the Nevado.

There was much head-scratching and pondering of what to do, with the simple-minded son of the farmer making some surprisingly practical suggestions. But no-one had a spare battery.

There was no alternative but to push – after all, it was pretty much downhill all the way to Ibagué. Jenny, in the driver's seat, sped off, and we could see the car lurching as she tried to jumpstart it every few metres. Fifteen minutes later, there she still was, far in the distance, still rolling downhill and still juddering as she let the clutch in and out.

We whiled away the time talking to the farmer's son. It turned out that when he said the guerrillas "hardly ever" came here, he meant that they actually appeared about once a month, to claim their "colaboración" (protection money). "Do they ever actually protect you, though?"

"Oh yes," said the boy. A few months ago, three cows had been stolen from El Silencio; the FARC were alerted, and a day later they returned with them. Well, they weren't actually the same cows, and it wasn't done to ask what had happened to the thief, but, shrugged the boy, who cared?

Meanwhile, a full 15 km down the hill and faced with the one uphill stretch of the entire run to Ibagué, Jenny had fortuitously encountered the lechero – the jeep that does a daily run up the valley to pick up milk and return empty churns. The driver transferred his battery into the Tercel, and started the engine; then the batteries were switched again, the dead battery replaced under our hood without the engine missing a beat.

"Everything will be fine as long as you don't stop the engine," said the lechero driver. "*No se preocupen.*" And then he added, after a nervous pause: "They say you are American spies."

Jenny gaped in incredulity and mystification. He pointed at our diplomatic plates. "So what are those, then?"

In fact everything did go fine, and I learned a good trick about basic car maintenance. It was evident that the battery needed distilled water. None available, of course. No problem. Every roadside stall in Colombia stocks Bretaña, fizzy clear mineral water. Open a bottle, drop in a small pebble; the fizzing stops instantly, and you have clean, good water.

11 Putumayo

Coke Is It

PUTUMAYO DEPARTMENT lies along the north bank of the wide and slow Putumayo River, an important tributary of the Amazon. Its only two significant towns, Puerto Asís and Mocoa, are linked to each other by a 150-kilometre north-south dirt road and to the outside world either by air (one strip in Puerto Asís), by perilous track through the Eastern Cordillera of the Andes, or by launch: fifteen days to Leticia, on the Amazon. There is not one kilometre of metalled road in the department and the largest town – Puerto Asís, pop. 40,000 – has no electricity: households make do on portable generators. What Putumayo does have going for it is its soil and climate, which are particularly suitable for the coca bush, first introduced here twenty years ago.

80 percent of the department's economically active population, i.e., 97 percent of the rural population, is directly engaged in one phase or another of the cocaine business. There is no stigma whatsoever attached to the business; most of the department's booming population came here expressly to grow coca, and the experts have yet to find a product that (in this region at least) can provide as lucrative a living.

Leaf pickers can earn up to US$500 a month (more than twice the minimum wage), but the objective of most cocaleros is to graduate to running a small lab and shipping out the refined product to Cali or the Cauca Valley at US$1,000 to US$1,200 a kilo.

Before I made my first visit to Putumayo in late 1997, the police had over the previous three years located and destroyed forty labs in the area and claimed to have eradicated four thousand hectares annually, but the total area under cultivation and the quantity of cocaine leaving the department continued to grow. One- and two-ton seizures were common, but forty tons of finest Putumayo cocaine still reached North America and Europe every year.

I didn't see it (understandably, no-one would take me), but I was told that the port area of Puerto Asís (a grandiloquent term for a square mile of redolent mud flats) was one night a week a scene out of the *Arabian Nights*. Cocaine growers, processors, and dealers from all over the department converged with their trucks and canoes, setting up tables and delicate scales. Buyers and connoisseurs went from table to table testing the consistency of the product and haggling over prices. All of this went on, romantically, by candle- and lamplight, the town being so starved of tax income that it could not afford a generating station. In a tacit understanding, neither the police nor the Army interfered with this souk-like spectacle.

This was not so much because the authorities had been bought off (although that did occur), but because, fundamentally, the commanders of neither force believed the battle on drugs could be won here. Even if Colonel Barinas of the police had the men and the equipment to wipe out the forty thousand hectares of crops, this would put nearly the entire population of the department out of work. There were no competitive substitutes (especially in light of the poor roads and infrastructure), and such crop substitution and loan programs that had been implemented under the government's PLANTE strategy had a serious inherent flaw: they applied only to active coca growers, not to those few campesinos who had resisted the lure of easy money. The greater your plantation of coca, the greater the loan you received – as long as you kept growing, harvesting, and periodically allowing destruction, you could benefit indefinitely from PLANTE.

Eradication campaigns had also led to serious human rights abuses: commonly, not only were crops burned but the houses of the cocaleros along with them. Nor were the police too patient with those who resis-

The waterfront, Puerto Asís

ted arrest; in the paper on the day I arrived, it was reported that three out of five cocaleros had been shot dead when the police intercepted an outward-bound truck shipment from Putumayo.

As the lucrative industry spread throughout the department in the early 1980s, so did the forces of the FARC, now organized into four fronts (numbers 2, 13, 32, and 48). The FARC typically stop short of shipping the product, but they tax every stage in the process: for every can of gasoline, sack of cement, and litre of ether or acetone that pass into their territory they exact carefully measured cash percentages. Similarly, for every kilo of refined cocaine that makes its way onto a light plane or river launch, they levy a further tax (currently US$35); exactly the same process is applied to legitimate businesses. It is not possible to undertake any business in this department without paying off the guerrillas.

The four fronts are subject to strict internal discipline and the typical pattern for the imposition of discipline on villages under their control is the classic "three strikes and you're out" ("out" being a shot in the back of the head). Commanders sometimes insist on the most unlikely sounding regimes – campesinos have been shot dead for the ecologically unsound practice of dynamiting streams for fish, and, more benignly, some revenue is raised by fining launch passengers for not wearing life jackets. Rebel troops are sometimes paid in cash (US$350 to US$500 a month), but the more usual pattern is that young men (as young as twelve) are lured in by the offer of uniforms, automatic weapons, and prestige; they are then kept loyal by threats that their family will be killed if they desert or – if they have participated in raids – that their name will be leaked to the police.

At the time of my visit, Franklin of Front 32 was the most prestigious of the four commanders in the region – the site of his jungle headquarters was widely known (indeed, I was offered a meeting), but neither the police nor the Army seemed particularly motivated to hunt him out. One person described Franklin's three-ring system of defences, with young children posted on the outer circle as scouts, and progressively more hardened veterans manning the other two circles.

Only the leaders had any grasp whatsoever of left-wing ideology – one guerrilla I spoke with had been frankly warned not to discuss Marxism in front of the junior ranks, presumably lest they perceive their commander's less-than-total grasp of the basic tenets of communist theology. In spite of the FARC's almost complete territorial dominance in Putumayo, they were not widely feared by the population; over the years, most villages had typically come to relatively comfortable arrangements. The scourges of the department were, instead, bands of heavily armed young delinquents – some were FARC deserters, others unemployed youths with one hand in the coca industry, still others (it was widely rumoured) off-duty or recently fired police. These gangs made travelling the department's principal road an ordeal not to be undertaken lightly.

My driver from Puerto Asís to Mocoa, where I was planning to visit a convent-run project, took it as a matter of course that, before setting off, we should go to his house and spend half an hour hiding my money in various difficult-of-access parts of the car; he then attached a CB radio that allowed him to check in with his base every ten minutes for the next few hours. For the final stage of my journey, three nuns bravely climbed in for my extra protection: it was widely considered that a nun in the car doubled your survival chances. The nuns (who were no wilting flowers) later told me that their entire community had been praying for my safety for two days. Returning to Puerto Asís, I

Army roadblock between Puerto Asís and Mocoa

nearly lost my money to fire, by stowing it in an air hose too close to the car's radiator.

The police and Army studiously avoided all deliberate contact with the guerrillas, eradicated only the exact amount of crops required by the DEA, and – although they searched all vehicles and passengers coming in and out of Mocoa and Puerto Asís – made no attempt to patrol the road. Where they were active at this time was in attempting to control the movement of the basic ingredients for the production of cocaine: gasoline, cement, ether, and acetone. However, like in San Pablo on the Magdalena, handwritten signs in Puerto Asís openly announced *We have gasoline* or *We have cement*: the police did not seem to be a major deterrent. Both forces also launched periodical raids on labs and clandestine airstrips, which certainly led at the very least to some rough handling of campesinos and at worst to shooting sprees. It was in the course of these raids that there sometimes occurred contacts with the guerrillas; the day before my arrival, the Army had lost a man at Puerto Vega when, immediately following the seizure of a gasoline shipment, they had been ambushed on the river by a rocket-equipped FARC contingent. Both police and Army kept a close eye on my visit and a small contingent toting machine guns came to ensure – in the friendliest possible fashion – that I boarded my scheduled flight out of Puerto Asís.

In this difficult context, foreign oil companies – tempted by the department's proven reserves – had also established a tentative footing. At this time they represented the only real economic alternative to coca, although the jobs currently on offer were short term and not especially well-paying. Among these companies was one from Calgary, which had gradually negotiated its way into arrangements with indigenous and other communities in a remote block of jungle to the northeast of Puerto Asís, accessible only by helicopter; it employed thirty to fifty local people in a camp guarded by eighty troops. It had taken the company three years to reach the point at which it felt comfortable with drilling its first exploratory well, and it estimated that it would be another three, all going well, before it could begin commercial extraction.

But back to the nuns. Correctly diagnosing that the children of Putumayo were perhaps the most tragically affected of all the victims of this climate of violence, the Sisters of the community of Villa Garzón organized in November 1997 a two-week workshop for peace that brought in four hundred children (aged five to twelve) from some of the most conflictive areas of the department. This project was funded largely by our own Canada Fund for Local Initiatives. Children were taught how to live together in a very real sense: through acting, sports, organized play, musical, and artistic expression. For many, it was literally the first time that they had ever played with other children. Out of a group of twenty grade-3 boys and girls with whom I met, eleven had lost a close relative (father, mother, sister, brother, aunt, or uncle) by murder.

When they saw a funeral going by (which was often), these children did not ask "Who died?" but rather "Who was killed?" Every single child with whom I met had heard shots fired in anger. Several, at the end of the workshop, did not want to go home again: ten-year-olds had already been promised by their brothers or fathers to the guerrillas. As I was almost everywhere in Colombia, I was impressed and moved by the bravery and heroism of the Church people who strove in anonymity and at great danger to themselves to make others' lives better.

Almost as vulnerable as the children were the indigenous inhabitants of the department. There were eleven ethnic groups represented here, organized on traditional lines into fifty-one cabildos, each with its governor; the indigenous population in the region totalled around eighteen

The children of Villa Garzón

thousand. A small number of these groups had traditionally used coca for medicinal purposes, but, as one indigenous leader said to me, "we never thought our medicine would end up killing us." The largest of the groups, the Paesa, had seen its population in the department decline by 50 percent in twenty-five years, the victim of sickness, of confrontations with external colonizers, of exploitation and recruitment by the guerrillas, and of army and police raids. Spiritually, indigenous communities had been devastated. Most of the ethnic groups here practiced a form of animism and believed that the jungle was inhabited by invisible beings: oil companies, power-line workers, and "coca colonizers" had historically shown scant respect for these beliefs. However, indigenous groups were increasingly well-organized and, following a controversial case elsewhere in the country that pitted Occidental Petroleum against the U'was, very well aware of their rights.

There were more problems. In the regional elections of 26 October 1997, Putumayo (in the face of guerrilla exhortations and threats) competed for the country's lowest participation rates. In Puerto Asís, 177 of the city's twenty thousand registered voters turned out; the mayor of La Hormiga was elected by a margin of ten votes to eight; department-wide, the participation rate was 14 percent. In three of thirteen municipalities, there was no voting at all – elections were rescheduled for 28 December (coincidentally, the Colombian equivalent of April Fools' Day). All those that were elected to office in October had been declared illegitimate by the guerrillas (an irony: the low participation meant they were indeed illegitimate, but this was a direct result of guerrilla threats ...) and were to be treated as "military objectives" as of 1 January 1998.

Few doubted the guerrillas meant business; the outgoing mayor of Villa Garzón was shot dead days before the elections, a councillor-elect was killed in December 1997, and the mayor-elect of Sibundoy escaped an assassination attempt two days before my arrival. Most forecast that January would be an exceedingly difficult month; Police Commander Colonel Barinas laughed when I asked him if he could guarantee the life of incoming officials; Barinas was actually much more interested in reminiscing about an RCMP course he had attended in Canada; he asked me if the CN Tower was still standing.

Quite apart from the electoral question, there was a another ticking time bomb in the so-called "Acuerdos de Orito": a wide-ranging set of social commitments signed by the government in late 1996 in the face of massive marches by coca workers protesting crop eradication. Even government sources admitted that next to none of the commitments had been met.

In spite of the blatant attacks by the guerrillas on democracy itself, most of the people I spoke to seemed blasé on the subject. Politicians in these parts had a reputation for being more corrupt than most; indeed, the current governor was at this time in preventive detention, waiting to be formally charged for embezzling a million dollars from the departmental civil service's pension fund. There was thus not a great deal of sympathy for the threatened mayors – most were perceived to have run for office only so as to be able to pillage the departmental coffers.

In late 1997, there was as yet no proven paramilitary presence in the department, although Medellín cartel mercenaries appeared here in the late 1980s and rumours now abounded of masked men in the night. More positively, there was a very small but growing network of social activists that were concerned with human rights, with the levels of violence in the state and with finding some way out of the cocaine stalemate, i.e., the authorities having found no alternative but to interdict and the locals knowing no alternative but to run the risks and continue to grow. This network was based on the Church – priests in Puerto Asís, notably, were acting as catalysts for a secular network of Peace Promoters and had formed an ad hoc Conciliation Committee to see if the threats of death hanging over political candidates could somehow be removed by negotiating with the guerrillas.

The municipal ombudsmen in both Mocoa and Puerto Asís were also energetic and active; the former organized for my benefit an impromptu meeting of the town's Human Rights Committee, in which seventeen institutions (including the Army and police) participated. Some human rights activists were from the most unlikely backgrounds; the amiable and articulate Sr Gilberto Sánchez, for example, had recently retired from seven lucrative years in the coca business to dedicate himself full-time to the defence of human rights. Although the minimum sentence for growing coca was four years, he had served no time in prison; I understood from others that such were his profits that he was able to buy his way out of any possible legal action.

Both the Army captain and the commander of police also came over as thoughtful individuals with a good appreciation of the issues at hand and a not-inconsiderable degree of sympathy for the average campesino of Putumayo. Both commented to me that, although their mandates were clear – respectively, to take on the guerrillas and narcotrafficking with the utmost vigour – it was neither practical nor wise that they be overzealous in carrying out their orders. The guerrillas and the cocaleros were occupying spaces that the state had been unable to fill – until it was in a position to do so, there seemed to be no point in taking ruthless action.

I was back again in early 1998, this time at the request of the Bogotá office of another Canadian oil company with operations in Putumayo. The aim was to bring together all agencies involved in development work in the department, share information, and – it was hoped – take the first steps towards integrating the social programs of oil companies with those of other agencies, including NGOs and the Catholic Church. Hitherto, such programs had typically been implemented on an ad hoc basis and with little regard to the plans of other agencies; for example, companies had built schoolhouses and then found that the Ministry of Education was unable to supply teachers.

Why did the oil companies want to be concerned with development work? In crude terms, this could buy them the peace and goodwill necessary for them to be able to drill and the acquiescence, if not the cooperation, of the guerrilla forces that dominated most rural parts of the department. It also allowed the companies to avoid the unpalatable and illegal option of paying off the guerrillas with cash "vaccinations." Three Canadian companies had interests in the area; according to Colombian legislation, all must work in partnership with Ecopetrol, Colombia's state-owned oil company.

Over the years, oil companies operating in this region, starting with Texaco in the late 1970s, had acquired a reputation of being at best indifferent. Social projects they had undertaken had tended to be of a paternalistic and short-term nature and had left few long-lasting beneficial effects. As one local put it: "If you needed some paint for your living room, you went to the company; if you wanted the bus fare to visit your relatives, you went to the company ..."

Firms now active or interested in tapping the still significant oil reserves in the region are saddled with suspicion, even hostility, before they begin operations. Yet, most people put the blame for the lack of visible benefits to Putumayo brought by oil as much on corruption and/or inefficiency on the part of local and federal authorities as on the companies.

The meeting between the oil companies and other stakeholders in development was only a limited success. Ecopetrol, apparently on account of bureaucratic difficulties, was not prepared to give even an outline of its intended strategies; its partners, no doubt feeling obliged to their big brother, were in the end similarly unforthcoming. Their silence was greeted with disappointment, not to say suspicion, by a number of those present, notably by the Church and the NGOs.

I found it significant that, next day, Padre Alcides, the parish priest of Puerto Caicedo – a nearby municipality under strong guerrilla influence – met with me for two hours but declined an invitation to meet with one of the Canadian companies. Most of the oil companies' community development projects in Putumayo, he said, were seen even by their direct beneficiaries as blatant and crude attempts to buy their loyalty, and some companies were quite knowingly paying off one or more of the armed groups.

I took advantage of my stay to take a few more general soundings. The department's new mayors, the bravest of whom had taken office on 1 January 1998 (others decided simply not to show up for work ...), had one priority and one only: negotiating their own lives with the guerrillas and, by extension, negotiating municipal programs that would be to the liking of the insurgents.

The new mayor of Puerto Asís had been visited by the guerrillas on 3 January; he managed to dissuade them from their initial plan of killing him but then had to endure a two-week kidnapping, a "forced vacation" as he wryly described it. In order to secure his own release, he had to agree to hand over all the accounts from the previous administration: ostensibly this was so that the guerrillas would know the financial situation facing his own administration, but reading between the lines it was clear that the aim of the FARC was to identify and pursue those responsible for perceived abuses under the previous government. Following the mayor's release the entire town council was summoned to a meeting with FARC leaders; a council member was understandably cagey when I asked him about the outcome of this meeting.

These negotiations were taking place against the background of a massive military operation that had seen three thousand federal troops poured into the Putumayo in search of eighteen soldiers taken captive by the rebels in a December 1997 assault on the mountaintop communications base of Patascoy. The soldiers were rumoured to be held in three groups of six, possibly on Ecuadorean soil. My arrival at Puerto Asís coincided with that of 150 soldiers by military transport from Bogotá and intense activity by a squadron of heavy Russian-built transport helicopters (known as Papayas on account of their soft skin, their weight, and their alleged tendency to fall out of the sky when the wind blew).

Antinarcotics operations had also been stepped up, no doubt in part because of the then-looming decertification process and also perhaps because the FARC were at this time more concerned with hiding their captives than with guarding coca plantations. I saw a flight of helicopters returning from what I later learned was a major raid on clandestine cocaine labs: one by one, the six transports, five of which were defended with a manned Gatling gun slung in their starboard doorways, spiralled down and unloaded eight or ten heavily armed, muddied, and evidently fatigued men. Incongruously, cheery salsa music blared out tinnily from the airport loudspeakers as the helicopters clattered down. Of the six helicopters I saw land, five – the armed (and presumably armoured) ones – were Bell 212s painted in green and white, the colours of the National Police, while the sixth was a grey 212 – the property of and flown by the DEA.

Complementing the Mirabel-built Bell equipment parked on the tarmac, a Canadian-built DASH-8 leased by the Aires regional airline made for something of an exhibition of the Canadian aerospace industry. Flying back to Bogotá I talked with the plane's engineer. He explained that it was not usual for an engineer to accompany every flight and that his presence was in no way due to any problems with the DASH-8. Rather, it was because three years ago a minor technical problem had stranded another Aires plane at nearby Puerto Leguízamo: the FARC had taken the opportunity to destroy it with one neatly placed rocket round. It was now company policy that every measure possible be taken to avoid having its DASHs stranded overnight in Southern Colombia. The garrulous engineer also commented that, barely a month previously and on the day following my own departure from Putumayo, he had sat exactly in this row of seats doing his best to tend to two seriously wounded army personnel, each of whom had taken several rounds in a FARC ambush on the river that morning. I agreed with him that it was a sad comment on the efficiency and equipment levels of the Colombian Armed Forces that they had to fly out their seriously wounded men by commercial flights. The engineer thought that one of the men, at least, had probably died soon after arrival in Bogotá.

Months later, in my office at the embassy in Bogotá, I received a man who had with him a scribbled note of introduction from the mayor of Puerto Asís. The young man worked as an air traffic controller at Puerto Asís airport. As such, he was privy to information regarding all incoming and outgoing flights, military and civilian.

A few weeks previously he had been briefly kidnapped by the local front of the FARC. Their aim was to recruit him as an informant. They took him to their encampment, on the southern bank of the Putumayo, showed him the corpse of a "traitor" executed that very morning, then promised they would reward him well for (a) explaining to them the jargon of air controllers (whom they routinely intercepted on their own surveillance equipment) and (b) supplying them with regular information regarding flight plans, the identity of incoming and outgoing military and police units, and the precise characteristics of different kinds of aircraft. As far as I could tell, the young man reluctantly complied, but passed on as little information as he thought he could get away with. He informed his superior in Bogotá of the situation in writing but was told, with regret, that he could not be replaced.

Then he became aware of the presence of paramilitaries in Puerto Asís: this fulfilling a long-time prediction of Putumayo-watchers. He told me he had seen four armed men in plainclothes descend from an Air Force Blackhawk helicopter and that a number of murders in Puerto Asís had since been attributed to these men.

Following the disappearance of the owner of the hotel in which the young man lived (an admitted cocalero close to the guerrillas), fatal shootings next door, and threats from both the guerrillas and the paramilitaries – delivered second-hand – the young man had now fled to Bogotá. He was still visibly shaken as he spoke to me. As he said, he now felt in danger of his life from both sides. I was inclined to believe him and recommended that his request for refugee status in Canada be considered favourably.

If you circulate long enough in the human rights and NGO world of Colombia, sooner or later people you know will turn up dead. It was with a certain sense of grim fulfillment that one day I found on an inside page of *El Espectador* a reference to the murder, the previous day, of Padre Alcides Jiménez, parish priest of Puerto Caicedo, Putumayo.

I recalled having lunch with the diminutive but dynamic priest on the plant-filled patio of his ramshackle church. He had been full of enthusiasm, of plans for his benighted parish. One project, Canada had agreed to support: the setting up of a small community radio transmitter, for programming on issues of health, agricultural development, adult literacy, and human rights. Some of the quiet sombrero-clad men to whom he had introduced me were probably guerrillas; I didn't ask – I knew that, if you wanted to work here, there was no way of avoiding them. I had met, too, his assistant Lilly – tall, young, black-haired – who had founded her own NGO, Nuevo Milenio, to administer the many social development projects that Alcides was constantly generating.

Lilly later explained to me what had happened. For two or three weeks, the priest had been using his Sunday sermons as an opportunity to preach for peace. He had roundly condemned all the actors in the conflict in Putumayo – the army, the police, the FARC, the paramilitaries – and had called upon the good people of Puerto Caicedo to publicly reject violence in all its forms by taking part in a march for peace.

Soon after, one Sunday morning, as the 11:00 AM service was drawing to a close and with some fifty people in the church, a motorbike drew up at the door of the church. A young man in a motorcycle helmet marched down the aisle, straight to where Alcides calmly awaited him. With a machine pistol, he pumped ten or twelve shots into the priest, turned around and strode out again. Lilly said that Alcides looked resigned, as if he had been expecting it.

Who did it? We never found out. Both the paras and the FARC had reason to wish to do away with a turbulent priest who preached peace. The least the embassy could do was help a terrified Lilly now to seek refuge in Canada and start her life over again.

12 Bogotá

PEARCHED ON A SHOULDER of the Eastern Cordillera at 2,650 metres, Bogotá at first acquaintance is far from the stereotypical Latin American capital. On a sunny and windy day in autumn, the sky is of a deep blue and the clouds a startling white never seen in Mexico City, Lima, or Santiago. The surrounding hills, which stand out sharply in the clear air, are of a deeper and richer green than you ever see at lower altitudes in the tropics. But more often the weather is of an English kind: lowering grey clouds and rain, with people scurrying across the streets under black umbrellas. Like in England, even when the sun is out you can never quite be sure that you won't need a sweater or a raincoat in a few minutes' time, and the altitude quickly puts a chill on you if you sit in the shade.

Crammed with honking buses that belch foul black smoke and obey no rules, the streets of Bogotá are typical of most big Latin American cities. There is no metro; every mayor discusses the idea, but the costs grow every year and the political benefits to the incumbent officials always seem so minimal that plans are invariably shelved. But, as if in sympathy with the weather, many parts of the city look strangely English: there are mock-Tudor mansions from the 1930s along the busy Carrera Séptima and heavily built but graceful red-brick houses in the leafy quarter of Teusaquillo. The bricks – still widely used, even in modern apartment blocks – all come from noisome and unsanitary family-run kilns in the hills to the north of the city; they lend a special character to this city, in an era when concrete otherwise dominates. And while Bogotá has a worldwide reputation as a dangerous place – indeed its very name always sounds to me hard and dismissive, like a guttural swearword – it can at times be the most gentle and civilized of places.

Take any Sunday or public holiday morning in the city centre. All the main avenues are closed off to traffic and dedicated only to cyclists and pedestrians. Bogotanos turn out by their thousands: serious mountain racers in gaudy spandex charge up the steep hill to La Calera and coast down again at terrifying speeds; entire families walk hand in hand clutching balloons and greasy stall-bought food; old men walk their dogs; joggers plod by. At a few well-known locations, great red and yellow tents are set up; there athletic young men and women lead the crowd in musical aerobics while grandmas gamely keep up with Shaquira, Ricky Martin, and "Livin' la Vida Loca." Everybody smiles to each other, and perfect strangers are greeted with a courteous "Buenos días" as they jog by.

Downtown and in the plush northern quarters, car parks are cleared out and become one-day flea-markets. Much of what they have to sell is dross, but if you're interested in having a large 1920s vintage chrome espresso machine, a real brass fire-extinguisher, or an early 1960s black and white TV, this is the place to look. And occasionally there are imaginative variations on the Ciclovía, as the now much-loved Sunday morning institution has come to be known.

One year, a Monday in September was decreed Green Day, and all private cars were completely banned from the roads throughout the city. Then-Mayor Enrique Peñalosa and cabinet ministers, many with their bodyguards wobbling behind them, rode to work on bicycles. Shortly after we left Colombia, I learned how his successor, one-time presidential candidate Antanas Mockus, had emulated Peñalosa by announcing Ladies' Night; in this vast seven-million-person metropolis where the macho rules supreme, from 6:00 PM to midnight only women were allowed to be out on the streets, in the bars, in the night clubs. The event filled the newspapers for days, but was a huge success, which the Bogotano male accepted with unexpected and unaccustomed good grace; crime rates (there are often up to twenty murders a night in Bogotá) fell spectacularly. Election days and other important days – such as Colombia's game with England in the 1998 World Cup – were decreed dry; although you could still get a glass of wine in upmarket restaurants such as the Canadian-owned Villa d'Este (by winkingly asking for a "tinto" – which means both red wine and black coffee), the rules were generally respected, and a dozen or so lives thus saved.

It's all very civilized and un-Latin American. And it's in complete and weird contrast with day-to-day Bogotá. On late weekday evenings, on the very same Carrera Séptima that on Sundays is thronged with fine citizens, you dare not stop your car at a red light lest you be immediately carjacked; indeed, official police advice is to run the lights at this hour. If you must venture out on foot, it's best to do so in company and after having divested yourself of most of your money, your watch, and any visible jewellery; even then, walk only in well-lit areas, look determined and as if you know where you're going, and on no account be distracted by people asking you the time or other apparently innocent questions. Don't venture anywhere south of Calle 0 – into the enormous no-go area that makes up the southern half of the city – "or you won't come out alive," so they say. If you're going to ride a taxi, only get into one that looks well-kept and whose driver (a) is alone and (b) seems courteous; demand to get out immediately if you sense you are being taken in wrong direction or you otherwise pick up bad vibes. And don't argue with him over the fare; he almost certainly has a gun under the seat and is prepared to use it. When all of the taxi drivers in the city went on strike, ostensibly demanding safer streets, a newspaper survey revealed that many more passengers had been attacked and killed by taxi drivers than vice versa; the strike soon collapsed.

I often found myself wondering which is the real Bogotano: the Suday jogger or the Thursday-night mugger? I think it's the former, for the simple and quite unscientific reason that I hardly ever met a Colombian whom – after getting well acquainted – I didn't end up liking. But violence, confrontation, and corruption have become the accepted and inevitable norm. Institutions like the Ciclovía and events like Ladies' Night – brief and tantalizing glimpses of a better, saner, and happier society – are like the 1914 Christmas Day truce in the trenches. They are warmly and enthusiastically welcomed, and enjoyed while they last, but no-one seriously believes that a daily life embodying that kind of civility could ever be attainable; cynicism has perhaps irretrievably possessed the souls of Bogotanos.

It's the same story when it comes to the eternal peace process, which always seems to be on the verge of a breakthrough but which never really gets anywhere. Moments of it are characterized by astounding civility. In early 2000, an unlikely joint team of government and FARC negotiators took a tour of Western Europe. The objective was to see how civilized and democratic societies manage things. And everything went off swimmingly. On their TV screens, war-weary Colombians beheld the strange spectacle of long-demonized FARC commanders wearing sports jackets and leaning against a bar in a Davos hotel, clinking their glasses with government Peace Commissioner Victor G. Ricardo and his team. Simón Trinidad, normally seen by TV viewers in camouflage fatigues and with ammunition around his neck, was seen giving an interview on a cold Geneva street, wearing a fashionable mohair bankers' overcoat, while his government counterpart looked genially on and then put his arm around Trinidad: fellow Colombians travelling in strange land. And a few weeks later María Emma Mejía famously flirted on TV with FARC supremo Manuel Marulanda.

Meanwhile, the killing was still going on. In fact, invariably, the next item on the news following reports of the European tour related some bloody confrontation in the Llanos or Putumayo, with government troops usually coming off the worse.

Much history has been made at the historic heart of Bogotá – composed of the enormous Plaza Bolívar and of the adjoining Spanish-looking La Candelaria barrio – and continues to be so. A couple of blocks to the east, as the streets of La Candelaria rise to the foot of Monserrate mountain, is the Palacio de San Carlos, now the Foreign Ministry, but once the presidential palace, and before that – in the 1820s – the home of Simón Bolívar. If you have the nerve, you can take advantage of some meeting with a Foreign Service official and ask to see Bolívar's bedroom. It is a small whitewashed room down a corridor to the right, off the red-carpeted entrance hall. Here are his small, hard bed, and an ornate leather riding saddle. But knowledgeable visitors head straight for the window and look out to the cobbled street. From this window

Bolívar famously leapt, on 25 September 1828, to escape an ambush by arch-rival General Santander; reputedly he was in bed with his mistress Manuelita at the time, although your Foreign Ministry guide will usually gloss over this delicately. The drop to the pavement is actually a disappointing fifty centimetres.

Down in Plaza Bolívar itself, on the north side, is the massive pale yellow granite Supreme Court building, just completed after a fifteen-year rebuild. In November 1985 it was taken by a squad of the M-19 guerrilla army, and all the court judges were held hostage. Controversially, President Belisario Betancur ordered in the Army, who literally drove their tanks up the front steps and blasted the hostage-takers into submission; most of the judges were killed in the process. The episode reverberates on: allegations have surfaced that the few rebels still alive when the Army finally reached the interior were executed summarily. Only a few days after this, with the population still reeling, came the eruption of the Nevado del Ruiz and the destruction of Armero.

Presidents are inaugurated here, political movements are launched, *Te Deums* are said, and there is the occasional lying in state. Instinctively, this is where the nation gathers at moments when history is being made, or a passing commemorated. One such moment came in the summer of 1999.

TV and radio humorist Jaime Garzón was shot dead as he drove to work at 5:45 AM on a Friday morning, only fifteen minutes before his daily satirical radio show was to begin. Garzón was widely known and very popular, famous most recently for his impersonation of a street-savvy shoeshine boy called Heriberto de la Calle. Leading politicians scrambled to have their shoes shined on the air by him, in much the same way as they might have sought to be roasted by Canada's *This Hour Has 22 Minutes*; Garzón's wit was often mordant, but to be "shined" by him and to have survived the ordeal had over the years become a sine qua non for political success. Garzón was also playing, at the time of his death, an increasingly prominent role in various peace-related initiatives; notably, he had just agreed to serve on a commission whose principal aim was to negotiate the liberation of a large group of hostages currently held by the rebel ELN.

The killing outraged blasé Colombians to an extent not witnessed since the assassination of then-presidential candidate Luis Carlos Galán almost exactly ten years previously. For three or four days, TV stations gave the event blanket coverage; as one commentator put it, "humour was one of the few things we had left: now they've even taken that away."

The funeral mass took place in the Plaza Bolívar, where he had already lain in state for twenty-four hours. The spectacle was both inspiring and sad. A crowd estimated at 200,000 carried tiny white flags that fluttered in the cold afternoon wind, and the enormous banners of the country's nascent peace movement, with its trademark green ribbon insignia, masked the imposing sandstone pillars of the Congress building. Just below the dais on which Garzón's open coffin stood, one individual clutched a large Colombian flag spattered with red paint and rent by mock bullet holes.

Flags all around the square flew at half-mast. On the rooftops, snipers scanned the square and squads of riot police, equipped with water cannons and dogs, filled every side street. But the afternoon was a peaceful one. The crowd listened respectfully, with many in tears, as Garzón's sister pleaded for this to be a turning point: "May Jaime's blood not have been shed in vain." There were some shouted slogans to the effect that the president was responsible: "*Si Señor, Cómo no, El Presidente Lo Hizo*" ("Yes sir, of course, the president did it"), this presumably a reference to a lawsuit against the government that Garzón had just won and for which payment was due on the very day of his funeral. But mostly people just stood and listened – a feeling of inarticulate despair filled the place. Thousands more, unable to get into the square, lined the streets along which Garzón's hearse passed en route to the city cemetery.

The funeral mass doubled as the latest in a crescendo of marches that had taken place across Colombia over the previous two months. The first – in Cali on 6 June 1999, shortly after the rebel ELN had abducted 180 churchgoers from a suburban Cali church – attracted 250,000 persons, far beyond the expectations of the organizers. The next had occurred in Medellín on 22 July, with nearly half a million persons – one quarter of the entire population of the city. The theme of all of the marches had been a simple one: "No more!" – a reference principally to kidnapping and forced disappearance, but by extension to violence in all its forms.

Meanwhile, there were few leads in the Garzón investigation. The most popular hypothesis was that this was the work of an extreme right-wing group intent on destabilizing the peace process and fomenting popular will for a military solution to the Colombian crisis. But, as most of the time, it could just as well have been the left.

There were happier moments here, too. Directed to spend the dawn of the new millennium in Bogotá – lest there be technical problems with the embassy's communications systems – Jenny and I bused down to Plaza Bolívar at about 7:00 PM on 31 December 1999. It had been dark for an hour or more and Carrera Séptima and the other main avenues were festooned with Christmas lights; on the vast brick facade of the Centro Andino shopping centre a Father Christmas mechanically rode back and forth, while "Jingle Bells" echoed out.

In the square were already half a million people. Laser beams played across the facades of the Congress and the Palace of Justice, and in front of the Cathedral a large stage had been set up. Technicians tested the sound system with sibilant "*Sí, sí, sí*"s, and "*Uno, dos, tres* ..." Whole families, with the small children wrapped up warmly against the cold, waited patiently, the children licking absently at huge candy-floss sticks or marveling at their fluorescent light sticks.

The star attraction tonight was media mogul and impresario Jorge Barón and his travelling *Show de las Estrellas*. For the past year or more, the suavely good-looking (in a Latin American way, that is) Barón had been taking his show to the most far-flung corners of Colombia: the troupe had even chartered three 727s and performed on a huge floating barge on the Orinoco at Puerto Inírida. The music was always classic Colombian salsas and cumbias, played with great energy – with the performers in colourful costumes – in front of open-air crowds in the tens of thousands. In the tropical towns, fire hoses would spray over the crowds to keep them cool, while Barón called out what had become his trademark: "*Agua para mi gente!*"

The shows were carried live on TV (on Barón's own channel) and repeated throughout the week; often they also featured Barón's identically clad small children, all confusingly called Jorge as well (legend had it that he called them all the same so as to guarantee that even if one of them died, his name would be carried on). For some small provincial towns, the arrival of Jorge Barón was the event of the decade, if not the century: he would be escorted in by a huge caravan from the airport, received by every dignitary imaginable, and the entire town would be given a holiday "for the duration." Once, I'd come across him in Apartadó, processing into town on a float like a head of state, preceded by Señorita Urabá, holding an enormous banana. When we visited Inírida a few months after the Barón phenomenon had passed through like a whirlwind, everyone was still talking about it and the main bar in town had been renamed *El Bar de Las Estrellas.* And when he took the show to San Vicente del Caguán, in the FARC-controlled demilitarized zone, hardened guerrilla commanders lined up like starstruck teenagers to have their picture taken with Barón or with their arm around one of his well-endowed dancing girls.

Barón had savvily caught the need of the people to occasionally have a really good time in the midst of all the depressing news, interspersing within his shows simple homilies on peace and tolerance, which were greeted with almost as much enthusiasm as *Iván y Sus Bam-Bam* or whoever the star attractions of the week were. There was even talk that Barón should run for president.

The millennium show in the Plaza Bolívar did not disappoint. For nearly three hours, frenetic Latin rhythms blared out and echoed off the historic floodlit facades, while Jorge himself preened in his shiny blue silk suit and his dancers waggled their sequined bottoms and breasts provocatively. At nine, ten, and eleven, there were pauses as a giant TV screen showed the millennium coming in across other time zones, and the ever-growing crowd joined in to chant in Spanish: "*Cinco, cuatro, tres, dos, uno, CEROOOOO!*"

Anti-climactically, we had to catch a bus back to the north end of the city at about 11:30 PM to turn off all the embassy's computers, then reboot them once more, as midnight came and went. But the ambassador had thoughtfully left a bottle of champagne in the server room, and we were able to watch from the plate-glass windows of the high-rise in which the embassy is located, as the sky over the south of the city was lit with a spectacular show of fireworks on the stroke of midnight.

13 News of a Kidnapping

LIFE AT THE EMBASSY in Bogotá was rarely dull. My files included the war, human rights, narcotrafficking, and more esoteric topics such as nuclear non-proliferation, desertification, and the Kyoto Protocol, which are the lot of Foreign Service political officers all around the world. But there was one area of work for which I had no training, which took up a huge amount of my time and on which, whether I liked it or not, I ended up being one of Canada's experts.

I had scarcely been in Bogotá a week, when Ida – our long-serving and highly reliable and wise locally engaged consular officer – phoned up with three words that I would come to hear again and again over the next few years: "*Tenemos un secuestro.*" We have a kidnapping. The first rule here is to let the relatives call the shots, but generally counsel patience and calm. I already knew that as long as you were prepared to pay and to wait, then sooner or later the chances were that your loved one would come out alive.

This case was not untypical. The victim was an experienced Canadian-Colombian gold-mining executive who knew the remotest parts of Colombia better than most and who had in his time doubtless run up against the guerrillas more than once. I will call him Neil.

Neil's Colombian wife was, as might be imagined, near hysterical. Her husband had failed to return from a visit to a remote prospecting site near Segovia in Antioquia Department, an area known to be largely under the domination of the ELN. But a few days after his disappearance one of the two men Neil was with reappeared – with a ransom demand and also with the bizarre request for all of the papers respecting the gold claim of Neil's company. What was she to do?

We reviewed all the normal procedures. Stay calm; don't pay anything to begin with – or the price will simply be raised; try to establish through other channels the whereabouts and well-being of the victim; consider finding a mediator – the local priest, for example. Unfortunately, the most recent case of a Canadian kidnapping was not encouraging: the ransom demand (again from the ELN) had started at US$10 million and only after many months and tedious Tom Clancy–like clandestine contacts had it been reduced to "only" two million and was that victim safely recovered.

With the initial help of the International Committee of the Red Cross, who in Colombia have a full-time staff who do nothing but assist in passing messages to kidnap victims, contact was established and delicate to-and-fro communication began – mainly between Neil's kidnappers and his business associate: a bow-tie-wearing white-haired Texan who inhabited a strangely dusty and rundown office in downtown Bogotá, its walls covered with certificates of establishment for a host of junior mining companies. When I sensed that discussions on money might have started, I decided the embassy's main role was over, for we could not formally sanction – as a government – the payment of ransom.

And relatively quickly – after about three months – Neil was out. He was extremely grateful to us but denied that any ransom had been paid; "It was a mutual misunderstanding" was all he would say, and I did not press him. He had lost weight but was otherwise in excellent health and spirits, with a number of anecdotes to tell.

Early in his captivity, for example, Neil had half-jokingly complained to his captors that he was going to miss seeing Colombia play a crucial World Cup qualifying game. They merely grunted in reply. But next morning at dawn, from the jungle clearing in which Neil and his captors had camped for the night, three of the young soldiers set off without a word. They were back at dusk. One carried a TV, one a generator, and one a can of diesel; they set up the equipment in the clearing, watched Colombia duly beat Ecuador, and then the TV was returned as quietly as it had come.

Another case involved another gold miner, Bill, who gave us a detailed debriefing in Bogotá when he finally emerged from his captivity. He had been taken at the mine site and, as is usual, kept on the move for weeks. Every day was a tough hike of fifteen or twenty kilometres, always in dense forest and usually far from any habitation; any time the group (which numbered a dozen in total) came near a village they would take the utmost care to detour around it undetected.

Initially, Bill was bound to a post in camp or confined to his tiny tent. But after a while he was trusted and could move around freely within the immediate confines of the camp. Escape was not that tempting, for by now he was totally disoriented and he had no idea where the nearest friendly habitation might be.

Most of his captors were still in their teens. Typically, they were illiterate, from large families of ten or more children, and had never known their fathers. They had a very basic grounding in Marxism, and the leader would periodically take the team through a kind of communist catechism, but Bill had the impression that this was more for his benefit rather than out of revolutionary fervour.

Bill taught them a little English, and they taught him some Spanish. They justified their action in stark, even childlike terms: "You were sucking our wealth up out of the earth – you must give us some of it before we can let you go." And as with Neil, Bill's captors took care to see that their investment did not depreciate excessively in value – when he showed symptoms that could be mistaken for yellow fever, a clearly terrified young nurse was found in some nearby village and brought in to administer a course of injections.

Of course, it's not just foreigners who are kidnapped – even though it's these cases that make for good introductory lines at diplomatic cocktails ("So how many have you had in this year?") and that capture the headlines abroad. By far the vast majority of the 2,500 or more persons who are reported kidnapped annually in Colombia (by most counts, more than half the world's total) are from middle-class Colombian families and – as an increasing number of couples make living will pacts that stipulate that if one is kidnapped, the other will not pay – kidnappers are turning more and more to children. For who can harden their heart and stonewall when the victim is five years old and an only child?

Mostly, the kidnappers are the FARC or ELN, although a good proportion are simply common criminals, who nevertheless may masquerade as guerrillas to inspire greater fear. Some kidnappings are meticulously prepared and researched. I once interviewed for political asylum a terrified bank clerk from a small rural bank in FARC-controlled territory. He had been called one day and asked to provide full details of the accounts and other holdings of a twenty-long list of local citizens. The purpose of the call was clear: the FARC wanted to know who was worth kidnapping and how high to pitch the initial ransom demand.

And while both the FARC and the ELN would repeatedly deny having executed specific kidnappings, the evidence was sometimes pathetically clear. A well-known TV presenter – Pacheco – was taken from his home near Choachí. A week later, the police intercepted radio calls between identified and well-known rebel commanders in which were discussed not only the kidnapping but also the brand of 4WD the victim was driving, how much it would be worth on the black market, and the precise extent of his farm and its potential resale value.

The government does what it can. It has set up a special office and named an anti-kidnapping czar. TV ads run constantly. An especially moving one simply shows a middle-class family morosely eating dinner: slowly the camera pans to an empty place setting, and the image then fades to a starker one of an old man chained to a bed, desperate. There is no need for commentary.

Media mogul Francisco Santos, himself kidnapped by Pablo Escobar in 1990 and later to become vice-president of the republic, for a time ran – and largely financed – a non-governmental organization called País Libre (Free Country), whose objective was to campaign against kidnapping and to provide advice and counselling to the family members of victims.

At various times, the government has attempted to enact legislation making the payment of ransom a punishable offence, in the hope that, if nobody pays, this will bring the phenomenon to an end. Indeed, well-known Colombian soccer player Rene Higuita was briefly and very publicly imprisoned for having mediated a release. But when it comes down to it, such a law is unenforceable: how can you tell a desperate wife that she must not pay to have her husband or child back and that if she does she will go to jail?

Then there were the cases of the hundreds of military and police officers captured by the rebels. It could be said that these men were in a way more "blameworthy" than civilian kidnap victims, but the human tragedies created by their disappearance were scarcely less heartrending.

By April 2000, it was estimated that some 530 police and Army (all of them men) were currently in the hands of the FARC and ELN (mostly of the former). Some of these men, seized during various military operations, had been in captivity for as long as three years. Although the FARC had periodically allowed letters and videos out, family members had been denied access.

It was all a huge embarrassment to the government. Nearly two years earlier there had been a flurry of activity that saw Congress enacting various pieces of legislation that would allow the government to exchange some of the FARC prisoners it had for the soldiers and police, but this gradually died down as the full implications of an eventual exchange dawned: it would have amounted to recognition of the FARC as "belligerents" in the international legal sense of the word, and it would also have been politically very difficult for the government simply to amnesty the FARC prisoners in question, many of whom were serving sentences for the most horrific of crimes. The media had only occasionally touched the question over the last eighteen months. A recent cartoon had an imprisoned soldier saying, on video: "It's good to know we are not all forgotten: some of us still have mothers who are alive." On 4 April 2000 a group of these mothers, calling themselves Asfamipaz (Association of Family Members for Peace), forcibly occupied a church in Southern Bogotá to draw the plight of their loved ones to the attention of the government and simultaneously announced that they were launching a movement encouraging all mothers and wives to stop their sons and husbands from enlisting with any of the armed groups, legitimate or otherwise.

I was asked to represent Canada – as a kind of international guarantor – at a ceremony during which Asfamipaz members agreed to vacate the church, the condition being that a coalition of NGOs and personalities now take up the cause of their loved ones. Most in the crowd of 250 or so women wore around their necks blow-up pictures of their children, husbands, or boyfriends; in many of the photos a young man would be proudly showing off his uniform on the day he signed up. Underneath would be a date and the name of the action in which he was captured: Miraflores, Mitú, Patascoy. Tellingly, nearly all the women here were unmistakably working class or campesino: just by looking at their worn, weather-beaten faces one could tell that this is a war being fought by the poor (and against the poor).

One woman showed me copies of a handwritten letter from her son for Mother's Day. Another simply clutched my hand and wept, unable to say a word. What particularly grated, said a third, was the fact that not even the commanders of the Armed Forces, let alone the president, would meet with the family members.

It was difficult to console them. History said that prisoner exchanges are one of the last issues to be negotiated in a peace process – which meant it would be years before these women saw their sons again, if ever.

Most Bogotanos would not dream of visiting Barrancabermeja or para-infested Urabá; run-of-the-mill urban violence, plus the nightly coverage of massacres on TV, is as close as most ever get to the war and this is understandably quite enough for them. Indeed, the upper middle classes go for years without ever leaving the city by land. Those who can afford it compensate by instead flying out every month or so to Miami and the Florida beaches (Colombians are the number one foreign real-estate holders in Miami, and by no means all of them are narcotraffickers). This gives the Bogotá-Miami route on a Friday something of the flavour of the Berlin Airlift, although the more politically incorrect term for the weekly exodus of the rich is The Jerusalem Express (a reflection of the relative wealth and importance of the Jewish community in the capital).

But the war or intra-narco vendettas occasionally strike home in Bogotá in a literal sense. I recall that on 11 November 1999 – Remembrance Day – the ambassador and I attended the annual wreath-laying ceremony at the British Cemetery. As a Colombian Army bugler waveringly played "The Last Post," we all simultaneously felt and heard a low, dull thump; a number of people glanced at each other and shrugged questioningly. While we were driving back to the embassy in Northern Bogotá, the police directed us around a long detour; the radio was already reporting that a powerful carbomb had exploded a few blocks to the west of the Canadian Embassy.

The episode proved to be isolated. It seemed that it was a protest on the part of organized narcotraffickers, aimed at conjuring up the terror of a decade ago when such occurrences were, almost daily, killing dozens and – specifically – at dissuading President Pastrana from signing what would be the first extradition order for a Colombian narcotrafficker in many years. The bomb in fact had the reverse effect: the president, to popular approval, responded by signing the order publicly and vowing that bombings of this kind would only reinforce his will to get tough on organized crime; indeed, so startling and sudden was Pastrana's response, that the conspiracy theorists said the bomb – which killed several passers-by – had been orchestrated by either the government or the USA.

There were other incidents we witnessed close to the embassy that were so typical and commonplace that they never made the news. One day I was standing in the open area of the Canadian Embassy secure section when I heard, above the low humming of the city traffic from the streets many floors below, three or four "pop-pop" sounds. I walked over to the plate glass windows and looked down to the side street west of us. A 4WD vehicle had collided with a plane tree on the side of the road, but there did not seem to be any great damage done. Fifty metres ahead, a motorcycle with two helmeted riders aboard was riding off, apparently oblivious to the accident.

It had been a drive-by killing, using the techniques perfected years before by Escobar's sicarios in Medellín: the motorcycle had followed the vehicle for several blocks and then, when the motorcycle driver saw clear space ahead, had pulled up to overtake; once he was level with the driver's seat, the pillion rider pulled out an Uzi and pumped a few rounds into the other driver, and they sped on. Both riders wore large helmets with opaque visors that masked their identities.

If you glanced out of the plate glass windows on the other side of the building, over the Hacienda Santa Bárbara shopping mall and the nearby residences of the Bogotano rich, you would be looking at the scenes of other dramas and tragedies. The talk of the neighbourhood in early 2000 was of the married couple and their live-in maid, who lived in one of the gated compounds here. For the couple, the maid was simply excellent: obedient, hard-working, and entirely satisfied with her quite low wages. But she was unusually silent about where she had come from, and the young couple began to feel that something was "up." One day, while she was out of the house on her morning off, they decided to look around in her bedroom for some clues. Under the bed, hardly concealed at all, was a machine pistol.

The couple were immediately in a quandary: whether to dismiss her and risk vengeance from the guerrillas or organized crime – whichever she was involved in – or simply to say nothing and hope for the best. They waited a week, then found a minor pretext and regretfully informed the maid that her services were no longer needed.

She called their bluff immediately: "It's about the gun, isn't it?" she said scornfully. "Well, don't worry, I'll go quietly. But you might like to know that there are a few dozen of us, just in this quarter ..."

Or, two or three houses down – you could clearly see the sharply sloping roof from here – there was another young couple, their four-year-old daughter, and, again, their maid. One morning, just after the couple had both gone to work, while the maid was getting the daughter ready for kindergarten, armed and masked men stormed in, held the maid at gunpoint, and rushed off with the child. The neighbours noticed nothing. Indeed, there was later some suspicion that the maid had been in on the whole operation. After about a month, the first ransom demand came in. Last I heard, the couple were selling everything to raise the cash needed.

German citizen Werner Mauss and his spouse Michaela have over the years made something of a profession out of negotiating the freedom of hostages: they have, for example, worked in Lebanon on a number of hostage cases in the 1980s, in Iraq to free German citizens at the time of Saddam Hussein's invasion of Kuwait, and in Thailand and Cambodia. It was thus natural that, in the 1990s, they turned to Colombia, the kidnapping mecca of the world.

However, in Colombia they became interested in more than just the freeing of kidnap victims. They developed close contacts with the rebel ELN. Just how close is a matter of debate: film footage obtained by TV Spiegel and shown repeatedly in Colombia certainly showed them in situations where they obviously enjoyed the friendship of guerrilla leaders. They also arranged for some twenty-one key ELN leaders to visit Germany, where they met with German State Minister Bernd Schmidbauer, an old Colombiaphile and good friend of Chancellor Kohl. All these activities (including the earlier hostage negotiations elsewhere in the world) were apparently undertaken with the full knowledge and support of the German government and in particular of Schmidbauer. Rumours that the Mausses might be less than neutral did not deter the former Interior Minister of President Samper, Horacio Serpa, in the course of a July 1996 visit to Germany, from suggesting to Schmidbauer that the Mausses be used to initiate a peace process between the Samper government and the ELN.

According to one version of events, the Mausses responded with enthusiasm to this idea. Schmidbauer facilitated the project by supplying the couple with false identities. The first step in the process was to be a gesture of good will by the ELN: the freeing of German kidnap victim Brigitte Schoene, wife of the president of BASF Colombia. The Mausses were successful in negotiating this – whether a ransom was paid is a matter of dispute – but were arrested in November 1996 when they were about to board a plane out of Bogotá with Ms Schoene.

The plot thickened. Colombian police (presumably defying Serpa) charged the Mausses not only with using false identities and with mediating in a kidnap rescue for financial gain (legally speaking, an offence, but not always prosecuted) but also with actually arranging this and other kidnappings in the first place. It was alleged that the Mausses had systematically been advising the ELN on individuals who carried heavy anti-kidnapping insurance and who would consequently be lucrative targets. Serpa and Schmidbauer found their dream of a negotiated peace falling apart.

In August 1997, after eight months of detention, the Mausses (often referred to in the Colombian media as spies) were released from custody – as a result of a technical irregularity in the manner in which they were charged – but not allowed to leave the country. In theory, most of the charges against them still stood, and it looked like they might be rearrested. Werner Mauss still insisted that his aim all the time was to begin a mediation process and that indeed this was still his objective. His spouse – tall, blonde, and invariably wearing dark glasses – had less to say in public and became the subject of melodramatic speculation in the media, which portrayed her as a latter-day Mata Hari.

Meanwhile, the months of the Mausses' detention and the embarrassment that the arrest caused to Germany led both governments to backtrack. President Samper, insisting he was misquoted in a German newspaper, ruled out any role for the Mausses in an eventual peace process, and the German foreign ministry issued a statement to the same effect. An official at the German Embassy in Bogotá admitted to me her great relief at the prospect of the affair dying down and said candidly that Schmidbauer had never enjoyed any kind of support for the initiative from within his department. She nevertheless insisted that the Mausses had the best of intentions.

On 23 March 1998 the FARC put in place, for some six hours, a road block on one of the main roads south out of Bogotá and proceeded to detain dozens of persons that the rebels apparently thought "interesting." Most of those originally seized were released within the following week, but the 53rd Front admitted to still holding some seven Colombian nationals, four Americans, and one Italian. The Italian citizen, alternately described in the media as a gemologist or a restaurant-owner, had been living in Colombia and had spent his holiday weekend fishing in the Llanos region; the four Americans were birdwatchers on vacation. One of the Colombians was the son of a well-known retired General. A total of eight persons (three civilians, five guerrilleros) died when the Army finally broke up the roadblock.

The FARC's regional commander, going by the name of Romaña and wanted for a multitude of crimes, gave several interviews in late March, including one to TV crews that arrived at the roadblock several hours before the Army. He indicated that if the FARC determined that the four Americans worked for the USA government or for any other international organization, "they will be tried and executed." Romaña recalled that the FARC had recently declared all USA government personnel living in Colombia as military objectives, on account of what the FARC described as increasing USA involvement in combatting the guerrillas. He added that, in any case, if any of the victims' personal fortunes was estimated at over US$1 million, the Americans would be "taxed."

Helicopters were meanwhile sweeping the hillsides where the kidnap victims were thought to be held. On 30 March, a large transport helicopter was hit by rebel fire but managed a forced landing with only three passengers injured. All the victims of this kidnapping were eventually released unharmed; it is not known what ransom, if any, was paid.

Kidnapping continues apace in Colombia. In a decree, the FARC have even "legalized" the forced detention of persons who, in possession of a fortune of at least one million dollars, refuse to pay "tax" to the guerrillas.

On a lighter note, kidnappings of cars and domestic appliances such as TVs and refrigerators have also become commonplace. One man became so irate when his car was seized three times, and "ransom" demanded for its return, that he wrote to the papers to complain. The FARC issued a public apology and stated that henceforth receipts would be issued, which could be produced in the event of attempts to "kidnap" the same item twice.

14 Lunch with Lucía

28 JUNE 2000. IT WAS a forty-five-minute flight between Bogotá and San Vicente del Caguán, the de facto capital of the demilitarized zone ceded to the FARC with the aim of providing a location for peace talks. Aircraft not authorized by the FARC ventured over this Switzerland-sized stretch of lowland jungle at their peril: the rebels were thought to have surface-to-air missiles.

Our turboprop plane, loaded down with the Government of Colombia's peace team, representatives of no less than twenty embassies and various UN agencies, wheezed its way over the Eastern Cordillera, across the barren Páramo de Sumapaz, and then steadily downwards into the humid lowlands. Our official mission: to meet as a group with both government and FARC representatives for an informal discussion on narcotrafficking and illicit crops – two of the thorniest topics in the sporadic talks that had been going on between the government and the rebels for the past two to three years. Unofficially, both our objective and that of the government was to create an international dimen-

Welcoming banner, San Vicente, 28 June 2000

sion to the talks and to expose the often blinkered-seeming FARC to international opinion and experiences from other transitions from civil war to peace.

Just as we had guessed and feared, the diplomatic games began almost as soon as the propellers wound down. Assembling outside the aircraft door was a FARC guard of honour comprised of FARC "Foreign Minister" Raúl Reyes and a host of senior military commanders, all loaded down in full battle gear. At the far end of a funnel of rebel troops, thirty or forty media reps, including from international TV, were waiting. And by peering out of the portholes we could see hanging on the control tower enormous banners with portraits of Simón Bolívar and FARC boss Manuel Marulanda. The intended impression was obvious: as we descended the stairs and the cameras began whirring, the image TV viewers would inevitably receive was one of diplomats visiting a foreign country, with full military honours.

Peace Commissioner Camilo Gómez grimaced as he prepared to be the first to step out. One by one, we followed him into the sunlight, to find ourselves inescapably bear-hugged by the beaming bandoleer-clad

Reyes, then thrust into double handshakes with rebel leaders Simón Trinidad, Joaquín Gómez, and Andrés París (all noms de guerre – punctilious reporters would list their names only in quotation marks). The cameras flashed and whirred. Score one to the FARC.

We were next taken by bus to the former headquarters of the Colombian Army's Cazadores (Hunters) Battalion – a modern, comfortable camp, ten minutes or so outside San Vicente del Caguán, capable of housing some one thousand troops. When the demilitarized zone had been created, the Army had been most reluctant to abandon this base, insisting for months that it be allowed at least to keep a token uniformed presence for the purposes of maintenance; but the FARC would not cut a deal, and the military still rankled at the humiliation.

On our first evening, we were able to spend an hour or two in San Vicente. To all appearances, everything was normal. Vallenato and ranchero music blared out from brightly lit bars, shops and stalls were open. A shopkeeper told us that life was remarkably tranquil, indeed that crime had declined dramatically since the government had pulled out (a function, I suspected, of the draconian and arbitrary justice system administered by the rebels, of which I had obtained a glimpse on an earlier visit).

I knew from previous visits why the FARC's military presence in town seemed to be so minimal: the rebel camps were instead located under dense forest cover in areas some distance from the main villages. The FARC were frank in admitting that they were not comfortable in urban settings, although one commander had told me that the main reason for their absence from the built-up areas was fear of a surprise aerial attack by government helicopters or bombers.

Next morning, we boarded our buses again and headed west along a dirt track for some ninety minutes to Nueva Colombia, the purpose-built site of the peace talks; every hundred metres or so along the dusty road, in another clear show of strength, there stood impassive armed sentries. There were newly painted signs everywhere: *Children on Road – FARC; No littering – FARC.*

The very remoteness of Nueva Colombia, an isolated complex the size of a small school, with a few tents in nearby fields, seemed a metaphor for the FARC themselves: as one wit on our bus remarked, "These are the Yanomani of Marxism-Leninism": the guerrillas that time forgot but who have been able – thanks to their incalculable income from narcotrafficking and kidnapping – to defy the tide of history.

Manuel Marulanda ("Sureshot") arrives with his escort

The diplomatic – or theatrical – games continued. The question on everyone's lips was whether Marulanda would appear in person. There was delay after delay – carefully orchestrated, I felt – and some of the ambassadors seated behind their country nameplates at the long rectangular table in the Nueva Colombia complex began to get restive. Then there was a stirring and a turning of heads.

In strode a lean, mean praetorian guard of some dozen heavily armed men, forming a scrum around The Man. Marulanda's arrival had an electrifying effect: all talking ceased and ambassadors, to their surprise, found that they had respectfully risen to their feet. With a casual whisk of the trademark white scarf he carried over one shoulder (for the purpose of swatting flies), Marulanda sat in a half-slouch and, without a word, signalled to a deferential Raúl Reyes that it was time to begin. I was reminded for a moment of Marlon Brando as Kurtz in *Apocalypse Now*.

Marulanda (another nom de guerre, taken from the small village in which he grew up) is – hate him or love him – a phenomenon. He proudly states that he was fighting in the jungles long before Fidel

Castro even landed in Cuba, and he has survived countless brushes with apparently certain death. Reputed to be a military genius – his nickname, Tirofijo, means Sureshot – he is a man of few words and looks to have survived as long as he has on account of his innate peasant caution and slyness. As I shook his hand, I felt slight guilt but also an undeniable tremor of excitement: more than that much better-known arch-villain Pablo Escobar ever had, this was the man who held Colombia in his thrall.

The talks, away from the cameras, ebbed back and forth and became increasingly frank. It was evident that the FARC's main agenda was to launch a blistering attack on the USA's much vaunted anti-drug strategy for Colombia, Plan Colombia, in the hope of enlisting at least the sympathy of some of the Europeans present, who were known to have serious reservations about the Plan. But we too had our agenda: if they wished to be taken seriously, the FARC must foreswear kidnapping, extortion, attacks on civilians, the recruitment of minors into their ranks, and involvement in the drug business.

At times, the rebel leaders seemed to be shaken by the virtually unanimous vehemence of the diplomats, who were not following the FARC's intended script. There were lame defences of kidnapping as "taxation of the oligarchy," and Joaquín Gómez – in a reference to the FARC's infamous Law 002, which decreed a tax of 10 percent on fortunes over US$1 million – triumphantly smirked, saying: "We have a law, so how can there be anything wrong with it?" Reyes, responding to the child soldier accusations, asked "Which is worse? A child sniffing glue under the bridges of Bogotá, or one with an AK-47 fighting for a better Colombia?" And those brutal and indiscriminate attacks on civilian populations with gas canister mortars? "We're working on refining our techniques." At one point Marulanda seemed to have walked out; to almost farcical relief, it turned out that he had needed urgently to go to the washroom (where he was besieged by breathless reporters who thought it was all over).

Lunch that day was a large chunk of beef, a boiled potato, and some greasy sausages eaten off paper plates as we sat on logs in a field adjoining the meeting room. I sat with Comandante Lucía, one of the FARC's more senior women commanders.

A FARC comandante talks to the press, Nueva Colombia

Lucía was in her late twenties or early thirties and had been with the FARC for ten years. She wore the FARC's standard battle fatigues, with rubber boots; "Lucía" was hand-painted in liquid paper on the top of each boot. She carried both a pistol and a large automatic weapon, which she tactfully kept pushing behind her back as we talked. She also wore lipstick, gold earrings and necklace, and a white silk scarf around her neck, with *FARC-EP* stencilled where one might expect to see *Dior*.

Lucía was from a small town in the Valle de Cauca Department, near Cali. She had never thought of becoming a guerrillera, but when she was a high school student some of her friends had older brothers and sisters in the FARC and she became interested. She hadn't joined for any ideological reason: at first it just seemed to be fun, rather exotic and dangerous, and it gave her a sense of belonging and camaraderie. She often wrote to her family and would occasionally even go home; her parents knew what she was doing. But her visits weren't that frequent: she got no leave as such, but could occasionally find an excuse to pass through her hometown.

There were only two ranks in the FARC, she said: comandantes and everyone else. And superficially there was no way of distinguishing a comandante from an "other rank." Salutations were usually "Comandante" or "Hermano/Hermana" (Brother/Sister); "Camarada" was also used. On formal and public occasions women wore white silk scarves and both men and women wore red, blue, and yellow armbands (the colours of the Colombian flag); the armbands were removed in combat. You were also permitted to decorate your headwear with a small pin or ornament: Che badges were very popular.

It was an extremely strict rule, Lucía told me, that you must carry your weapon with you at all times, even to the bathroom; Marulanda carried a pistol only, but many would also carry a larger calibre automatic weapon. (I observed that there was no predominant model.) A few carried rocket-propelled grenades in their top pockets "for good measure."

Lucía, when pressed, admitted that she had been in combat "a few times." Women, she went on, were treated almost identically to men within FARC ranks and had to perform similar duties. Did this mean that the men cooked and cleaned as well? "Of course!" But I had noticed that it had been young female guerrilleras that had done all the serving of iced water, coffee, and food throughout our visit; I let the question pass.

Formal marriage was not allowed, but informal liaisons were permitted. Transfers from one unit to another, so as to accompany one's partner, were in theory not possible, but, Lucía smiled, "You can always find an excuse." Guerrilleras were discouraged from getting pregnant and were issued, on request, with contraceptive pills, but they might occasionally be given leave to have a baby, after which they would be expected to return to the ranks.

In their spare time in camp, the middle to junior ranks listened to the radio (the FARC had two FM transmitters of their own) or watched TV. There were also many organized activities. Most evenings an hour was set aside for political discussions, usually led by a comandante; often there would be readings from oeuvres such as *Das Kapital*.

"So what, in a word, does the FARC believe in?" I asked. Lucía looked at me in surprise. "We are a Marxist-Leninist revolutionary movement, a People's Army ..."

"Does this mean, for instance, that you are against private property?"

"Of course ..."

"And foreign investment?"

"Not necessarily."

"Concretely, what's your ambition?" I asked.

"To take over the Government of Colombia and install a dictatorship of the proletariat."

"And would you, say in three or four years' time, call elections?"

"Elections in Colombia," frowned Lucía, "have never produced a true government of the people ... And look what happened to the Sandinistas when they decided to go that way ... No, I don't think so."

I wondered if there was any group or individual after whom the FARC modelled themselves. "No, not really ... We try to take a little bit here, a little there."

"What went wrong in the Soviet Union?"

"They became corrupt. So did the Sandinistas. We're especially strict about that sort of thing. Any corruption or theft in the ranks, and the penalty is very severe indeed ..."

"But do you actually think you are ready to take over government by force?"

"No, not yet. But we're certainly on schedule. In 1982, the central command set certain strategic targets, and those we have fully met. We now have the principal cities of the country encircled. It will be a few more years yet, but we will take power, you can be sure of that."

I hesitated how to phrase my next question in a sufficiently delicate manner. "Is there not a risk," I ventured, "that your military strength may be outrunning your political support, even so?"

"No. There is no danger of that. The people are with us. We know this. And we plan to double our strength over the next couple of years. You'll see."

They were calling us back to the next session now. Quickly, I asked, "But why are you bothering to participate in these peace talks?"

"Well, this is like an alternative strategy, a Plan B if you like. We don't have a problem with talking to the government, if that's what they want, but that doesn't mean we're going to change our objectives at all."

We trudged over to the large covered area that was to be the setting for the afternoon's hearings. The forty-five non-stop presentations were interrupted at one point when a large brown and white dog sat down in front of the speakers' podium and began to stretch and yawn at what seemed to be particularly appropriate moments. In the midst of a dry presentation on biodiversity in Amazonia a small child walked out and fed the dog a cheese sandwich. There were constant interruptions from claques at the back of the auditorium: most were anti-USA or anti-Plan Colombia, vindicating the decision of the American delegation not to show. At the chant of "*Plan Colombia – patas arriba!*" (Plan Colombia – belly up!), the brown dog duly obliged.

At a duller moment, I was startled suddenly to find myself looking right into the long telephoto lens of Lucía's Nikon. She clicked, then looked up and winked.

15 Just Another Day at the Office

DESPITE THE HORRORS of violence, war, corruption, and kidnapping that plague Colombia, at the Hacienda Santa Bárbara or the Centro Andino you can shop for Gucci goods, browse in a huge Tower Records, or watch the latest Hollywood movies in English and go out for a Big Mac afterwards. The diplomatic circuit goes on much as it does anywhere. There is the occasional summons – more under the Pastrana administration than in beleaguered Samper's time – to the Foreign Ministry to meet formally with incoming Foreign Ministers or Heads of State. Once every few months, there are ceremonies at the parade grounds of the army, where medals are handed out, generals promoted to new heights, troops inspected, and exhortations made to ever greater efforts in the war; such occasions are always useful for cornering key commanders for a firsthand reading of the military situation or for the careful passing of key concerns on human rights.

Every week or so an embassy hosts its National Day reception, while on one or two evenings a week there's a cocktail event in honour of a visiting dignitary or official. Most popular, as everywhere, are the Queen's birthday celebrations in the beautiful grounds of the British Residence, which usually attract a sprinkling of ministers, maybe even the president, and the even larger 4 July celebrations at the USA Embassy (once organized by the ebullient and nationally notorious Ambassador Myles Frechette and now by his much more discreet successor, Curtis Kamman).

At such events, it's not considered good protocol to bring your bodyguards into the reception with you. Thus at the larger events – and even at one or two I hosted in my apartment, which were graced by the presence of ministers – the sidewalks for several streets around are half-blocked with heavily armoured vehicles (usually Suburbans) while burly men in sunglasses and sharp suits lounge around and exchange the latest gossip about the security world.

A regular event organized partly by the Canadian Embassy, but principally by the resident community of Canadians and Canada-philes, is the annual Terry Fox Run, a fundraiser for local cancer research. Running to raise funds for charity was something new when the embassy first introduced this idea in 1996, but by 1999 it had taken hold and the Carrera Terry Fox, which took place every autumn in the Parque Simón Bolívar, had become a regular fixture. Certain adaptations, of course, had to be made for Colombia. The ambassador would energetically jog his ten kilometres around the park, to the applause of the crowd, but a few metres behind him would be trailing his puffing bodyguards – on one memorable occasion in suits and ties, as they had not quite realized what they were in for. And while the sponsorship of several multinational oil companies was a welcome boost to the Terry Fox coffers, British Petroleum baseball caps did not exactly go like hot cakes; as was seriously pointed out to a number of still-innocent expats who wore them for the event, this was akin to wearing a "kidnap me" sign.

As a rule, the Canadian Embassy did not go in for National Day receptions – austerity orders from Ottawa – but in 1999 we made an exception: in the spring we had moved into a new chancery, further north than the old one, and in a brand-new office block. It seemed a good moment for a celebration.

In the week leading up to 1 July we organized several low-budget but high-profile events in the neighbourhood close to the Canadian Embassy. A series of classic Canadian movies – *The Grey Fox*, *Jesus of Montreal* – were shown while, at the Hacienda Santa Bárbara, Canadian rock videos ran around the clock. A group of native dancers from Duncan, Vancouver Island, performed three or four shows daily and – perhaps the highlight of the week – two native carvers, also from BC, carved a specially designed totem pole from West Coast cedar in a roped-off public area of the shopping mall. Importing the cedar log had been a nightmare, necessitating urgent phone calls and the cashing in of a considerable amount of credit with the airport authorities at the last minute, but, to our delight, the carvers never had fewer than twenty fascinated persons crowded around them; under the guiding hand of the experts, small children were encouraged to take a chip with the chisel and were allowed to keep the fragrant cedar shavings. Another big hit were the two uniformed Mounties who stood guard at various locations and for one afternoon strutted round on horses lent by the local police academy (I was disappointed to learn that one of the Mounties had actually never been on a horse before).

The culmination of these events was a noon-time reception on Canada Day. We had had word that the president himself would attend – a rare honour – and careful plans were drawn up; offices were tidied, best suits and dresses put on, minute-by-minute schedules drawn up, speeches rehearsed. Twenty minutes before twelve the presidential guard arrived, in their traditional uniforms and gleaming silver plumed helmets, and drew themselves up in a double line outside the plate-glass doors over which hung an enormous Canadian flag. We were told that he would arrive by helicopter at a military base one kilometre to the south and then proceed here by limousine.

At ten to twelve, other guests started to arrive and, a little embarrassed by the grand reception committee, made their way up the funnel of guards and to the elevators. There was the clattering of a helicopter overhead, but no-one looked up: traffic-control helicopters were routine, as were military aircraft coming and going. Then it became apparent there was some restiveness inside the foyer. I hurried in to smooth things over and found an irate crowd of fifty or sixty people standing in front of closed elevator doors and arguing with the building administration. The Indian Ambassador huffed and puffed, turned on me and said it was intolerable to be kept waiting in this manner, and strode out again, presumably to take his lunch at home. It was impossible to find out what was going on, and it was nearly half past twelve before the elevator doors opened again and the by now distinctly irritated party-goers were able finally to advance on the canapés and champagne.

It turned out that the president had changed his mind at the last minute and had ordered his helicopter to land directly on the roof of the building. As a security precaution, all other access to the tower had been shut off while Mr and Mrs Pastrana smilingly toured the embassy's two floors and greeted the flustered staff, who had not quite expected things to happen so quickly (and who were still tidying their offices). As one of the hosts, I let the first flights of elevators leave without me, but – squeezed into the back of a subsequent load – thus missed what would have been one of the highlights of my posting here: making the formal introduction of the president, in Spanish, and serving as master of ceremonies. Instead, a rather surprised but nevertheless cool intern called Vanessa – the daughter of the national deputy ombudsman, who had been volunteering with us for the week's events – stood in and handled everything in impeccable Spanish, but occasionally faltering English and French.

My last day at work in Colombia was 14 July 2000. At the French Embassy, some twenty or thirty blocks to the south of ours and near my apartment, a band had just played the Marseillaise and a crowd of several hundred people, who had been impatiently awaiting the off for nearly half an hour, was now able to launch itself on the Camembert and Chablis. Then my cellphone rang. I was tempted to turn it off, but I could see from the caller ID that it was my wife Jenny – back at the embassy, holding the fort almost alone – and that accordingly it might be important.

"There's a crowd of about a hundred people outside the building," she said. "They're carrying banners, shouting, and their spokesman says he wants to speak to you."

I signalled to the ambassador, who was by this time attacking a baguette on the far side of the crammed hall, and – along with the other embassy invitees – we drew up a plan. I would enter the building in one car, via the underground car park, and check out the situation from inside, while the ambassador drove stealthily to the adjoining Radisson Hotel and stayed in contact by cellphone.

Inside the building, things were a little tense. The front doors had been locked, but the crowd was pressing against them dangerously, and one or two rocks had been thrown. Most of the building had now been evacuated, and I immediately sent home all staff except our embassy security guard, Joe Mochilan, using the underground car-park route of which the crowd did not seem aware. The building management had called in a squad of riot police, and at this time they were assembling in a vacant lot at a discreet distance away.

I made my way around to the front of the building and asked for the leader of the group. There was much to-ing and fro-ing, and initially the leaders – whoever they were – said they would not talk unless they were admitted to the foyer itself. The building management was understandably nervous about opening the doors to permit this, lest the entire building be overwhelmed, but eventually a compromise was reached by which most of the crowd stood back and a small delegation of five was admitted for initial negotiations.

The whole affair had in reality nothing to do with the Canadian Embassy. The crowd consisted very largely of street salesmen and -women who had been served eviction orders by the city authorities. Although they had been offered alternative facilities in a nearby market, they were not happy with the prospect of uprooting their makeshift stalls and were demonstrating to this effect; their purpose in coming to the embassy was on the one hand to gain some publicity – an embassy siege could always be guaranteed to draw in the media – and on the other to ask us to serve as go-betweens in negotiations with the authorities. I knew one or two of the leaders of the group through earlier contacts with the trade union and labour rights movement, and this was why they had asked for me personally.

Talks dragged on all afternoon, with the riot police (by now massed in the underground car park but occasionally popping up in an elevator, to be surreptitiously pushed down again) itching to wade into the crowd and disperse them by violent means. But TV cameras had arrived by now, and even if I had felt disposed to such a course of action, the negative publicity of the evening CM& news program showing people being beaten up in front of the Canadian coat of arms was not something I relished. At one point I was negotiating on two fronts: with the ever-more-unruly demonstrators, and with the police in their gas masks and body armour.

At last, ninety minutes after I had summoned him by cellphone, a visibly nervous city ombudsman arrived, Deep Throat style, through the car park. I explained the situation to him and, after much hesitation, he agreed to meet with a small delegation in one of the building's public rooms that, for the purposes of this meeting only, we would pass off as embassy premises. The ambassador and I would sit in on the beginning of the meeting to formally guarantee it; we would then discreetly withdraw.

All went more or less according to plan, although there were some tense moments at around 9:00 PM when the crowds outside, under the mistaken impression that their delegation had been arrested and carried off, started pressing rhythmically against the plate-glass doors and also threw a few bricks. The glass held.

By about 10:30 PM, things were at last defused. Drained, those few of the embassy staff who had remained throughout the ordeal sent out Pablo, the ambassador's bodyguard, for Big Macs and Cokes from across the road; we sat eating them in the embassy entrance area, under the gaze of our new totem. I hadn't had the opportunity to say goodbye to anyone at the embassy, and in fact my office was still in disorder. But it had been a memorable final day at work.

Epilogue

When I visited Medellín in late 1997, I paid a courtesy call on the then governor of Antioqia Department, Alvaro Uribe Vélez. He shook my hand vigorously and immediately sat me down at a small folding card table in an adjoining office, laid with silver and white linen. As I bemusedly ploughed through one dish after another, which was served by a discreet waiter in a white jacket, Uribe switched off the lights and projected a PowerPoint presentation onto the wall, detailing both his achievements and his plans for his remaining time in office; he strode around the room frenetically, punctuating every telling statistic with stabs of his finger and repeatedly looking me in the eye, calling me by my first name. Uribe was manic, driven, but impressive.

Five years later, with Andrés Pastrana's term of office coming to a close and peace negotiations with the both the ELN and the FARC clearly going nowhere, kidnappings still rising, crime as out of hand as ever, the mood of the country was truculent and combative – "Give war a chance," people seemed to be saying. In February 2002 the president, with explicit international support, ordered the retaking from the

FARC of the demilitarized zone, a de facto admission of the failure of his term of office. Alvaro Uribe, who had in the meantime taken time out to do a degree at Oxford (I met him once more, at the Heathrow airport car-park, and helped him with the ticket machine), now strode onto the national political stage.

In May 2002, in the first round of the presidential elections, standing as an independent and notwithstanding his reputation as a hardliner, including allegations of undesirable proximity to the paramilitary movement (Uribe's father was killed by the FARC in 1983, and he made no secret of his personal bitterness with the guerrillas), he outdistanced perennial Liberal challenger Horacio Serpa by the astounding margin of 20 percent; Noemí Sanín was left in the dust as well; for the first time in recent Colombian history, the Conservatives – Pastrana's party – did not mount a challenge. In August, Uribe was inaugurated as president.

In December he announced that while the war against the guerrillas would be pursued aggressively pending a more "serious" approach to peace talks by the FARC and ELN leadership, he would in parallel negotiate with the paramilitary movement their own dissolution. The move was met with horror in the human rights world, where many insisted there could be no negotiation with common criminals, but Uribe persevered; while attacks on trade unionists and other activists continued, the overall level of paramilitary abuse did decline and by the latest count one thousand paras have handed over their weapons. The process was suddenly thrown into doubt by the mysterious April 2004 disappearance of para leader Carlos Castaño, following a shootout between rival para factions.

Uribe also took a tough stand on kidnapping and laid down firmer conditions for eventual talks about an exchange of FARC prisoners for captured military personnel; he was severely critical of an ill-conceived and unauthorized attempt sponsored by French Foreign Minister Dominique de Villepin to rescue from captivity one of Villepin's erstwhile students and minor presidential candidate Ingrid Betancourt, stating – to widespread public sympathy – that there were no "star" kidnap victims in Colombia, that every single kidnapping was a crime against humanity, and that every victim deserved equal consideration.

By mid-2004 Uribe was still pulling in public approval ratings of 70 to 80 percent, apparently on account of the average Colombian's appreciation that security had improved; a movement was growing to amend the Constitution so as to allow him to compete for a second presidential term in 2006.

Andrés Pastrana went to live in Spain. His Peace Commissioner – Victor G. Ricardo – was posted as Ambassador to London, and then to Pretoria; I met him again in early 2004 when he hosted a Colombian film festival in Cape Town. Former Foreign Minister and vice-presidential candidate María Emma Mejía ran unsuccessfully for mayor of Bogotá in 2003.

Peace Brigades International are as active as ever in Colombia and still saving lives; new recruits are welcome. At Renacer, Timothy Ross, Stella, and all of the staff continue to do miracles with street children and young prostitutes; but they are in desperate need of funds; all proceeds from the sale of this book will go towards their work.

And the Canadian Embassy still supports the efforts of the displaced of Cacarica and San José de Apartadó to re-establish themselves in their homes and to live in peace. I was moved when in March 2004 one of my successors copied me on a report from Urabá, prefacing it with the remark "people still remember you over there"; certainly I will never forget them.

Index